Sensational
Kids

G. P. Putnam's Sons

New York

Sensational Kids

Kids

Hope and Help for Children with
Sensory Processing Disorder (SPD)

LUCY JANE MILLER, PH.D., OTR
with DORIS A. FULLER

G. P. PUTNAM'S SONS
Publishers Since 1838
Published by the Penguin Group
Penguin Group (USA) Inc., 375 Hudson Street, New York, New York 10014, USA • Penguin Group
(Canada), 90 Eglinton Avenue East, Suite 700, Toronto, Ontario M4P 2Y3, Canada (a division of
Pearson Penguin Canada Inc.) • Penguin Books Ltd, 80 Strand, London WC2R 0RL, England •
Penguin Ireland, 25 St Stephen's Green, Dublin 2, Ireland (a division of Penguin Books Ltd) •
Penguin Group (Australia), 250 Camberwell Road, Camberwell, Victoria 3124, Australia (a division
of Pearson Australia Group Pty Ltd) • Penguin Books India Pvt Ltd, 11 Community Centre,
Panchsheel Park, New Delhi–110 017, India • Penguin Group (NZ), Cnr Airborne and Rosedale
Roads, Albany, Auckland 1310, New Zealand (a division of Pearson New Zealand Ltd) •
Penguin Books (South Africa) (Pty) Ltd, 24 Sturdee Avenue, Rosebank, Johannesburg 2196,
South Africa

Penguin Books Ltd, Registered Offices: 80 Strand, London WC2R 0RL, England

Library of Congress Cataloging-in-Publication Data

Miller, Lucy J.
Sensational kids : hope and help for children with sensory processing disorder / Lucy Jane Miller with
Doris A. Fuller ; foreword by Carol Stock Kranowitz
p.   cm.
Includes bibliographical references and index.
ISBN 0-399-15337-3
1. Sensory integration dysfunction in children.   I. Fuller, Doris A.   II. Title.
RJ496.S44M55   2006   2005056490
618.92'8—dc22

Printed in the United States of America
10 9 8 7 6 5 4 3 2 1

Book design by Sarah Maya Gubkin

Research about sensory integration dysfunction is ongoing and subject to interpretation. Although all
reasonable efforts have been made to include the most up-to-date and accurate information in this book,
there can be no guarantee that what we know about this complex subject won't change with time. Read-
ers with concerns about the neurological development of their children should consult a qualified professional. Neither the publisher, the author, nor the producer takes any responsibility for any possible
consequences from any treatment or action by any person reading or following the information in this
book.

While the authors have made every effort to provide accurate telephone numbers and Internet
addresses at the time of publication, neither the publisher nor the authors assume any responsibility for
errors, or for changes that occur after publication. Further, the publisher does not have any control over
and does not assume any responsibility for author or third-party websites or their content.

Some names and identifying characteristics have been changed to protect the privacy of the individuals involved.

TO MY COURAGEOUS *and amazing parents, Edie and Marty, whose lives were an embodiment of Margaret Mead's statement:* "Never doubt that a small group of thoughtful, committed citizens can change the world. . . . Indeed, it's the only thing that ever has."

AND TO THE REST *of my sensational family, whose support enables me to keep going: Bill, Coles, and Marita; Katy, Greg, Tasha, Alex, and Abby; Mike, Laura, Matt, Andy, Joey, and Jonny; Dan, Shell, Sarah, Ryan, and Jordan; and Phil, Phyllis, Barbara, and Karen.*

AND MOST OF ALL *to BMBB, who convinced me long ago that I could succeed—and who still believes in me.*

CONTENTS

Part I. The Basics

Part II. Living with Sensational Kids

Part III. Beyond the Basics

Checklists, Figures, and Charts

FOREWORD

When Lucy Jane Miller and I first met at the 1998 American Occupational Therapy Association conference in Baltimore, I knew enough about her to be awed. As a preschool teacher, I was not in the field of OT but rather buzzed around it because of my interest in children with sensory-processing problems. Of course, I knew Lucy's name—her reputation was well established as an extraordinary occupational therapist, as a student of research pioneer A. Jean Ayres, and as the only full-time researcher in Sensory Processing Disorder (SPD). Nobody alive knew more about SPD than this small, beautiful, modest dynamo. To me, she was the "Queen Bee."

At the conference, I was introduced to Lucy as the author of the just published *The Out-of-Sync Child*, the first book for parents about Sensory Processing Disorder (then called "sensory integration dysfunction"). I felt awkward because I was aware that a book written by a layperson about a neurological disorder might not be accepted by professionals. I stood there, uncharacteristically speechless to be meeting one of my personal heroes.

But Lucy smiled at me kindly. "Thank you so much for writing your book," she said. "It is a huge contribution. I'll feature it on my website and recommend it to all the parents I see at the STAR Center, where we're doing research with kids."

I was flattered beyond belief. Lucy Jane Miller liked my book! She liked it! Receiving her approbation was as good as it gets.

Within a few months, my book was flying off the shelves. Parent to parent and teacher to teacher, word got out that a book was available to answer basic questions about sensory-processing problems. Frustrated parents and bewildered teachers deluged me with questions, such as:

"How can my kid be oversensitive to touch but under-sensitive to movement?"

"Can SPD be cured? Is there a medicine to fix it?"

"What will become of my child as a teenager and adult?"

"How can I include this child in my classroom?"

"Who is the 'go-to' person for this disorder?"

To answer questions, I put together an FAQ letter, which included information about Lucy's STAR Center—where intervention for children and adults occurs—and her nonprofit organization, the KID Foundation, which focuses on advocacy, education, research, and parent support. Although I was reluctant to impose on her jam-packed schedule, I realized that I needed more of her expertise. One afternoon, I took a deep breath and called her up.

When Lucy answered the phone, I reintroduced myself. "Carol," she said, "how did you know I would be home? I just ran back for something. I'm never home during the day! I don't even have an answering machine on this telephone, so I would have missed your call altogether."

The timing was magic, we agreed. She gave me the information I needed for my FAQ letter and much more. We talked for almost an hour about her research, her quest for funding to support studies of "sensational kids," her compassion for struggling families, and her goal to spread awareness of SPD. I told her about my zeal to get "out there" and spread the word. She said, "Once the dream begins, you just have to pursue it, right?"

Thus, our friendship began.

Meanwhile, I had entered the lecture circuit, speaking about the basics of SPD and demonstrating strategies for young children that I had developed as a teacher. Wherever I appeared, parents and professionals besieged me with questions, and I, in turn, besieged Lucy for answers.

Via telephone and e-mail, she supplied them. Patiently, she provided meticulous definitions and explained complicated concepts. Generously, she gave me her time and attention. I wanted to understand SPD, and Lucy knew that I needed to understand it better so I could teach parents, educators, and others when I lectured. We were *in sync*, committed to the same cause. Lucy became my private partner on the lecture circuit, tirelessly answering my never-ending questions and always at my side in spirit if not in fact.

As interest in SPD blossomed around the country, I urged Lucy to lecture with me. I knew audiences would benefit tremendously if we were public as well as private presentation partners. At first, she declined, saying, "The most important contribution I can make is to learn what causes the disorder and how to best treat the symptoms. I need to stay focused on advancing the research for this to happen. If I start speaking at conferences, I'm afraid it will take me away from finding the answers that are central to helping these kids."

By 2002, I was doing sixteen presentations a year for the seminar company Sensory Resources, which wanted to feature Lucy as much as I did. When Sensory Resources offered to donate her speaking fees to the KID Foundation to support SPD research, Lucy finally relented. We began teaching together, making daylong presentations to parents, teachers, occupational therapists, and other pediatric professionals, from coast to coast. Onstage, I would suggest a fun activity for children, and Lucy would explain what was going on inside the child's central nervous system that made the activity work. I would tell therapists what educators need in order to help children with SPD in the classroom, and Lucy would tell the therapists how to meet those needs. She provided research-grounded and understandable answers to the most pressing questions for those who live and work with children who have SPD.

Until now, Lucy's answers have been available only to audiences at these presentations and to families who visit the KID Foundation website or take their child to the STAR Center in Denver. But no resource is as thorough or durable as a book in hand. Now, with *Sensational Kids*, Lucy's research and wisdom are available to parents, teachers, and therapists everywhere—in rereadable, underlinable, read-out-loudable, repeatable print.

Sensational Kids is the perfect complement to *The Out-of-Sync Child.* My book introduced Sensory Processing Disorder from the point of view of an early-childhood educator; *Sensational Kids* provides in-depth information about the underlying mechanisms of the disorder and strategies for dealing with common issues as only the leading researcher in the field of SPD can. What's more, Lucy does it all through vivid stories that bring alive the challenges and opportunities for families, teachers, and therapists with children who have SPD.

At last, the most renowned researcher and practitioner—the person everyone goes to for answers—shares her body of knowledge with all of us. Our wait for the authoritative book on Sensory Processing Disorder is over.

Thank you, Lucy!

CAROL STOCK KRANOWITZ, M.A.

The diagnosis was Sensory Processing Disorder. What exactly was that? Was there something wrong with my son's brain? Was it a disease? What caused it? Would he grow out of it? Is there a medicine for it? Is it my fault? Do a lot of children have this? Do adults have it? Can he get better? How can I help him?

A thousand questions, a thousand fears. When I first heard Michael might have SPD, I was overwhelmed with worry, confusion, and guilt. As I continued to ask questions, everything began to make sense, one answer at a time.

MICHELLE MORRIS AND HER
SENSATIONAL SON, MICHAEL

INTRODUCTION

When I was sixteen years old, I stopped seeing things the way other people do.

Literally.

Without contact lenses, my vision was growing blurrier and blurrier. With contacts, I could see, but my eyes ached unbearably. Just a few months earlier, I'd been making plans for college, for the summer, and for all the other things typical sixteen-year-old girls think about. When my sense of sight began to fail, my whole world shifted. My parents took me to a local ophthalmologist, but he brushed aside my complaints. "There's nothing the matter with her eyes," he told us. "It's all in her head."

It was three years before we found out why my vision was failing—years that I now realize led me to the world of the sensational kids this book is about.

With sensational kids, sensory abilities are impaired by a complex neurological disorder, not by a disease, as my vision was. *Sensory Processing Disorder* (SPD) is the current name for the condition that affects at least one in twenty children. (You may also have heard the disorder referred to as sensory integration dysfunction, SI dysfunction, SID, or DSI, to name a few alternative labels.) Children with SPD experience touch, taste, sound, smell, movement, and other sensations differently from typical children. Some feel sensations more intensely, others feel them less intensely, and some just don't get sensory information "right"—"up" feels the same as "down," or a penny feels the same as a button.

Because they don't process sensory information the way other children do, sensational kids don't behave the way other kids do, either. Activities people think ought to come naturally—dressing, eating, making friends, taking a spelling test, going to the movies, responding to a hug, and a thousand other everyday activities—are a struggle, and social, emotional, personal, and/or academic problems can result.

If you are a parent of one of these children, you already know what I'm talking about. Perhaps your son or daughter—

is two years old and refuses to wear new clothes until you've washed them dozens of times, or

is four years old and has already been labeled a "troublemaker" because he's constantly running into other children and knocking them down, or

is six years old and doesn't seem to notice when he falls down and cuts his knee, even if he's bleeding, or

is eight years old and still can't tie his shoes, or

is a teenager and doesn't have any friends.

When your child was a baby or a toddler, the atypical behaviors might have seemed like inexplicable quirks, but at some point you began to worry, and you started asking questions.

Most likely, you started with your health care provider, but satisfactory answers may have been hard to come by. When your child was quite young, you might have been told, "Don't worry, he'll grow out of it." Friends and maybe even your spouse may have scoffed at your concerns. Parents of sensational children hear a lot of, "He's just being a boy," or "If you'd just stop being so overprotective, everything would be fine." Maybe you even heard what my family heard when I worried about my eyes—that the symptoms were all in your head.

Eventually your child's differences became harder to ignore, and you were presented with a new set of theories. If the symptoms were

severe, you may have been given grim-sounding explanations—
"Failure to Thrive," "Oppositional Defiant Disorder," "Infantile
Anorexia," "Obsessive-Compulsive Disorder." If the symptoms were
milder, it's possible you were told the problem was *you!* . . . as in, "You
just need to be more firm." It didn't help when blunter friends or even
total strangers scolded you with admonitions like, "You ought to stop
coddling that child," or "Don't you think it's time your child learned
some manners?" or "This child should be on medication!"

But these suggestions never seemed right, either, and when you
tried the "firm" approach, it didn't help at all. In fact, nothing has
helped much, and now you're seeing signs that your child feels different, isolated, and more than a little anxious—the way I felt before
my sensory condition was diagnosed and treated. You watch your son
or daughter struggle to perform tasks that come so easily to other kids
and realize that *something* is disrupting your child's life, but you don't
have a name for it. You want desperately to help, but you don't know
where to start. On far too many nights, you spend sleepless hours star-
ing into the dark and wondering what's wrong, fearing that your child
will never be happy, and thinking the critics are probably right—it's
all your fault.

It is for you that I have written *Sensational Kids.*

I was in college before we solved the mystery of my fading vision.
By then, wearing contact lenses had become agony, and even enormous shapes were fuzzy without them. It was my alarmed freshman
roommate who insisted I see a doctor at the school clinic, triggering
a series of referrals that finally brought answers and help. I was diagnosed with advanced keratoconus, a disease that distorts the corneas
and—without treatment—eventually leads to blindness.

The diagnosis was grave, but it also came as a relief. My vision
problems weren't in my head after all! The symptoms were real and
they had a name. I finally knew what I was fighting and could make
a plan for fighting it.

This was in 1971, when the cure for the disease was bilateral corneal transplants, a procedure performed by only two doctors in the United States. My name went on a waiting list for donor corneas, and I doubled up on classes so I could finish college before my surgery. I learned Braille and practiced with a cane, in case the cure didn't work and I lost what was left of my eyesight. Eventually, I reached the top of the list for my transplants. During the first two-hour surgery, the bad right cornea was replaced by a new donated cornea that was stitched to my eyeball with sixteen sutures. For the next three months, I wore patches on both eyes and lived on morphine for the pain. Nine months later, the process was repeated with my left eye.

The operation was a success, but I felt lost in my carefully maintained darkness. The endless stream of doctors, fellows, residents, and medical students who gazed admiringly at my eye murmured, "Beautiful, beautiful," but I didn't feel beautiful at all. I couldn't see, I made a mess when I tried to eat, I couldn't perform basic personal hygiene tasks, and, after a lifetime of *seeing* people when I talked to them, it didn't feel like communication when I talked in the dark. What's more, the experts seemed to care only about my beautiful new eye. I felt reduced to a single sensory organ—an eyeball.

Then someone new entered my life. She was a young occupational therapy student doing her internship, and she had been assigned to teach me how to feed, dress, and otherwise take care of myself. She was about my age and showed absolutely no interest in my eyeball. Instead, she talked to *me,* Lucy Jane Miller, and listened to what I said. She always wanted to know how *I*—not my eye—was doing. She told me little things about her life so that we had a real relationship, even though I couldn't see her. I referred to her as "Angel" and imagined her with long blond hair, blue eyes, a perfect Olympian body, and a halo, of course. I learned to identify her footsteps and detect her scent so I could say, "Hi, Angel!" just as she came into my room.

Finally, the day came when Angel chanced into the room when

my patches were being changed, and I finally glimpsed my rescuer with my eyes as well as with my other senses. The sight astonished me. Angel was a polio survivor. Half her face and body had been paralyzed and left sagging by the disease. In my darkness, Angel was beautiful because I could only "see" the beauty that was inside.

In the fog of recuperation, my future came into focus. While still in my eye patches, I applied to occupational therapy school. Two days after the last stitches were removed following my second transplant, I started graduate school.

One of the first books I read with my new eyes was the work of the pioneering occupational therapist and neuroscientist A. Jean Ayres. In *Sensory Integration and Learning Disabilities*, Dr. Ayres wrote about the behavioral, social, and emotional issues that arise when a child's sensory foundation is not firmly established early in life. She stressed the importance of early diagnosis and described in detail how occupational therapy (OT) was helping children.

Fresh as I was from my own darkness, Dr. Ayres's words resonated instantly. Demoralized and disabled by the long-term repercussions of a doctor's proclamation that my symptoms were all in my head, I knew how critical accurate and early diagnosis was. Barely out of my teens, I knew the humiliation of being unable to perform normal, everyday routines like other people my age. Grateful for Angel's care, I was a firm believer in how dramatically OT could address sensory issues and improve a person's life. Before my first semester ended, I decided to spend my life promoting the understanding, accurate diagnosis, and effective treatment of the sensory-integrative disorders that Dr. Ayres described.

Sensational Kids is the fruit of that commitment.

In the pages that follow, I take you into the homes, classrooms, and communities of children with Sensory Processing Disorder and share what more than thirty years of work with children has taught me about SPD.

Part I covers the basics of the disorder: symptoms, diagnosis, treatment, the role of the occupational therapist, and other fundamentals. Here you'll find first-person accounts of real families living with SPD and learn about A SECRET—an acronym I developed for the strategy I teach others to help sensational kids succeed at home and in the community.

Part II consists of portraits of five fictional children—five vivid "day in the life" chapters. Each chapter includes a running commentary explaining the child's behaviors and provides A SECRET suggestion for modifying those behaviors. Although each story-chapter describes a child with a particular set of symptoms, you'll probably recognize your child and find helpful strategies in all the chapters. Likewise, parents of children diagnosed with other childhood disorders that have a sensory component—Attention-Deficit/Hyperactivity Disorder or autism, among others—may find useful information about the sensory aspect of their children's problems.

Finally, Part III takes you "beyond the basics" to the emerging science of SPD, my current professional focus. Rigorous research is the key to increasing awareness and understanding of SPD, and the field is on the brink of an information revolution. The final section of the book gives you an overview of the discoveries scientists are making and a glimpse of promising new directions for research.

Occupational therapy is a recurring theme. Even though some professionals in other fields receive training in sensory issues, occupational therapists have specialized in treating SPD since Dr. Ayres first coined the term "sensory integration dysfunction." (OTs will be referred to as "she" or "her" and sensational children in general as "he" or "him" purely to avoid reader confusion.)

The passage between a family's first recognition that something about their child is "different" and a final, accurate diagnosis can be brief and straightforward or long and discouraging. Whether you're a parent, teacher, physician, or therapist, *Sensational Kids* offers the information you need to make the journey more swiftly and smoothly.

Today the keratoconus that overshadowed my teen years is much more commonly diagnosed and corneal transplants are performed as an outpatient procedure by ophthalmologists who can readily be found in any major city and many smaller ones. The understanding and treatment of the disease has advanced to a point where patients no longer have to endure the painful, scary years that I did.

My hope for sensational families everywhere is that knowledge about and treatment for Sensory Processing Disorder will continue to grow so that the millions of sensational children currently "muddling through" daily life will enjoy the same hope and help that research and recognition already have bestowed on countless other conditions that once baffled science and disrupted lives.

LUCY JANE MILLER, PH.D., OTR

PART 1

The Basics

A parent's realization that something is different about his or her child's development is followed by intense questioning. When this questioning leads to recognition of sensory problems, the questions become more specific and concerns can grow.

Getting Started:

If You Think Your Child Might Have SPD

___ Try to stay calm and organized! Remember, at least one in twenty children has SPD. You are not alone.

—— Talk to your child's pediatrician or your family physician about the signs and symptoms you see. You and your child need a supportive "medical home."

___ If a medical examination does not produce an explanation for your child's behaviors, ask for a referral or locate specialists trained in sensory processing who can screen your child and determine if a full SPD evaluation is needed.

—— If screening warrants it, have your child evaluated for SPD, ideally by a multidisciplinary team. Become informed about screening and evaluation services available to you at little or no cost through your local school district.

—— If your child is diagnosed with SPD, make sure you get a written copy of the evaluation results for future reference by you and others.

—— If your child receives professional intervention, make sure you start intervention with a written treatment plan that identifies the goals and expected duration of treatment.

—— Attempt to get insurance reimbursement. Ask your clinician to help; experienced clinicians know many strategies to qualify your child's treatment for insurance coverage.

—— Never give up! If your intuition tells you something isn't right with your child, trust your perceptions. Nobody knows your sensational child as well as you do!

And remember: There *is* help and hope for sensational kids!

*I am frustrated to the point of tears. It's so hard to see your child strug-
gling, failing, trying again, failing again. I want to do everything I can
to make things easier for my daughter so she'll be successful and feel good,
but I can't seem to find the right things—if there are any. When we are
so exhausted from just getting through each day, it is nearly impossible to
see what she needs and do something about it.*

*Yesterday, Emma said, "Mom, maybe I shouldn't have gotten born. My
brain isn't like other people's. What's wrong with me?"*

CONTRIBUTED BY TERRI REINHART AND DAUGHTER EMMA

Chapter 1

What Is Sensory Processing Disorder?

When Emma Reinhart was born twelve weeks early, weighing
barely two pounds, the Reinharts were warned that prematurity
might result in some developmental delays. They were concerned, of
course, but so encouraged by the way their little fighter overcame
those touch-and-go early months that they just knew she'd triumph
over whatever hurdles lay ahead. When Emma didn't act like other babies her age, they comforted themselves with the certainty that many
preemies need time to catch up.

But Emma didn't catch up. As time went by, she fell further and
further behind her age-mates. Once she stepped into the social whirl
of preschool, the differences became painfully obvious. While other

children played outside, Emma would stand behind a tree and watch, unable to join in. The most basic transitions—from one classroom to another, from one activity to the next—caused her to fall apart. At home, she had trouble taking baths, eating regular foods, even listening to her brother play his violin. Having her toenails cut was an ordeal.

The Reinharts' initial optimism gradually gave way to alarm. Something in Emma clearly wasn't working the way it should, but what was it? Emma was becoming more and more isolated, and she seemed so unhappy. Some observers hinted that the Reinharts' parenting style was to blame; others suggested that Emma had been put in the "wrong" school. The pediatrician said the fearful preschooler might have an anxiety disorder or, at least, "Failure to Thrive." Terri and her husband, Chris, didn't believe any of the labels fit, but they didn't have a better one.

By the time I met the family, Emma was five years old and so defensive about every new sensation that we could not even test her in our specialized "spaceship" laboratory—a testing room specially designed to put sensational kids at ease. I interviewed the Reinharts about their daughter's history and development and discussed Emma's medical background with her pediatrician. When the multidisciplinary team at the clinic conducted a comprehensive evaluation, they concluded that the little girl had been right all along.

Emma's brain wasn't like other people's. Emma had Sensory Processing Disorder.

Sensory Processing and SPD

Sensory processing is a term that refers to the way the nervous system receives sensory messages and turns them into responses.

All of us are constantly managing sensory messages. Sight, sound, touch, taste, smell—the five familiar senses that let us hear the clock ticking in the background, feel the breeze blowing in the window, smell the cookies baking in the oven—come instantly to mind, but we're also constantly managing sensory messages from two less familiar sensory sources. Sometimes called the "hidden" senses, the proprioceptive and vestibular senses give us our perceptions of speed, movement, pressure on our joints and muscles, and the position of our bodies. It is your sense of vision enabling you to see the words on this page, your vestibular sense signaling that you are sitting upright while you read, and your proprioceptive sense letting you know how much resistance is needed to hold up the book.

Most of us are born with the ability to receive sensory messages and organize them effortlessly into the "right" behavioral and physiological responses. If that yummy cookie aroma coming from the kitchen turns into the smell of something burning, we don't have to stop and think about what to do. We automatically translate the olfactory (smell) message into the behavioral response of dropping the book we were reading and rushing to the kitchen. At the same time, the nervous system produces a physiological response—an uptick in heart rate, a rise in blood pressure, the outbreak of a fine sweat.

Sensory Processing Disorder exists when sensory signals don't get organized into appropriate responses and a child's daily routines and activities are disrupted as a result. Let's say a boy is at play in the park when a ball careens toward his head. If the boy doesn't connect the ball with danger and duck or raise an arm in self-defense, he could get hurt.

If this child consistently fails to organize similar messages, chances are he will have problems in other areas that rely on the same sensory and motor foundations. If the problem is that he can't plan the motor action of ducking, he might also struggle with putting on his socks or making his way through crowded spaces. If he sees the ball coming but can't judge how close it is, he may struggle with spacing letters and words. If he sees the ball and knows it's close but isn't alert enough to take action, it's probable that he'll miss a lot of other sensory messages important to everyday activities such as passing easily through a doorway or reaching directly for his milk glass.

As problems like these recur in multiple areas, it would be easy for this child to start feeling awkward, stupid, or just plain "different" because he can't do the simple things all the other kids can do so effortlessly. If other children begin ridiculing him, he might have trouble making and keeping friends and feeling good about himself. His parents would become worried or frustrated. No matter what his gifts and strengths are, life would be hard.

The Legacy of Dr. A. Jean Ayres

The condition increasingly known as Sensory Processing Disorder was first recognized in the mid-1900s and was originally called sensory integration dysfunction. Dr. A. Jean Ayres was an American occupational therapist, educational psychologist, and neuroscientist who pioneered the study of the disorder. Dr. Ayres is famous for exploring the association between sensory processing and the behavior of children with disabilities in her groundbreaking 1972 book, *Sensory Integration and Learning Disabilities*.* She theorized that when sensory processing is impaired in a child—when there is a "sensory integrative dysfunction"—social, emotional, motor, and/or functional problems can result. She devoted the rest of her career to investigating this theory.

I arranged to spend the summer after my first year of graduate school studying under Dr. Ayres at her clinic. Our first lecture started promptly at eight A.M., and she lectured for precisely fifty minutes. Then she stopped. "Now you will ask me questions for ten minutes and then I will continue," she said. I was speechless! "I don't know

---

* Ayres, A. J. *Sensory Integration and Learning Disabilities*. Los Angeles: Western Psychological Services, 1972.

enough yet to ask questions," I stammered. Dr. Ayres brushed off my objection without a trace of sympathy. "If you can't question me, you can't question yourself," she said. "You must question yourself if you wish to become a true researcher."

What I Do

Throughout this book, it may appear that I wear a lot of hats. That's because I do!

I began my career in 1974 with a wonderful opportunity to care for children in a position that included providing occupational therapy in an early-intervention program, consulting in a preschool, and working in Head Start. Next, I directed a preschool for children with emotional problems, which offered me the extraordinary benefit of mentorship by experts from the Psychoanalytic Institute of Boston. The occupational therapy services I provided at these settings were much like the intervention that many children described in this book receive. Treating these kids taught me that OT intervention is not a one-size-fits-all formula, but rather a therapeutic approach at its best when each child is recognized as a unique individual. From the start, I not only practiced but taught—training and certifying therapists nationwide to give and interpret the first diagnostic test Dr. A. Jean Ayres developed.

However, because I had studied under Dr. Ayres before I was even a certified OT, it was research that was my passion. People who knew me then say that I was always asking questions: "What diagnosis does that child really have?" and "What's the real difference between this treatment and that one?" and "Why does that type of treatment work?" I saw that identifying children when they were younger prevented secondary problems like low self-esteem, and I decided to develop a test that would identify sensory-processing problems in children from two and a half to five years

old—younger than Dr. Ayres's test allowed. In 1979, I founded the
KID Foundation, a nonprofit charity, to fund that project and others. My first nationally standardized scale, the Miller Assessment
for Preschoolers (MAP), was published in 1982 and again in 1988
by The Psychological Corporation, which also publishes others of
the seven nationally norm-referenced scales I have developed. All
of these tests are based on play so that children can receive evaluations in a fun and culturally fair manner.

Eventually I added a social advocacy hat to my collection, serving three terms on the Colorado Governor's Council for IDEA
(Individuals with Disabilities Education Act). Through my work on
the council, I learned the importance of family-centered care—
what parents called the "Copernicus Revolution," an approach in
which families are no longer the "planets" revolving around their
children's care providers but instead the center of the universe
around whom the professionals need to orbit. Later, I joined medical school faculties, first at Washington University and then at the
Health Sciences Center in Colorado, settings that brought me in
contact with students who raised questions of their own about
young children with disabilities. When I added the lecturer hat that
my friend and colleague Carol Stock Kranowitz describes in the
foreword, I was able to take the message about Sensory Processing
Disorder to national and international audiences as well.

Over the years, no matter which of my hats I was wearing, I
was always humbled by the recognition of how little was known
about Sensory Processing Disorder and how frequently children
with SPD were overlooked or didn't "qualify" for intervention. I saw
children who started as winners falling further behind and being
isolated from other children until the joy and innocence of childhood left them, and they became "failures." I vowed to advance
what we know about children with Sensory Processing Disorder
and to champion as long and hard as necessary until SPD be-

came formally recognized as a "real" diagnosis by the medical establishment. To amplify my own efforts, I recruited two national multisite collaborative research groups to bring together researchers with the same goals. Those two groups and other researchers are hard at work filling in answers to the many remaining questions about SPD.

Today, most of my hats can be found hanging at either STAR (Sensory Therapies And Research) Center in Denver—where family-centered care for children and adults with sensory-processing, learning, attention, behavior, and motor challenges is offered—or at the KID (Knowledge in Development) Foundation, where I direct the Research Institute. From its initial goal of developing an early-childhood test for SPD, KID has bloomed into a multifaceted organization that is one of the best friends a family with a sensational kid can have. KID's mission includes:

- *Parent Support:* organizing local support groups for parents, called SPD Parent Connections, now in almost a hundred cities and seven countries
- *Education:* sponsoring scientific and educational conferences and operating an extensive website, the main source of information on SPD for thousands of parents and professionals worldwide
- *Networking:* maintaining the SPD Resource Directory, where parents can find health care, education, and resources that cater to sensational kids in their own communities
- *Advocacy:* working with committees responsible for revisions of standard medical diagnostic manuals to advocate for inclusion of SPD
- *Research:* conducting ongoing scientific research and providing consultation to other professionals who are conducting SPD research

When I'm not wearing my hats at STAR or KID, or on the road lecturing, I breathe deeply the pure Colorado mountain air and dream of a future in which comprehensive and appropriate services exist for all sensational kids and where parents' hopes for their sensational children are fulfilled. I work, I teach, I care about "my" kids, and I wonder . . . *Where does SPD come from? What parts of the brain are involved? How can it be defined? What treatments work best? How does it change as a child gets older?* Eventually, over time, an ever-growing village of parents and professionals will answer these and other questions . . . together.

Though Dr. Ayres's remarkable career ended with her death in 1988, her probing approach and the body of research she produced continues to serve as the cornerstone of study into Sensory Processing Disorder. When I meet with parents whose children have SPD, I urge them to ask questions the way Dr. Ayres asked questions—until they find satisfactory answers. *What are the symptoms of Sensory Processing Disorder? How do symptoms change with age? What kinds of treatments seem to help?*

These are just some of the important questions this book addresses. As research continues to expand our knowledge of SPD, parents will continue asking questions for years to come, obtaining more answers along the way.

Behavior and SPD

"Look at your son's desk," Mrs. Estes said. The cardboard box that held Billy's supplies was exploding, its sides ripped, crayons broken, and all the pencils missing erasers.

My heart sank. I had been happily anticipating my very first parent-teacher conference. My son was a big boy now (called "William") in the first grade. I couldn't wait for his teacher to tell me how bright he was! What a good reader he was! How well he got along with the other children! What a pleasure he was to have in class!

We sat in little-people chairs, facing each other. "When it's time to get in line, Billy runs pell-mell through the classroom, charging into desks and chairs and plowing into others," the teacher continued. "He crashes into the line, knocking over all the other kids like dominoes. Then he says he didn't do it. What he means is that he didn't mean to do it."

I tried to swallow the lump in my throat and blink away the tears in my eyes. Apparently, my son was not a joy to have in the classroom after all. As I struggled to hide my dismay, Mrs. Estes said I might want to find out about Sensory Processing Disorder.

"What's that?" I asked. I was worried, but I tried not to let the worry show.

CONTRIBUTED BY WILLIAM'S MOM

There are children who can't organize their desks and children who crave organization in everything, right down to the food on their plates.

Children who can barely arouse themselves to leave their beds and children who can't calm down enough to sleep.

Children who have trouble sitting up straight and children who can execute amazing feats of physical derring-do.

So many children. So many behaviors.

It would be wonderfully convenient if Sensory Processing Disorder produced one or two patterns of unusual behavior that always looked the same, but this is not the case. SPD produces three classic symptom clusters that may occur independently or in combination with one another and that can range in severity from mild to severe. While each symptom cluster has a sensory basis, the resulting behaviors are as diverse as Emma shrinking from other children, Billy crashing into them, and other children engaging in actions that are equally dissimilar.

I'll describe the patterns of SPD and their symptoms in detail a little bit later, but the following shorthand definitions will get us started:

- *Sensory Modulation Disorder* (SMD) is a problem with turning sensory messages into controlled behaviors that match the nature and intensity of the sensory information. Both Emma and Billy have types of SMD.
- *Sensory-Based Motor Disorder* (SBMD) is a problem with stabilizing, moving, or planning a series of movements in response to sensory demands.
- *Sensory Discrimination Disorder* (SDD) is a problem with sensing similarities and differences between sensations.

Within each of the major patterns, subtypes have been identified. Figure 1.1 provides a snapshot of how the major patterns and subtypes fit under the umbrella of Sensory Processing Disorder.

It's important to remember that *all* of us experience sensory problems occasionally, and some of us experience them regularly. For example, I am sensitive to labels against my skin, so I always cut them out of my clothes. This doesn't mean I have SPD. My label aversion is an isolated oversensitivity that doesn't get in the way of my daily life.

It would be quite another matter if I were a child so sensitive to the light touch of clothing that I resisted wearing shoes or refused to wear any clothes except one old, well-washed sweatsuit. Soon, my life would be affected at every level, from the most basic activities of getting dressed to the more complex ones of fitting in with classmates who wore "regular" kid clothes. I would undoubtedly have problems in other areas where the sense of touch was involved. In other words,

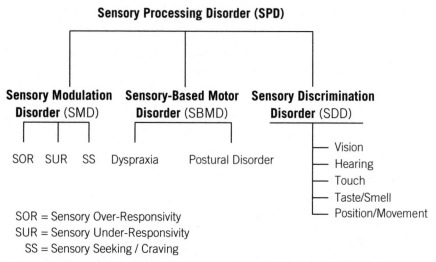

Figure 1.1. Classification of Sensory Processing Disorder Patterns and Subtypes

I would be a child whose everyday activities and social interactions were being disrupted.

The hallmark of children with Sensory Processing Disorder is that their sensory difficulties are *chronic* and *disrupt* their everyday life. Children with SPD get "stuck." And no matter what strategies a determined parent uses—stickers on a chart, praise, discipline, or some technique another parent said worked magic for them—kids with SPD stay stuck. Parents of sensational kids often say it seems like their children have no control over their bodies. Well . . . guess what? They don't. Children with SPD behave differently from typically developing children because their brains really are different.

The degree of difference varies, as it does with any condition. Some children are affected in only one sensory system; others in multiple systems. Symptoms of the same subtype may be severe enough to raise parents' alarm from birth or so mild that it takes years to recognize that something about their child's functioning isn't quite right. A great many children exhibit symptoms of SPD *and* another disorder, such as autism or Attention-Deficit/Hyperactivity Disorder

(ADHD),* a phenomenon that Chapter 12, "Beyond the Types," will cover in detail.

No matter where a child's symptoms fall on the continuum of severity, Sensory Processing Disorder needs to be identified as early as possible. When symptoms affect children but don't greatly affect people around them, it's easy for the problems to be missed. But Sensory Processing Disorder *always* deprives children of the sensory information and experience they need in order to learn and develop. Whether sensory issues are mild or severe, a child's social, emotional, motor, and academic development can be impaired unless timely help in overcoming and/or adapting to the disorder is received.

Context and Sensory Processing Disorder

When Brogan was four, we attended Mass at our local church, bringing crayons and coloring books to keep him and his sister entertained. They were doing fine until the choir began to sing toward the end of the service. We noticed Brogan covering his ears and assumed the volume was uncomfortable for him. Then he crawled onto my lap and began crying, which soon escalated into uncontrollable sobbing. "What is wrong?" I whispered. Tears rolling down his face, he moaned, "The music is so sad." We tried to explain to him that it wasn't really sad, but he was crying so hard and was so inconsolable that we had to carry him out of the church and go home.

The next week as we prepared to attend Mass, Brogan asked, "Where are we going?" I told him we were going to church. Immediately he began to cry. "I don't want to go, Mommy," he said.

---

* Attention Deficit Disorder was renamed Attention-Deficit/Hyperactivity Disorder (ADHD) in *Diagnostic and Statistical Manual-IV* (commonly called the *DSM-IV*). However, the term ADD is still widely used and is useful as a descriptive umbrella for a disorder in which attention deficit *with* hyperactivity is only one of three subtypes. Because the acronym ADHD has largely replaced ADD in popular literature, it is used throughout this book to encompass all three subtypes of attention disorders in the *DSM-IV.*

"Please don't make me go hear that sad music again." He was so frightened about becoming sad that we eventually said, *"Okay, you don't have to go."* After that, my husband and I took turns going to Mass and staying home with our son.

CONTRIBUTED BY LAURA HENEGHAN AND SON BROGAN

Brogan's reaction to the powerful music during Mass illustrates another characteristic of Sensory Processing Disorder, a highly variable element called "context."

Regardless of the pattern or the severity of SPD, the disorder's symptoms are the by-product of many factors: the time of day, the setting, the child's level of stress or fatigue, and the specific sensation involved. Brogan, for example, was able to sit quite successfully through the long church service. It was only when the service included heavy music—in other words, when his context was modified by a sensory change—that he fell apart.

Every one of us lives in a "context." My personal context includes my nuclear family and extended family, who all live nearby and congregate for birthdays and holidays; my team at work, whom I see and collaborate with almost daily; and my exercise buddies, with whom I "power walk" whenever I can. Each context has its own standards and expectations. For example, at work we dress rather formally, but with my exercise partners I wear workout clothes. At family gatherings, everyone talks at the same time, but on the job people take turns. In each context, I have different relationships and perform tasks of different kinds.

Brogan's context included being part of a religiously observant family that went regularly to Mass where somber music was played. A typically developing child might find the long church service tedious and grow fidgety, but he would not melt down when the organ started to play. Because Brogan's sensory processing is impaired (he was eventually diagnosed with sensory over-responsivity in the auditory system), the sadness of the music was exaggerated until it overflowed the boy's emotional capacity to handle the sound, and he lost control. Mass in a church with a soaring pipe organ, it turned out, was a bad fit for this particular child.

All of us function most efficiently when there is a "just right" fit between our context and our innate personal characteristics—the aspects of personality, temperament, intelligence, attentional, emotional, and sensory capacities and all the other qualities that make us each unique. When children with typical sensory-processing skills find themselves in a context they don't like, they might whine or complain, but they usually can adapt as needed to achieve a good fit. They cope.

Because children with SPD aren't processing sensory information naturally and efficiently, the just-right fit is generally harder for them to achieve. Rambunctious Billy would also be uncomfortable in the long church service but for a different reason. With his appetite for physical movement thwarted, Billy would have trouble sitting still. However, Emma—a child who finds bright lights and sudden sounds alarming—might actually thrive on the melodic music, quiet atmosphere, and low lighting of the church, doing much better in the long service than in her more stimulating kindergarten environment.

Looking at children in context helps parents and others appreciate that a sensory processing difficulty is not like a broken bone, which is pretty much the same all day long, but more like eyesight, which is affected by available light, visual task, and fatigue. Context explains why the same child may be totally competent in one setting or at certain times of day and utterly lost in other ones. Looking at children with SPD in their contexts enables us to develop new ways of helping them.

When a just-right fit consistently eludes children and everyday life is disrupted, a developmental red flag has gone up. Fortunately, there are well-tested methods of identifying and addressing sensory issues if warning signs are present. For sensational families, learning that a child has Sensory Processing Disorder usually comes as a relief. They weren't imagining things after all! Their child has a condition that is real and has a name. At last they know what they're facing, and can develop a plan for fighting it.

Emma—Five Years Later

It is difficult to remember those incredibly challenging years when Emma was in preschool. Today, she is a nearly "normal" eleven-year-old, attending a normal fifth-grade class. She still has her challenges with noise, with balance, and with anxiety, and it is still nearly impossible for her to be in a room by herself. However, she has attended a theater camp at the Denver Center, actively participating the entire time. It was like watching someone prepare to climb Mount Everest every morning, but she did it and her confidence has gone way up. She has started playing violin and trumpet in the school orchestra. She has dreams of learning to ride a unicycle, and she has even started to learn juggling!

What she has done has taken a tremendous amount of work, both on the part of her teachers and therapists. She now recognizes what her part is and what she needs to work on, and she suggests her own ways of moving forward. Emma has developed a real sense of WILL and knows that if she works hard, she can accomplish whatever she wants.

CONTRIBUTED BY TERRI REINHART AND DAUGHTER EMMA

Why "Sensory Processing Disorder"?

A logical question to be asking yourself right now is, "Why does Dr. Miller call this problem *Sensory Processing Disorder* when Dr. Ayres called it *sensory integration dysfunction* and when other SI-linked names for it are common?"

The answer is that, to scientists and many physicians, "sensory integration" refers to a neurological process at the cellular level, not to behavior, which is the topic parents and therapists are usually discussing. Describing behavioral symptoms with a term that already has a specific scientific and medical meaning has led to widespread confusion and misunderstanding about SPD and complicates communication between parents, physicians, therapists, and even scientists working at different research centers. The existence of multiple terms also makes it hard for parents looking for books and articles about their child's sensory issues to know whether they're reading about the same problem or a different one.

"Sensory Processing Disorder" gives us all—parents, therapists, teachers, researchers, physicians, and others—an accurate, descriptive term that distinguishes the disorder from its theory and treatment and simplifies communication about the heart of SPD: the children themselves.

Joshua weighed ten pounds, nine ounces when he was born, and by the time he was three months old, I was worried. Our pediatrician told us he wasn't developing as fast as other infants because he was a "big baby." At his four-month appointment he weighed eighteen pounds, nine ounces, and I was concerned because he wasn't lifting his head or trying to roll over. The doctor said, "Don't worry! He'll come around." This went on for his whole first year.

CONTRIBUTED BY VALERIE DOME AND SON JOSHUA

Chapter 2

Symptoms and Warning Signs

When Joshua Dome was born, his parents were experienced veterans thanks to their three-year-old daughter, so red flags went up quickly when their son didn't hit the motor milestones—rolling over, creeping, crawling, cruising—anytime close to when typical babies reach them.

"It's true he was a large baby, but why would his weight have anything to do with his muscles and their development?" Valerie recalls thinking. "I could understand maybe a month or two delay but certainly not more. By the time he was twelve months old, the only things he could do were sit up, eat, and hoot like an owl."

At the same age, his older sister had been close to walking.

Everyone kept telling the Domes not to worry and not to compare Joshua to his sister. "He'll develop in his own time," they were told.

"I didn't believe them," Valerie says now. "Deep down, I knew there was something wrong with my son."

Red Flags and Early Warnings

Parents are in the best position to know when their child has a sensory problem, but their observations are often discounted because they are "just the parents." If the family's health care provider isn't familiar with SPD, the clues that triggered the parents' alarm may be overlooked, misinterpreted, or dismissed. The parents may be scolded for overreacting or they may be offered assurances, as the Domes were, that their child is "just a little delayed" or "going through a phase" or "showing his personality." The child may be misdiagnosed and even treated for another disorder that is familiar to the doctor rather than for the real culprit, Sensory Processing Disorder.

By the time I meet families like the Domes through the KID Foundation, at the STAR Center in metropolitan Denver, or in one of the workshops I teach, the parents are often near despair because they have tried and failed to convince somebody that red flag symptoms exist and are disrupting their child's life in basic ways. Like Valerie Dome, they know something isn't right, but they are intimidated, frustrated, or downright discouraged because nobody believes them.

If you are a parent in this situation, you need to assure yourself that when it comes to your child, *you are an expert!* Just because your concerns are brushed off by others does not mean you are wrong. Until Sensory Processing Disorder is more widely recognized and accepted in the medical and educational communities, you will continue to be your child's best—and perhaps only—advocate, and you must persevere. Familiarizing yourself with the symptoms of the disorder will help you sound the alarm earlier and more effectively on your child's behalf.

To begin the process, let's take a look at the three classic forms of Sensory Processing Disorder and their most common subtypes.

Sensory Modulation Disorder (SMD)

> *One evening when my son was three, he was playing in the living room while I was in the kitchen. I was just taking the casserole out of the oven when Jordan started to scream one of those blood-curdling screams that is every parent's worst fear. I raced to the living room but couldn't immediately see what was the matter.*
>
> *Only after I got Jordan into better light did I understand. The inside of every finger on his right hand was red and blistering. I froze, trying to figure out how in the world this had happened in my own child-safe living room, but the burn was so bad that I didn't have time to look for answers. I cried to my husband that we had to go to the emergency room, where doctors found second-degree burns on Jordan's palm and fingers. It turned out he had grabbed a lightbulb and didn't let go of it right away. By the time the sense of heat reached him, it was already too late.*
>
> CONTRIBUTED BY LORI FANKHANEL AND SON JORDAN

Jordan's delayed withdrawal from the hot lightbulb is a symptom of Sensory Modulation Disorder (SMD), a chronic and severe problem turning sensory information into behaviors that match the nature and intensity of the message. Children with SMD may under-respond, like Jordan did when he touched the light bulb, or over-respond. Some do neither, instead seeking sensation with a single-minded determination.

Three distinct subtypes of SMD have been identified: sensory over-responsivity, sensory under-responsivity, and sensory seeking.

Sensory Over-Responsivity

> *We never could sing around Tanner, not even "Happy Birthday."*
> *He cries intensely and incessantly at any sound. Sometimes his weep-*
> *ing from hearing sounds gets so loud and constant that he throws up.*
> *So our house and our family are very quiet. We never sing when he is*
> *around, and we try not to make any noise. This is especially hard for*
> *his six-year-old brother. Ever since Tanner was able to say any words,*
> *he has screamed, "Off! Off!" whenever we take him out. When we try*
> *to go to a store or a restaurant, he screams, "Off! Off!" like he wants*
> *me to "turn off" the store or "turn off" the restaurant the way I turn*
> *off the sound of the TV or radio.*

CONTRIBUTED BY KAREN DE WOODY AND SON TANNER

Children with sensory over-responsivity (sometimes called "sensory defensiveness") respond to sensory messages more intensely, more quickly, and/or for a longer time than children with normal sensory responsivity. Unlike Jordan, who could hold on to a lightbulb long enough to be burned, a child who is over-responsive might grow nervous merely sitting on the sofa next to a hot lamp. Anxiety or discomfort in situations that don't faze other children is common. As they did to Tanner, sensations that others find innocuous or even pleasant may provoke feelings of "Off! Off!"

Over-responsivity may occur in just one of the senses or in a combination of two or more. A child who is over-responsive to the sense of touch might be fussy about the texture of the sheets and pillows on his bed, while a child who is over-responsive to the sense of sight might shrink from going outdoors in bright sunshine. One little boy's parents came to see me because everything smelled bad to their son. "He's getting in trouble at school," they told me. "He keeps poking the girl who sits in front of him. When we asked him *why*, he said, 'Because her hair smells funny.' " This was a boy who was over-responsive to olfactory sensations.

Most children with over-responsivity are enormously challenged by transitions. Parents may see this at home in a child who fights such basic changes as getting out of or into bed, or moving between locations, such as from the house to the car. Teachers see it at school in students who object strenuously to moving from activity to activity, such as from circle time to recess. Children with over-responsivity create a comfort zone in an overstimulating world by avoiding change, which always holds the potential of leading to some new insult to their senses. This need is so great that compulsive and perfectionist habits are common. An over-responder might refuse to eat two different foods that were allowed to touch on the plate or reject a toy that wasn't located in the exact spot on the shelf where it had been carefully placed the day before.

Children with sensory over-responsivity are among those most likely to set off parental alarms because their behaviors are typically so dramatic and noisy that they can't be ignored. Babies with over-responsivity may cry or scream when their diapers or clothes are changed or when they are moved around. Toddlers may show an almost obsessive aversion to anything messy, refusing to participate in preschool activities like finger painting. Children with over-responsivity may also have serious difficulties falling asleep and/or dislike being held or rocked. One mother told me her toddler son rejected snuggling with the words "Too much Mommy," making it clear that what he meant was, "There's too much of you!" Children with over-responsivity may become aggressive or severely withdrawn, depending on the strategy they use for dealing with the constant experience of "too much" sensation. Some "fight" sensation, others take "flight," and still others "freeze" in the face of uncomfortable sensory messages.

Some symptoms of sensory over-responsivity are listed in the checklist below. If your early warning system recognizes several of the behaviors listed below, you may want to have your child evaluated for a Sensory Modulation Disorder.

Red Flags of Sensory Over-Responsivity

My child's sensory responses include being frequently bothered by:

___ Fuzzy or furry textures (wool clothing, animal fur, textured blankets)
___ Mud or glue on his hands
___ Crawling or walking barefoot on a coarse carpet or grass
___ Feeling crumbs around his mouth
___ Having his hair, fingernails, or toenails cut
___ Fragrance from perfume or bath products
___ Food textures
___ Background noises when he is trying to concentrate
___ Noise in a restaurant, mall, or large gymnasium
___ Any loud, unexpected sounds, such as sirens, school bells, an engine backfiring
___ Playing on swings and slides
___ Bright lights or sunshine
___ Being upside down, as when turning a somersault

My child's behaviors frequently include being:

___ Aggressive or impulsive when overwhelmed by sensory stimulation
___ Irritable, fussy, moody

_____ Unsociable; avoids group activities and has trouble form-
ing relationships

_____ Excessively cautious and afraid to try new things

_____ Upset by transitions and unexpected changes

Sensory Under-Responsivity

> *When Jacob was a little over two years old, he fell down a flight
> of thirteen hardwood steps headfirst and landed on his right cheek. He
> picked himself up, only a little shaken, rubbed his cheek, and smiled
> at me from the bottom of the staircase. I was in shock. Over time, I
> grew accustomed to his high tolerance for pain and assumed that kids
> who cried when they fell down weren't "typical."*

CONTRIBUTED BY IDA ZELAYA AND SON JACOB

Children with sensory under-responsivity exhibit *less* of a response
to sensory information than the situation demands, taking *longer* to
react and/or requiring relatively intense or long-lasting sensory messages before they are moved to action. Like Jordan's failure to sense the
dangerous heat of the lightbulb until he had burned himself, Jacob's
high tolerance for pain is a symptom of sensory under-responsivity.
Under-responders often fail to notice when they bump or bruise themselves and can be slow to notice cold as well as heat. Parents sometimes
report they have to be vigilant to prevent their children from going
outside barefoot in the snow.

Children with under-responsivity are usually socially withdrawn,
preferring solitary games to playmates or not playing at all. Given a
choice, they will stay indoors even on the most inviting days, preferring to play alone on the computer or read. They rarely complain
about missing the company of other children or of being "bored." If

other children try to draw them into games, they often react with indifference, sometimes even failing to notice that somebody is trying to get their attention.

Because children with sensory under-responsivity are often quiet and self-contained, this is one of those subtle patterns that may go overlooked or undetected. In infancy, under-responsivity is often seen simply as the sign of a quiet personality and may even be viewed by parents and caregivers as a plus—the mark of a "good baby." Often it is only in toddlerhood or even later—when under-responsivity manifests in toilet-training problems, "low and slow" activity levels, and limited social interactions—that parents realize there is more going on than a mild disposition.

Some symptoms of sensory under-responsivity are listed in the checklist below. If several of them describe your child, an evaluation for SMD may be warranted.

Red Flags of Sensory Under-Responsivity

My child has these sensory symptoms:

____ Doesn't cry when seriously hurt and isn't bothered by minor injuries

____ Doesn't seem to notice when someone touches him

____ Dislikes trying new physical activities and rarely initiates them

____ Nearly always prefers sedentary activities like computer time to active physical games

____ Was slow or unmotivated to learn to dress and/or feed himself

____ Often seems unaware of what's going on around him; doesn't hear his name being called

___ Often seems unaware of body sensations such as hunger, hot or cold

___ Is or was unaware of the need to use the toilet

___ Is not able to use his hands for a task without watching them

___ Does not notice noxious smells

___ Does not notice food or liquid left on his lips

My child's behaviors frequently include being:

___ Passive, quiet, withdrawn

___ Difficult to engage in conversation or other social interactions

___ Easily lost in his own fantasy world

___ Apathetic and easily exhausted

___ Excessively slow to respond to directions or complete assignments

___ Without inner drive to get involved in the world around him; uninterested in exploring games or objects

Sensory Seeking

The boy can climb anything, leaping into space with no regard for the crash at the bottom. He repeatedly zeros in on dangerous attractions, like electrical outlets and busy streets. No amount of redirection, coaxing, or sternness has any effect. He can take apart everything, including child locks and baby gates. Our home is bare of all objects and furniture that are not child-proof. He bangs his head in frustration and vomits when he's upset. My husband and I know something is wrong, but we just don't know what.

CONTRIBUTED BY MICHELLE MORRIS AND SON MICHAEL

Michael's behavior illustrates the third subtype of SMD: sensory seeking. Children like Michael have a nearly insatiable craving for sensory experiences and actively seek sensation, often in ways that are socially unacceptable.

Some degree of sensory seeking is normal in children as they learn, grow, and try to master new challenges, but children like Michael are extreme in their quest. On a playground or in an amusement park, they may seek out a scary ride that other children approach with apprehension, and then gleefully return to it over and over, as if they can't get enough stimulation. At school, they clown around by throwing themselves against a wall and falling to the floor with such violence that supervising adults worry they'll hurt themselves. When their quest for sensation is thwarted, children who crave sensation can become extremely demanding—even explosive or aggressive. Most children can be a little wild at times, but the thrill-seeking of these children is well beyond average, and labels such as "troublemaker," "bad," and even "dangerous" are commonly applied to them. These children often are ejected from private preschools and frequently get in trouble for disciplinary problems very early in elementary school. Because they are overly active and appear to have limited ability to control their impulses, their symptoms are easily confused with better-known ADHD (see Chapter 12, "Beyond the Types").

The quest for sensation in children like Michael extends beyond the realm of motor activity. Kids who are sensory seeking may prefer food with spices and flavors that children typically reject, like Tabasco sauce and jalapeño-flavored corn chips. They may find that no noise is ever "too loud," and play their CDs or the TV at volumes people around them find ear-splitting. Their social interactions tend to be invasive—they crowd people and touch them, knock other kids over or go down the slide too fast and overtake the child in front of them because they're so excited. All this nonstop movement can be so exhausting that they may fall into a deep sleep during the day and then be too rested to sleep through the night.

Some symptoms of sensory seeking are listed in the checklist below. If several of them describe your child, you may want to seek a professional evaluation for SMD.

Red Flags of Sensory Seeking

My child has these sensory symptoms:

____ Is on the move constantly

____ Likes crashing, bashing, bumping, jumping, and rough-housing

____ Shows a strong preference for excessive spinning, swinging, or rolling

____ Constantly touches objects; touches and/or intrudes on people

____ Seems unable to stop talking and has trouble taking his turn in conversations

____ Takes excessive risks during play; climbs high into trees, jumps off tall furniture

____ Loves to play music and television at extremely high volume

____ Seeks opportunities to feel vibrations, such as by leaning against stereo speakers or appliances like the washer and dryer

____ Frequently fixates visually on objects such as reflections of the sun in the side-view mirrors of the car

____ Prefers foods with strong flavors/tastes (bitter, sour, spicy)

____ Often licks, sucks, or chews on non-food items such as hair, pencils, clothing

____ Is nearly impossible to take to the movies, church, or into other settings that don't allow him to move around

____ Is unable to sit still in a chair
____ Smells or tastes objects when playing with them

My child's behaviors frequently include being:

____ Angry or even explosive when he is required to sit still or
stop what he's doing
____ Intense, demanding, hard to calm
____ Prone to create situations others perceive as "bad" or
"dangerous"
____ Excessively affectionate physically

Sensory-Based Motor Disorder (SBMD)

"He can't ride a bike yet, and it's your fault!"

The words of José's father still ring in my ears. "He picks up your fears, and that's why he won't even try!"

It's been a never-ending argument. José's dad thinks our son should have learned how to ride a bike when he was five years old, but now he's close to eight and has shown no interest in bike riding. I bought a fancy bike with training wheels and took him for trial runs. We did this over and over, but José didn't have the balance, coordination, or the desire to ride a bike. He seemed to hold it against me that I kept making him try. At least once a month I took out the bike and tried it with him, but it was always the same. I finally gave up. Maybe his dad is right. Maybe it's because of me.

CONTRIBUTED BY JOSÉ'S MOM

Sensory-Based Motor Disorder (SBMD), the second classic pattern of SPD, describes the dysfunction that occurs when the "hidden" proprioceptive and vestibular senses that allow our bodies to move and sense our position are impaired. The proprioceptive system is the sense that tells us where our body parts are in relation to each other and signals how much we have to contract our muscles in order to move. We use this sense when we feel how heavy a box is or decide how much pressure to apply with our legs and feet when we walk upstairs. The vestibular system is the sense that tells us where we are in space (specifically, how much we are tilted away from the pull of the earth's gravity). It's how we know that we are standing upright even when we get out of bed in the dark and can't see our bodies.

Children with SBMD have trouble with stabilizing, moving, or performing movement sequences, such as opening the car door and getting into the car seat. Two subtypes exist: dyspraxia and postural disorder.

Dyspraxia

My twelve-year-old Sean tried to play team sports like soccer, baseball, and basketball until it became painfully obvious that he could not keep up with the other kids. Next he tried karate and came home in tears, afraid that people were laughing at him because he made so many mistakes. Then came ice skating, but that required too much flexibility. A brief flirtation with team hockey was too rough and demanding. We tried Boy Scouts for a while, but all those merit badges were also too physically demanding. Finally, we quit trying. "I'm just a loner, Mom," he told me.

CONTRIBUTED BY ANDREA MILLER AND SON SEAN

Children with dyspraxia have difficulty translating sensory information into physical movement, unfamiliar movements, or movements with multiple steps, such as planning how to move through a crowded classroom in order to put an assignment into the teacher's tray. The dyspraxia subtype can manifest as dysfunction in gross-motor (large movements), fine-motor (small movements of the fingers and hands), or oral-motor (movements of the mouth) problems, or in a combination of these, with any one dominating.

Dyspraxic children with gross-motor involvement often are awkward and clumsy. As babies and toddlers, they may be slow to reach milestones such as crawling, walking, and running. Riding a bike is almost always problematic because it requires not only unfamiliar movements such as pedaling, but the coordination of multiple movements such as pedaling in conjunction with steering and watching for traffic (yes, José has dyspraxia). Children with dyspraxia often struggle with playground games and sports because they cannot perform the necessary movement sequences. Recess and physical education class are likely to be miserable, and social isolation can result from being unable to keep up. Because they lack a natural sense of where their bodies are in space or in relation to objects and other people, they also trip or bump into things frequently.

Fine-motor dyspraxia generally becomes evident from about twelve months of age, when children begin to exhibit difficulties reaching for objects, holding small objects such as a single Cheerio, and/or letting go of objects when they want to. As preschoolers, these children have trouble coloring inside the lines; in elementary school, their handwriting may be nearly impossible to read. They may struggle with self-care activities that require coordinated movement, such as dressing, combing their hair, and bathing. Unless someone at home helps them put on their clothes, they often arrive at school looking disheveled because they can't arrange their clothing properly, even well into childhood.

Oral-motor dyspraxia creates challenges involving use of the mouth, tongue, and lips. Infants whose dyspraxia takes this form may not be able to suck, swallow, or breathe deeply, problems that may make feeding an ordeal. As they get older, they go on to have trouble chewing and eating. Their jaws may hang open, causing them to drool. Oral-motor dyspraxia can also affect speech, making it hard for them to coordinate their lips and tongues to form words.

Children with dyspraxia often have a low tolerance for frustration and may suffer low self-esteem because of their chronic failure to perform basic motor activities. Social rejection is common because symptoms such as drooling, dishevelment, or being a "klutz" visibly sets these children apart from their age-mates. Some dyspraxic children develop dazzling verbal creativity to compensate, becoming "bossy" and telling playmates what to do because they can conceptualize a game but lack the physical ability to play an active part.

Some symptoms of dyspraxia are listed in the checklist below. If several of them describe your child, an evaluation for a Sensory-Based Motor Disorder may be appropriate.

Red Flags of Dyspraxia

My child has these sensory-based motor symptoms:

____ Was slow to sit up, roll, crawl, walk, and/or run
____ Has difficulty with motor activities that require more than one step, such as opening a carton and then pouring a glass of milk
____ Has difficulty learning new motor skills, such as riding a bicycle, tricycle, or big wheels
____ Is clumsy, awkward, and/or accident-prone
____ Often trips or bumps into other people or things
____ Frequently breaks toys and other objects unintentionally
____ Takes a long time to write things down and to do tasks that involve following a series of directions
____ Has trouble with self-care activities that require multiple steps, such as getting dressed

___ Struggles with multistep assignments in school, like making a collage or assembling a binder

___ Has difficulty keeping personal spaces organized, such as a school desk or bedroom

___ Has trouble playing with manipulatives, such as blocks and beads

___ Has poor skills in ball activities and other sports

My child's behaviors frequently include:

___ Preference for fantasy games or talking to actually "doing" things

___ Preference for sedentary activities rather than active play

___ Messy or sloppy eating

___ A disheveled appearance

___ Frustration when unable to complete tasks due to poor motor skills

Postural Disorder

> *Connor is four years old, but he has such low muscle tone that he is pretty unstable on his feet. However, he's very bright. His doctor said he will never be an Olympic runner, but he may very well be an astrophysicist.*
>
> CONTRIBUTED BY KATHY HUTTON AND SON CONNOR

Children with postural disorder have difficulty maintaining enough control of their bodies to meet the demands of a given motor task. For example, they may have such poor muscle tone that they can't sit up straight to write at a desk. Their penmanship may be illegible, just like a dyspraxic child's, but the cause of the problem is different.

Children with dyspraxia have messy handwriting because they can't plan where to put the letter on the page, how big it should be, or how much space should appear between one letter and the next. Writing *cat*, the dyspraxic child may use a little *c,* a big *A,* and put the *t* halfway down the next line. But children with postural disorder have messy handwriting because they lack the muscle tone in their shoulders and upper bodies to stabilize themselves in an upright position while their fingers keep a just-right grip on the pencil.

Postural disorder is frequently seen in combination with other subtypes of Sensory Processing Disorder. For example, Emma, the little girl who hid behind trees at recess, has a postural disorder in addition to her sensory over-responsivity. On the rare occasions in kindergarten when she joined her classmates in active play, her postural disorder made it hard for her to succeed—or even to keep up. If the teacher finally convinced her to play Red Rover, Emma could never break through the opposing line of children because she did not have the ability to contract her muscles and exert the force required to push herself through the barrier formed by the children holding hands. She also had trouble adjusting her body appropriately to perform specific tasks. For example, she couldn't swing because she couldn't stabilize her body while she pumped her legs. Her core upper-body muscles were so weak that she would fall off the swing.

Some symptoms of postural disorder are listed in the checklist below. If several of them fit your child, an evaluation for a Sensory-Based Motor Disorder may be warranted.

Red Flags of Postural Disorder

My child has these sensory-based motor symptoms:

____ Poor muscle tone and/or seems weak compared to other children

___ Often slumps over at a desk when writing

___ Is unable to contract muscles and pull against another force needed for activities such as chin-ups

___ Does not automatically move as necessary to complete physical tasks; for example, does not shift to catch a ball thrown to one side

___ Has difficulty using both hands at the same time; for example, can't use a rolling pin or roll out a ball of clay with two hands

___ Has difficulty crossing the middle of his body to complete a task; for example, uses his left hand to write on left side of a piece of paper and his right hand for the right side of paper

___ Has poor balance and falls over easily, sometimes even when seated

___ Has poor endurance and gets tired easily

___ Does not consistently use his dominant hand

___ Has difficulty climbing a jungle gym or dangling from a bar with his arms

My child's behaviors frequently include:

___ Appearing lazy

___ Appearing unmotivated or indifferent

___ Appearing weak and limp

___ Tiring easily or appearing tired most of the time

___ Difficulty holding his own in games like tug-of-war

Sensory Discrimination Disorder (SDD)

> *One time when I was cutting vegetables for dinner, my son came into the kitchen to speak to me. I turned to reply, knife in hand. He*

stepped back, clearly frightened. "Did that knife cut me, Mom?" he asked. He couldn't tell! The knife was a good three feet away from him, but he could not judge the distance of the knife, and he had no clue whether he had actually come into contact with it. No wonder he's afraid so much of the time.

CONTRIBUTED BY MARIE RAWLINSON AND SON DAVID

Sensory discrimination is the ability to interpret and distinguish messages within sensory systems. Tactile sensory discrimination is what enables a child to tie a knot or zip a zipper without watching his fingers do the job. Auditory sensory discrimination helps him hear the difference between a spoken *g* and *k* or in the words *bag* and *back*. Visual sensory discrimination is what allows him to distinguish between a written *p* and *q* or to locate objects that are mixed up with others, e.g., find a specific toy in a toy box.

In Sensory Discrimination Disorder, the third and final classic pattern of SPD, the ability to distinguish between similar sensations is impaired in one or more of several systems: touch, vision, hearing, taste, smell, or perception of body movement (vestibular and/or proprioceptive). José, the eight-year-old who couldn't ride a bike, also has a tactile Sensory Discrimination Disorder. When his teacher says, "Students, take out your pencils," José is still feeling around inside his desk when everyone else has started writing because he lacks the tactile discrimination to recognize the pencil without seeing it. Eventually he has to lean over so he can visually locate the pencil. This sequence leaves him behind on the assignment before he even gets started, which makes him feel "stupid."

Children with SDD often need extra time to process sensory information because they have trouble figuring out what they are perceiving as quickly and naturally as other children do. This difficulty may make them appear cognitively delayed and result in negative stereotyping that handicaps them in the classroom and at play. Self-esteem issues can result.

Some symptoms of Sensory Discrimination Disorder are listed in the checklist below. If several of them describe your child, you may want to seek a professional evaluation.

Red Flags of Sensory Discrimination Disorder

My child has difficulties with these sensory tasks:

___ Telling what is in his hands without looking
___ Distinguishing exactly what is touching him and/or where on his body
___ Judging how much force is required for a task, such as how firmly to hold a pencil
___ Detecting whether or not he is in motion
___ Identifying and distinguishing between different sounds
___ Hearing what is said to him if there is background noise
___ Finding his way around buildings and other environments
___ Recognizing objects by their shape
___ Organizing writing on a page, such as spacing between letters or words
___ Seating self in chair; may overshoot or sit too hard
___ Differentiating textures of food
___ Differentiating smells

My child's behaviors frequently include:

___ Difficulty following directions; gets lost easily
___ Aversion to playing with puzzles or other visual games

____ Frustration when unable to differentiate visual or auditory signals

____ A need for directions to be repeated

____ A need for more time than other children to perform assigned tasks

When Red Flags Go Up

Just because you've recognized your child in one or more of the checklists above doesn't mean he or she has Sensory Processing Disorder. Like me with discomfort with my clothing labels, an isolated sensitivity may exist. It's possible that a medical condition or a non-sensory disorder is present. Some children arrive later at the milestones than others; yours may be one of them.

False Alarms

Not every child who is late reaching developmental milestones or who behaves somewhat differently from his peers has Sensory Processing Disorder or another malady. My daughter Marty walked at seven months, but her older sister Nicole didn't walk until she was two. Both girls were in the "normal" range. Nicole just wasn't as motivated to walk as she was to do other activities. What sets children with SPD apart is that their sensory issues make fully experiencing and enjoying everyday life impossible.

However, when a pattern of atypical behavior persists *and* the pattern interferes with the child's ability to develop and enjoy a normal, active childhood, questions need to be asked and answers found—the sooner the better. Early diagnosis is one of the keys to effective intervention in children with SPD.

The road to diagnosis must begin with your child's physician. Certain diseases, other medical conditions, and/or mental health disorders need to be ruled out before SPD can be considered. What's more, your child needs a supportive medical "home"—and so do you. Finding a pediatrician, family doctor, nurse practitioner, or other health care provider who listens to you and believes what you say will smooth the passage from red flags to diagnosis and intervention. Good doctors listen and believe parents. Committed physicians will be curious to learn more about a disorder that may affect significant numbers of children.

If your reports of red flags are met with platitudes, if your expertise about your child is dismissed, if your information about Sensory Processing Disorder is met with skepticism or derision, *find a new health care provider!* The time you spend in the search may well speed your arrival to the next step: evaluation and diagnosis.

> *My search for the right doctor for my baby began while I was pregnant. After Jake was born and we knew he had special requirements, my approach became more hard-nosed. I interviewed the nurses and doctors in my area. I called and expected these health care providers to call me back. I asked for appointments to meet the doctors so I could discuss my child's special needs before it was time for a checkup or an emergency presented itself.*
>
> *Doors were closed in my face! Receptionists politely stated their "office policies." All the good doctors were not accepting new patients. Discouraged, I talked with my husband about finding a doctor much farther away.*
>
> *At last I heard about a local doctor with a fantastic reputation. I called his office expecting to hear that his patient list was full, too. I explained my needs to the receptionist and left my name and number. To my surprise, I received a wonderful return phone call from the*

doctor himself, and we chatted for about a half hour. I interviewed him and he asked questions about SPD. He had heard about it—that was a huge plus—and he was happy to learn about the progress my son had made with occupational therapy.

At the end of the conversation I said, "Are you willing for me to teach you everything I know about SPD?" His reply was an enthusiastic, "Yes!" Since then, he has supported the therapy my son so badly needed and, with his added effort, Jake has become a happy, healthy, thriving first-grader, a Cub Scout, a loving brother, and a friend.

I say this with the conviction that comes from a successful experience: Finding out about SPD, finding the right doctor, and never taking no for an answer can save your child's life.

CONTRIBUTED BY LAURIE RENKE AND SON JAKE

Rachel and I went in for her second visit to the neurologist, where I shared my general concerns regarding some of the possible diagnoses other doctors had given me. When I said, "One doctor told me it might be sensory integration . . . ," the neurologist just stopped me dead. "Telling me that she has SI is like saying she has a headache," he said.

I was dumbfounded, confused, and upset. This was a person in authority. He should know more than other doctors. And he should believe me—after all, I'm the one who lives with Rachel day in and day out. It made me feel stupid and inferior. His attitude toward SPD was not only casual but condescending. More important, I took his statement as a dismissal of Rachel's sensory issues. I felt lost. Why didn't he believe me?

CONTRIBUTED BY CINDY HURT AND DAUGHTER RACHEL

Chapter 3

Assessment and Diagnosis

When I first met Cindy at an SPD Parent Connections* meeting, she was still confused and upset by her encounter with the neurologist. The dismissive doctor had probably been talking about the neurological process of sensory integration at the cellular level—not Rachel's distressing behaviors—but Cindy had no way of knowing that.

* SPD Parent Connections is a grassroots organization sponsored by the KID Foundation to provide support, information, and understanding to anyone who lives with a child who has a Sensory Processing Disorder (SPD). Chapters operate nationwide in the United States and in several other countries. Information is available at www.SPDNetwork.org/parent-connection.

What Cindy did know was that her daughter was two years old and had oral sensitivities so severe that the taste and texture of food were unbearable. Though her parents had made the heart-wrenching decision to have a gastrointestinal tube implanted in their daughter's stomach when she was nine months old—a drastic measure required only in the most extreme cases—Rachel was still just a wisp of a child and not getting bigger very fast.

What's more, the toddler was not developing the food-related social skills so critical to being a full participant in daily life. Preschool snack time, playmate birthday parties, family meals, even being in the kitchen when her mother cooked—these and other routine life experiences were closed to her. In fact, all sensory experiences were problematic for Rachel, who was happy only in those rare moments when everything in her environment was "just right" and nothing was tripping her sensory alarms.

By the time I met her, Rachel had been evaluated by a neurologist, an endocrinologist, a geneticist, a metabolic specialist, and a gastroenterologist. "We were searching for medical answers because Rachel had completely stopped growing and would not eat anything," Cindy told me. The pediatrician labeled Rachel "failure to thrive," the metabolic specialist diagnosed "infant anorexia," and other specialists offered other explanations. But the Hurts thought something more must be behind their daughter's severe reactions to food and other sensations.

Then Cindy read Carol Stock Kranowitz's *The Out-of-Sync Child** and recognized Rachel in its descriptions of children with Sensory Processing Disorder. "That turned my life and Rachel's around," she says. "We had already made progress understanding the medical side of our daughter's problems. Once we learned about SPD, we were ready to help the whole child."

---

* Kranowitz, C. S. *The Out-of-Sync Child: Recognizing and Coping with Sensory Integration Dysfunction.* New York: Perigee Books, 1998.

The severity of Rachel's Sensory Processing Disorder was extreme, but the frustrating and frightening road the Hurt family traveled was not. Sensational children whose symptoms are quickly identified are the exceptions. The rest are like Rachel and her family—slogging along on a treadmill of appointments and referrals that lead nowhere. When a child has SPD, the treadmill stops only when an accurate diagnosis of the sensory-processing issues is made.

Early Diagnosis

> *Why do so many parents wait to get their children therapy until the kids are in school? Why aren't doctors recommending therapy sooner? I just don't understand it. SPD should be treated as soon as possible. If you think your child might have a delay, DON'T WAIT! Do what you can do as early as possible before your child gets older. Most likely your first instinct that something is wrong is right. Mine was.*

CONTRIBUTED BY VALERIE DOME AND SON JOSHUA

Diagnosis is the clinical fact-finding mission that must take place before sensational children can begin intervention or treatment for their sensory issues. If you spot the red flags of SPD in your infant or toddler, the case for seeking immediate diagnostic services is powerful.

- *Early diagnosis leads to early intervention.*
  The sooner an accurate diagnosis is made, the sooner intervention can begin. Many children and their families suffer needlessly for years because of sensory issues that could have been addressed if a sound, professional evaluation had determined that Sensory Processing Disorder was present and treatment had begun sooner.

● *Early diagnosis increases the chances of successful intervention.* The immature brains of younger children are more "plastic," which enables them to change more easily. This makes intervention more effective for them. Older children still benefit, but the benefits may take longer to achieve and may be based on cultivating coping skills rather than on modifying the brain, as early intervention is believed to do.

● *Early diagnosis lays the groundwork for better school experiences.*
Children who receive intervention at younger ages—as infants or preschoolers—acquire the skills they will need to succeed in school sooner and usually have better experiences once they enter school. This is why federal law requires and funds the screening and, if indicated by the screening, evaluation of preschool-aged children with suspected disabilities (see "IDEA—What the Law Says").

IDEA—What the Law Says

The federal Individuals with Disabilities Education Act (IDEA) requires that children under the age of six who have or are at risk of developing school-related problems be screened for potential disabilities. A child may be referred for screening by parents, physicians, educators, or others who are concerned.

If your child is under age three, check with your local early intervention program (generally run by the Department of Education or the Department of Health). Typically children must demonstrate delayed development to be admitted into the program for further assessment and then for treatment. For children with Sensory Processing Disorder, the delays must be shown in motor or social-emotional activities, or activities of daily living (called adaptive) because "sensory" is not a recognized area. IDEA mandates that these assessments be free to the family, although your health insurance may be billed.

If your child is age three or older, contact your local school district. Ask for the Child Find program or for preschool special education. Assessments for children between the ages of three and five are mandated under IDEA but may be provided by a variety of programs, including the local school district, the local early intervention program, or others, depending on where you live. Your local school will be able to help you determine the correct place to go for an initial screening and assessment.

Eligibility requirements apply. For more detailed information, see Appendix D, "Eligibility Requirements for Screening/Evaluation Under IDEA."

CONTRIBUTED BY SHARON RAY, SC.D., OTR

● *Early diagnosis can prevent secondary problems from developing.*
Children who perceive themselves as "failing" at activities that most children perform effortlessly are at risk for other problems, such as social difficulties, academic underachievement, acting-out behaviors, and/or low self-esteem and self-confidence. When children are diagnosed and treated at younger ages, they are more likely to escape this defeating cycle.

● *Early diagnosis provides correct labeling for unusual behaviors.*
Because of their atypical behaviors, children with SPD often attract negative labels such as "aggressive," "withdrawn," "weird," "hyper," "out of it," and others from peers and adults. With early diagnosis, these behaviors get

labeled early for what they really are—symptoms of an underlying neurological disorder. Undeserved and undesirable stereotyping, punishment, and other consequences are minimized or avoided.

- *Early diagnosis improves family life.*
  The stress on the families living with sensational children can be devastating. The understanding that comes with diagnosis helps parents avoid such common traps as assigning blame to each other for their child's behavior or disagreeing over discipline. A diagnosis also gives parents an explanation they can use to address the criticism and disapproval that is often directed at them as well as at their child.

The arguments for early diagnosis are strong, but *don't worry if you are the parent of an older child!* A correct diagnosis of SPD fosters understanding at *any* age, even in adulthood, and many elementary-school children and adolescents benefit from occupational or other therapy after diagnosis later in childhood. No matter what age your child is or where on the spectrum of severity his or her disorder falls, perseverance pays off.

Screening for SPD

We went to anyone and everyone we thought might help. Overall, the diagnoses have been many, from ADHD to "nonverbal learning disability" to "low-seizure threshold." We have been told lots of nasty and discouraging things by professionals, some of whom were so cruel that it was hard to believe what they were telling us. It was an occupational therapist who finally gave us help. She will be in our hearts forever.

CONTRIBUTED BY DAWNE ROY AND SON BRAD

Evaluation for SPD often begins with *screening* to determine whether differences in development exist and are sufficient to warrant a more comprehensive assessment.* Screening is basically a professional search for red flags that varies in sophistication, format, and setting. Sometimes a round-robin system at a "kindergarten round-up" takes place, and your child sees several specialists—perhaps an occupational therapist, a physical therapist, and a speech/language therapist—for a few minutes apiece, with each one looking at a different area of development. In other cases, a single evaluator such as a pediatrician or another professional may screen all your child's developmental markers using a standardized tool such as the First STEP (Screening Test for Evaluating Preschoolers). Screening may occur at school, in your doctor's office, or at a private practice clinic. In any of the formats or settings, you are likely to be asked to fill out one or more parent checklists and a developmental history to supplement the observations of the evaluators.

Even if a test is objective in nature, evaluation always involves some subjective judgments. Different evaluators often draw the line between "typical" and "atypical" in different places. Ultimately, however, the point of all screening is the same: to determine whether your child's development is sufficiently different from well-established norms to suggest a comprehensive assessment.

Screening will produce one of three findings:

- Your child does not need further evaluation.
- Your child should be watched and re-screened at a later date.
- Your child needs a comprehensive evaluation.

* When a physician or other professional has already determined that a problem exists, the screening step has already taken place, and the child begins the assessment phase without being screened further.

If the finding is that a comprehensive evaluation is warranted, your next step will be to find the best professionals to conduct it.

The Multidisciplinary Team

Perhaps the most frustrating part of the initial evaluation process for me was hearing one professional after another tell me that my son couldn't do this, couldn't do that—when I knew full well that he could. I remember thinking over and over, "Why won't he show them what he knows? Why won't he talk to them like he does at home?"

Then one day, I took him to a therapist who specialized in sorting out sensory-based developmental differences. The room we were in for the session was quiet, uncluttered, and well organized. David was allowed to roam freely while the therapist and I talked. No performance demands were placed on him for at least fifteen minutes and . . . he responded to this approach beautifully.

CONTRIBUTED BY MARIE RAWLINSON AND SON DAVID

If a screening has determined that a comprehensive evaluation is warranted, it's best to enlist a qualified multidisciplinary team to perform a thorough assessment (see also Appendix E, "Locating a Multidisciplinary Team"). At a minimum, a strong multidisciplinary team includes these members:

- *a pediatrician, family doctor, or other physician* to evaluate your child's general health and physical symptoms and determine whether medical conditions exist that may explain them. The doctor will also refer you to any specialists you may need, such as an ophthalmologist or a neurologist;
- *a psychologist* (preferably a child clinical psychologist with special training in the assessment of children) to admin-

ister standardized tests that will evaluate your child's intelligence and other cognitive abilities related to learning and memory;

- *a psychiatrist, psychologist, or other mental health professional* to assess your child's social and emotional well-being;
- *an occupational therapist* to serve as the team's expert on Sensory Processing Disorder.

If the team doesn't include an OT or another sensory specialist, you need to gently insist that one be incorporated. Sometimes a physical therapist or another allied health professional trained in Sensory Processing Disorder can be included instead of an occupational therapist, but in general the OT will be the health care provider who has studied and been trained in sensory integration theory and assessment for SPD.

If your child has a problem in a specific developmental area, expanding the team to include relevant specialists will be necessary. These specialists might include:

- *a speech/language pathologist* to evaluate your child's communication;
- *a physical therapist* to evaluate motor control, muscle tone, and movement issues;
- *a pediatric neurologist** to evaluate neurological disorders such as epilepsy, cerebral palsy, and various syndromes;
- *a developmental optometrist* to evaluate visual perceptual problems and/or a *pediatric ophthalmologist** to assess whether something is physically wrong with the eyes;
- *a learning specialist* (e.g., a neuropsychologist or other educational specialist) to evaluate learning disabilities and learning style.

---

* Typically seen only upon referral by the primary physician.

Especially in rural areas where fewer specialists practice, parents may find health care professionals from one field conducting the examinations in another field. Services provided across professional lines in this manner are called "transdisciplinary."

A comprehensive multidisciplinary evaluation for Sensory Processing Disorder can be expensive, but treatment is also expensive, and treating the wrong disorder wastes not only money but time. What you pay will be determined by where you live, the comprehensiveness of the testing, whether some of the testing can be administered by your school district personnel, and other factors (see also Appendix F, "What Will a Team Evaluation Cost?").

When it comes to the cost of evaluation, knowledge is power. By learning as much as you can *before* you begin, you can avoid paying for services you might obtain at little or no cost. Consulting the special education office of your local school district, closely studying your medical insurance plan, and networking with parents who have already gone through a team assessment with their children are excellent ways to begin expanding your knowledge.

The OT Evaluation

The first time Heather was assessed at age five, she was misdiagnosed with ADHD and possible Anxiety Disorder by a team that didn't believe in Sensory Processing Disorder. Even though the occupational therapy department was one floor away from the multidisciplinary team, not one professional on my daughter's team knew what OTs evaluate, so an OT evaluation was not included in the assessment. Because the evaluators missed the sensory basis of Heather's problems, she didn't receive the treatment she needed. More years elapsed without improvement.

CONTRIBUTED BY JENNIFER JO, PH.D.,

AND DAUGHTER HEATHER

What happens if there are no multidisciplinary teams where you live and traveling isn't possible for you? Even if a multidisciplinary team is available in your community, what if the increased cost of working with multiple professionals is more than you can afford, or your local teams don't include sensory experts? Or what if the available team doesn't "believe in" SPD, like the one Dr. Jo encountered? If you must rely on a limited number of specialists to evaluate and diagnose your child, where do you turn?

Once your primary physician has ruled out a medical explanation for your child's behavior and you have determined that testing services are not available from your school district, you should ask for two referrals.

One referral will be to a psychologist. The psychologist will administer intelligence tests to identify your child's cognitive strengths and weaknesses—information that is needed to interpret the other standardized tests your child will take. Additionally, a well-trained psychologist will be able to rule out other childhood developmental and behavioral disorders such as ADHD and learning disabilities.

What Is OT, Anyway?

Occupational therapy was defined as a field of work nearly a hundred years ago. Old though the field is, many people are unfamiliar with the profession, especially as it relates to children. Even some health care providers labor under the out-of-date misconception that physical therapists work with gross-motor problems while OTs work with fine-motor issues. This is not true.

Occupational therapists specialize in assisting people with the everyday activities (called "occupations") that make life meaningful and productive. In pediatrics, the OT's goals typically include improving daily life tasks and routines such as sleeping, eating, learning, playing, relating, and developing, as well as the complex activities needed for academic success at school. This holistic therapy addresses behavioral, physical, and cognitive abilities as well as psychological functioning and the child's context.

Occupational therapy is a health care specialty that requires a bachelor of science degree (until 2007) or a master of science degree (from 2007 and thereafter) as well as certification/registration by the National Board of Occupational Therapy (OTR), and—in most states—licensure (OTR/L).

The second referral should be to an occupational therapist or another health professional specifically trained to diagnose sensory-based disorders (see Appendix G, "Locating and Choosing a Qualified Occupational Therapist"). The importance of consulting a professional skilled in sensory-based evaluation is poignantly illustrated by Jennifer Jo's long and frustrating search for the cause of Heather's sensitivities. As a psychologist, Jennifer had never encountered sensory integration during her studies. When she found a team to assess Heather's problems, nobody on the team was familiar with Sensory Processing Disorder. Today Dr. Jo feels the team's lack of a specialist in sensory issues was the primary reason Heather's SPD went misdiagnosed and untreated for so long.

Whether an occupational therapist is on your child's multidisciplinary team or is evaluating your child independently, the sensory-based evaluation follows a typical protocol that usually includes an initial interview without your child present, casual observation of your child at play in the clinic's waiting area or where he is relaxed, standardized testing, and clinical evaluation in the OT gym. These measures may be supplemented by observation of your child at school or at home and by interviews with teachers and others. In general, the evaluation will last about two hours.*

It's important for everyone involved to remember that an evaluation provides only a snapshot of how a child feels on *that* day in *that* situation—not a complete picture of the child's daily life. Sociologist Uri Bronfenbrenner has described assessment as "the science of the strange behavior of children in strange situations with strange adults for the briefest possible period of time," which nicely sums up the limitations of the evaluative process. To minimize these shortcomings, keep diaries of your child's daily behavior for a couple of weeks before the evaluation and bring them to testing sessions. If your child is on any medications, provide complete medication information, including history and dosages. Make sure the evaluator has copies of all relevant reports that other professionals have given you, including laboratory results, report cards, and standardized test scores. I always suggest to families that they make a notebook just to hold all this material because, believe me, there will be reams of it.

Once your child's evaluation is complete and you've received a written report, make sure you schedule a face-to-face feedback session with the evaluator. This will give you an opportunity to ask questions about points that are unclear after you've had an opportunity to read the report, digest the information, and look up any jargon you don't understand. To make this session as worthwhile as possible, prepare your questions in advance. If your child does have SPD, a sensory-based evaluation is the gateway to help for your child. Making sure you understand the assessment results thoroughly is essential if you're to pass through successfully to the intervention that waits beyond.

* If your child is being given the Sensory Integration and Praxis Test (SIPT), evaluation will take more time. The SIPT is not given in all settings because it is quite long and expensive, can be given only by a clinician certified to administer it, and can be given only to children who are cooperative and within the scale's age and IQ ranges. Additionally, the SIPT is indicated only for children with Sensory-Based Motor Disorder or Sensory Discrimination Disorder, not for those with Sensory Modulation Disorder alone.

Diagnosis

I finally decided I'd had enough! I would no longer listen to other people just because they had more experience than me or held degrees of higher status.

Why had I been so hesitant to follow my own instincts? How did I, a psychologist, allow myself to be led astray? Whenever I came close to speaking out about the evaluation process, I was told—even by friends and colleagues—to "stay in the role of the mother and let everybody else do the assessing." I wish I had realized that particularly in the role of the mother, one should never step back.

CONTRIBUTED BY JENNIFER JO, PH.D.,

AND DAUGHTER HEATHER

Whether your child is evaluated by a multidisciplinary team or by an individual clinician, there is one final member of the multidisciplinary assessment team I need to talk about: YOU.

Later in this book, I'll discuss at length the crucial role of families in the treatment of their children, but families are vital to the diagnostic process as well. If Jennifer Jo, with her Ph.D. in psychology, could be intimidated, any parent is vulnerable to being intimidated by the knowledge and authority of health care professionals. Like Dr. Jo, you need to fight the temptation to remain silent and be "nice." *Don't* be passive! *Do* speak up! The clearer you are about what you want from the evaluation, the more likely it will produce the information you want. The more concrete your questions, the more concrete the answers will be.

If your child is being evaluated by a team, the team members will confer before you are given a diagnosis. Often just one of them will be selected to explain the findings to you. If the diagnosis is sensory-based, the occupational therapist will probably be the one to talk to you after the evaluation process is complete. Whoever presents the diagnosis, the diagnostic report should include the following:

- the probable diagnosis;
- a clear description of your child's strengths and limitations, including where Sensory Processing Disorder fits into them, if at all;
- what interventions are recommended, if any, and why; and
- a plan of action for moving forward.

As a parent, you may never know definitively that a diagnosis is "right," but as the expert on your child, you will very likely have a strong gut feeling about the diagnostic label your child is given. If you have doubts, ask to see the criteria upon which the diagnosis is based. Request an explanation of anything you don't understand, do research on the Internet, or go to the library. Decide for yourself if the description seems right.

Parents sometimes hope or expect to emerge from the assessment process with a complete treatment plan. This is not realistic. As you go through evaluation with your child, you need to remember that diagnosis is not treatment. Nor is evaluation a one-time deal. Even if your child does have SPD, no professional, no matter how qualified, can understand your child's symptoms and their causes in just a few hours. That will take time, and the time comes in the next step toward your child's fuller and happier life—during intervention.

Jack is three today. He still has a long way to go, but we have been amazed at the huge changes that took place so quickly once he was accurately diagnosed and began intervention. In retrospect, I have three wishes for our family and all families who live with Sensory Processing Disorder: I wish our pediatrician had been better informed. I wish all OTs were certified to assess SPD. I wish I had found the SPD Network earlier.

Early intervention is so important, but without early diagnosis it can't happen. Diagnosis was the door between having our lives turned upside down by Jack's sensory-based behaviors and getting him the help he needed to behave differently. Until we passed through that door, we couldn't get to the better place on the other side.

CONTRIBUTED BY PAMELA CARDIN AND SON JACK

OT is fun! First, the therapist establishes a bond as a friend with your child. Together they giggle and play, with the child leading the way, showing the therapist what he likes to do. They cavort on swings and climb imaginary mountains. They huddle in tents and search for goodies under pillows, pretending it's the sea. As trust grows and bonding follows, the therapist adds new elements that address the child's challenges: games to strengthen weak muscles, toys to stimulate sensory experiences. Swings, whistles, deep pressure. Michael loves his therapists. I think he always will. They are his family. And ours.

CONTRIBUTED BY MICHELLE MORRIS AND SON MICHAEL

Chapter 4

Treatment and Strategies

When I was a young therapist, a four-year-old who wasn't toilet trained was referred to me. I spent hours working with this little boy and his family on toilet training, but at the end of a year of therapy, he still wasn't toilet trained. That's when I learned that the parents *didn't care* if their son was toilet trained! In their culture, it didn't matter. They had a lot of goals for their son about moving and reading and other skills, but toilet training wasn't on their list.

The specific behaviors parents hope to change with therapy vary with the values of each family. One family might set a high priority on having their child enjoy noisy birthday parties, another on going to the movies with the family, and yet another on having the confidence to ask questions out loud in class.

Research shows that parents whose search for answers about their sensational kids leads them to occupational therapy consistently express three hopes for their children and two for their families or themselves.* For their children, parents desire:

- *Social participation and acceptance*
  Parents want their children to behave in a way that enables them to make and keep friends, to "fit in," and to be accepted by their communities. They don't want their children being ostracized for their differences.

- *Self-regulation*
  Parents want their children to be aware of their own sensory needs in everyday settings and situations so they can control their impulses and regulate themselves—to get up when it's time to get up, sit still when it's time to be still, sleep when it's time to sleep.

- *Self-esteem and confidence*
  Parents want their children to feel good about themselves. When children can't manage simple tasks that all the other kids seem to be doing, they often end up feeling like failures. The more convinced children become that they can't do things, the less likely they are to try. Unresolved, a sense of incompetence can become a self-fulfilling prophecy.

---

* Cohn E., L. J. Miller, and L. Tickle-Degnen. "Parental hopes for therapy outcomes: children with sensory modulation disorders," *The American Journal of Occupational Therapy* 54.1 (2000): 36–43. The findings of this study were specific to children with Sensory Modulation Disorder but can be extended to parents of children with other patterns of Sensory Processing Disorder.

Family-Centered Care

I am scared for my child. He has such outbursts and rage when he gets too much stimulation. What is going to happen to him when he is older? His IQ is 157 and he is very social and verbal, but his fine-motor skills are at the level of a one-year-old. He struggles to button and zip. He's not eating like he should either.

It's an endless fight to get our son what he needs, and this causes conflict between my husband and me. Sometimes it seems no one understands SPD. How many people go through this? What is the prognosis for children like Jakob?

I am so sad. I know this isn't our fault or his. I know he was born with this, but I'm afraid he will always struggle. I want him to be happy, and a lot of the time he is not.

CONTRIBUTED BY JAMIE RIDDICK AND SON JAKOB

Parents have goals for themselves as well as for their children, and the therapist in family-centered care considers these as well in planning treatment. Parents typically say they want:

- *Strategies for success*
  Parents know their children are struggling desperately and want to help them but typically end up feeling inadequate. They long to understand why their children act in atypical ways and they want reliable techniques for changing those behaviors. They need what occupational therapist Diana Henry* calls a "toolbox" to help them get through their days and especially through situations where their children are likely to melt down in public.

---

* *Tools for Parents Handbook.* Youngtown, AZ: Henry OT Services, 2001 (www.teach-about.com).

● *Personal validation*

Parents who are living with sensational children need support. They want confirmation that their children's problems are real and difficult to live with and are not the parents' fault. They yearn to hear that they are doing a good job and that their efforts on behalf of their children are important. Parents of children with visible handicaps get a lot of support. Parents who have a child with the "hidden handicap" of SPD need support, too, but are likely to be met with stares and demeaning comments when their children act differently than other children.

In family-centered care, parents and therapists become partners who assume different but essential roles. The parents identify priorities and are the experts on their child; the therapists measure progress toward the established goals and are the experts in therapeutic technique. Using a family-centered model, parents and therapists together use a specialized way of thinking about everyday life in order to achieve the goals that reflect the family's culture and values.

You may encounter professionals following a more therapist-centered model. If you find a clinician who has no experience in family-centered intervention but otherwise is a good fit for your family and is open to trying a new approach, perhaps you can learn together. Just keep in mind that family-centered treatment is the standard of care for intervention and is widely available. There is no reason to settle for less.

The Role of Intervention

One of the most important things I learned from OT was that if Sammy said something was hard for him, I needed to believe him! Especially with kids who are bright and look "normal," the inexplica-

*ble inability to do things that seem simple—tie their shoes, ride a bike,
go to a noisy birthday party—can seem like such stubbornness. My attitude toward my son instantly changed. My frustration level dropped
and I focused on finding ways to help him instead of prodding him.*

CONTRIBUTED BY VICKY MYLENIC AND SON SAMMY

The everyday term for intervention is *treatment*, which I'll use
throughout this book because it's a familiar word even if it's an im-
perfect one. The trouble with *treatment* is that it evokes images of a
quick and complete fix in the way antibiotics "fix" infections.
Occupational therapy is not a quick "fix." It is a therapeutic program
designed to improve the quality of your child's life by increasing his
or her daily living skills in the three occupations central to childhood:

- *work*, such as going to school, reading, writing, doing
  homework, practicing a musical instrument, and/or other
  "productive" activities;
- *play*, such as recess at school, birthday parties, team sports;
  other movement activities (e.g., dance, gymnastics, martial arts); make-believe and pretend games; movies and
  other recreational outings;
- *daily living and self-care routines*, such as sleeping, eating,
  getting dressed, going to the bathroom, and family chores.

Treatment by occupational therapists and other professionals specially trained in sensory-based therapies can take place in a number
of settings: public schools, hospitals and outpatient clinics, and private practices. In all these settings, the role of intervention will be to
improve your child's daily living skills. However, therapeutic methods
and the purpose of public and private therapy are different, and your
child's treatment experience will be significantly influenced by the
setting of the therapy.

In the school system, the role of the OT is to facilitate educationally relevant adaptations and accommodations to improve children's performance at school. For example, the school OT might arrange to change your child's seating in the classroom, recommend organizational techniques, consult with a PE teacher, or otherwise address the external elements of his school context—the environment, relationships, and tasks. Rarely are children pulled out of the classroom for one-on-one OT to work on internal problems with attention, emotion, or sensation. Parents sometimes grow frustrated or angry when school OTs do not provide individual therapy, but treating the underlying neurophysiological impairment of SPD and symptoms that are not obviously relevant to education is not the school's role or its legal responsibility.*

Nearly always, it is the private or hospital/clinic-based therapist who delivers what is known as "direct therapy" in one-on-one sessions. The mother's description of OT at the beginning of this chapter is a description of this type of therapy, and most of the stories of intervention that appear throughout this book refer to direct therapy. Although private therapists may also advocate for accommodations with the schools, the primary focus of direct occupational therapy is to modify the underlying neurological systems believed to impair motor functioning and behavior. Additionally, children learn to recognize and verbalize the sensations that create problems for them. For example, many occupational therapists teach the concept of "engine speed"—"Is your engine running too fast, too slow, or just right?"— to help children describe and monitor their inner state of alertness.†

---

* The Individuals with Disabilities Education Act has what is called a "least restrictive environment" mandate. This means services may *not* involve direct occupational therapy or other therapies unless those services are essential to enable a child to *participate* in school. Because the link between sensory-based OT and school participation is indirect, most schools do not provide this type of OT service. That is why many parents opt for a combination of school services and direct services from a qualified provider outside the school setting.

† Williams, M. S., and S. Shellenberger. *How Does Your Engine Run? A Leader's Guide to the Alert Program For Self-Regulation.* Albuquerque, NM: Therapy Works, 1994.

In direct therapy, parents and children both learn how the child's context influences behavior and how to manipulate context in order to improve functioning. Besides a "toolbox" of specific techniques for daily life, parents learn more general strategies for problem solving.

Therapists may also teach parents to "reframe" their child for themselves and others by seeing the child's behaviors as a symptom of sensory impairment rather than as an act of will. Reframing helps people understand that the behavior of a child with SPD is "physical, NOT parental," as one mom puts it. Understanding typically brings relief from the stress, anxiety, and guilt common among sensational parents. Family relationships tend to improve. When I asked one parent about the changes her child had made in treatment, she said, "You're asking the wrong question. Sure he's changed, but what really changed was our whole family."

More information about the methods used to achieve change through therapy can be found in Chapter 14, "Intervention Methods and Treatment Effectiveness."

How Parent Priorities Become Treatment Goals

Our goals are simple: William is a boy who loves others and wants others to love him, and we want them to love him as we do. We look for ways to have fun each day, and we always find a part of our day that is funny and gives us a reason to laugh. We seek to help others and we want our son to help others, too. As a parent, I do not foresee William having a life void of opportunities just because of his sensory problems. Instead, I see him as a boy blessed with some extra childhood years that will bless me, too, as a father who loves his son very much.

CONTRIBUTED BY W. JAMES JONAS III
AND SON WILLIAM JAMES JONAS IV

My toilet-training failure with the four-year-old may not have changed the little boy's behavior, but it certainly changed mine. In one unforgettable lesson, I learned how critical it is to identify clear, attainable parent goals right from the beginning of therapy. Now I schedule at least an hour to meet with the parents without their child present before intervention even begins. At the end of the interview, I always close with, "Later on, when we're sitting here after treatment is over and you have made this great effort to bring your child to therapy two or three times a week, how will we know if the treatment worked? What are some goals we can set that might be achievable, and how will we know they've been met?"

There are many ways to measure progress in therapy. You will know intuitively that things are better because your child's daily life will show concrete improvement and your life should become easier. However, measurement is essential to validate and make a record of your impressions. The following are among the measurement techniques I have found most useful.

- "Report card"—a graph filled out daily or weekly by the parents and reviewed regularly by the therapist and parents together in order to monitor change. The sample in Figure 4.1 shows how progress on parent priorities in three areas of behavior might be monitored with a report card.
- Goal Attainment Scale—a chart recording the child's level of functional ability at the beginning of therapy and the change during therapy. The Goal Attainment Scale in Figure 4.2 shows how progress toward going outside in rain and wind might be monitored. At some pre-agreed interval in treatment, perhaps after fifteen or twenty appointments, the therapist and the parents would revisit the scale to see how far the child has progressed toward the established goals.

DAILY "REPORT CARD"

Make a mark at the place between 0 and 100 that you feel summarizes your child's function or behavior for today.

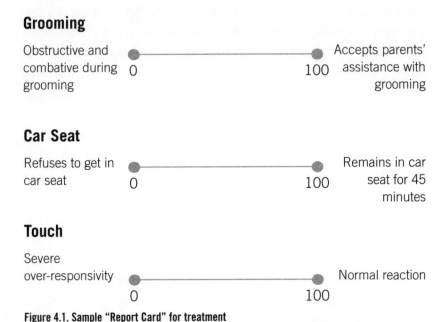

Grooming

Obstructive and
combative during   0
grooming

100   Accepts parents'
      assistance with
      grooming

Car Seat

Refuses to get in
car seat   0

100   Remains in car
      seat for 45
      minutes

Touch

Severe
over-responsivity

0   100

Normal reaction

Figure 4.1. Sample "Report Card" for treatment

- Standardized testing—tests can measure a host of childhood behaviors and abilities, including academic achievement, motor development, peer relationships, aggression, self-esteem, and many more. A child can be tested at the outset of treatment to develop "baseline" data after which tests can be used later to monitor progress.
- Anecdote—stories that describe the child in specific situations before he started therapy and at the end of therapy can be provided by the parents and examined as a way of assessing change. Most of the first-person stories you read

Rank	GOALS	1	2	3	4	5
	To be comfortable going outside in various environmental conditions (wind, flying insects, snow) and playfully engage in activities	Child will completely refuse to go outside to play in any conditions	With significant coaxing from adult, child will go outside briefly but continually request to go back in	With sensory diet preparation, child will stay outside for up to 5 minutes with adult support	With sensory diet preparation, child will stay outside without adult support for up to 20 minutes	Child will playfully engage in outdoor activities in a variety of environmental conditions, including wind, snow, and insects for 30+ minutes

Figure 4.2. Sample Goal Attainment Scale for treatment

in this book are anecdotes collected in the process of measuring progress.

- Videotape—one of my personal favorites. If a picture is worth a thousand words, a moving picture may be worth a million. Making a videotape of the child engaged in a specific activity at home, such as eating dinner or playing with a friend, both before intervention starts and again after treatment, provides a dramatic record of change. Even if the therapist can't personally videotape a child, parents can make a video on their own and bring it to the final session to view and evaluate progress along with the therapist.

Therapists each have their own methods for helping parents identify goals for intervention. It's extremely helpful to find a professional who sets measurable goals with you and monitors your child's progress toward those goals. If geographic, insurance, or other constraints leave you without access to a clinician who uses goal-setting, you *can* write up your own. However, having expert help projecting realistic goals so you can monitor progress is preferable. If goals are realistic and measurable, everyone involved—your child, your family, and even your therapist—will end up feeling successful.

A Sensational SECRET

Through OT, we became aware of Mac's needs and learned ways to minimize the impact of his sensitivities on all our lives. For example, if smells are intense in a restaurant, we learned to get ourselves moved. If lights are too bright, we make sure he can wear a cap, even at school. We always have a Game Boy in his backpack because tuning into that helps him tune out other things going on around him when he starts to feel overwhelmed. Now that we know how to change things around our son to make his sensitivities affect him less, we are all able to deal with his SPD issues pretty well.

CONTRIBUTED BY SONJA ROSE AND SON MACKENZIE

One of the desires nearly all parents voice for therapy is for strategies to improve daily life with their sensational kids. A toolbox of techniques for specific priorities is indispensable, but parents also need broader strategies to help them address sensory and behavioral issues that can be variable, contradictory, and baffling.

In the therapeutic setting, the strategy therapists use is an approach called "clinical reasoning," a creative and flexible way of looking at a child's personal characteristics and context and then making the modifications that will help him function more successfully. Rather than a rigid formula for what to *do*, clinical reasoning is an elastic way to *think*.

I created the acronym A SECRET to give parents and children—because eventually the goal is to show children how to modify situations as needed—an easy way to remember and use the same fundamentals in their everyday lives. Your OT may not be familiar with the acronym A SECRET, but every well-trained therapist uses clinical reasoning to help children with sensory problems. A SECRET has seven elements:

A	Attention
S	Sensation
E	Emotion regulation
C	Culture
R	Relationships
E	Environment
T	Tasks

The first three elements—attention, sensation, and emotion regulation—are the individual characteristics that influence your child internally. The last four—culture, relationships, environment, and tasks—are the contextual elements that influence him externally.

Any elements of a child's context can be manipulated by parents to address sensory issues and behavioral problems wherever and whenever they arise—at home, in school, or in the larger community. Let's say you're on a grocery run and your over-responsive child keeps telling you that he has to go to the bathroom even though he went right before you left home. You've learned by now that this behavior is really his way of saying, "Get me out of here, Mom! There's way too much sensation for me to handle."

The parent who knows A SECRET or an equivalent method of clinical reasoning asks herself:

- **A**ttention: Is there a way I can draw my child's *attention* away from his anxiety?
- **S**ensation: Is there a *sensation* that is alarming my child right now? If so, what is it, and can it be modified? Can I use another sensation to override the alarming one?
- **E**motion: What *emotion* is my child experiencing, and what techniques do I know that work best when he feels this way?
- **C**ulture: What part of our family's shopping *culture* can be changed to avoid situations like this in the future? Can I shop without my child, or can we shop at a smaller market or at a time of day when fewer people are shopping?
- **R**elationship: Is there something in his *relationship* with me or someone else right now that's causing him to act this way? What can I do about it?
- **E**nvironment: What in the *environment* is setting my child off? How can I change it?
- **T**ask: What is troubling my child about the *task* at hand? How can the task be modified so that it is not so prob-

lematic for my child? Is there another task I can substitute now that will provide a calming influence?

The most obvious way to address your child's sensory overload would be to leave the supermarket environment. If leaving the market is not practical, go through each of the SECRET elements and ask yourself, "What can I change in my child's context or how can I influence his internal state?"

You might give him a task: "Can you cross off each item on the shopping list when I find it?" You could alter your relationship at that moment—picking him up and carrying him through the store if he's little or introducing an interactive game: "Let's see who can find the most yellow boxes in this row." You might provide sensory input with a hard, calming hug or a drink he could suck through a straw while you shop.

Learning A SECRET is like finding the proverbial gift that keeps on giving. Whether your child is an infant, a teenager, or somewhere in between, you will have acquired an elastic strategy that grows with him. I'll provide numerous examples of how A SECRET works when we spend a day with the sensational children in Part II.

In therapy, good take-home strategies are offered for use with your family's routines—getting up in the morning, eating, going to school and work, coming home, doing homework, ending the day. Regardless of how your child's therapist presents strategies for everyday living, you should expect to leave therapy with specific intervention techniques and ways of thinking that are realistic and easy to put to work, *not* a long home program that feels like a mountain you have to climb.

Treatment Frequency and Duration

As a child with severe SPD, David spent much of his time confused. The confusion bred fear, and the fear triggered fight/flight

*reactions, either of which made it difficult for our son to move for-
ward in positive ways. Therapy was a way out of the confusion, a
bridge to the world.*

CONTRIBUTED BY MARIE RAWLINSON AND SON DAVID

The frequency and duration of therapy varies, often—sadly—
depending on the family's insurance coverage. In a perfect world,
children with SPD would all be seen more often over a shorter period of time, followed by a break for the therapy to "sink in." In
other words, your child would go to therapy two or three times a
week until he reached a plateau—the point at which he mastered
a chunk of ability with tasks that were previously difficult. Then
he would practice this mastery in everyday life until he reached a
new developmental level or challenge that he couldn't handle on
his own.

My experience suggests that children do much better if they get
treatment this way, in bursts of therapy called "intensives," that are followed by respites. It's as if children's brains need time to organize what
they have learned to do in therapy and to make these new skills automatic in the real world.

However, even as few as one session a week for six weeks (a common insurance coverage limit) appears to help somewhat, and the
common limitation of twenty visits per year is often enough to provide a good, solid foundation for improvement (see Chapter 14,
"Intervention Methods and Treatment Effectiveness"). Many families
say it's easier to fit therapy into their lives and take time away from
other scheduled activities when therapy is made the top priority for a
short intensive stretch, such as twenty sessions in seven to ten weeks,
rather than for an extended period of time, such as once a week for
twenty weeks.

Knowing when it is time to end therapy can be hard for parents
and therapists alike. Most kids can always continue to get a little bet-

ter, and it's possible to keep going virtually forever in hopes of moving one more step forward. Nonetheless, therapy eventually comes to an end. Sometimes the reason is pragmatic: insurance coverage or private resources run out. In other cases, the progress that remains to be made is not enough to justify the continued time, effort, and expense.

Personally, I like to plan the end of therapy from the beginning of therapy. If you stop because you're forced to stop, everyone ends up feeling unsatisfied. On the other hand, if you plan in advance to stop when the child makes a predetermined developmental gain or after a certain amount of time, everyone is able to finish with a feeling of success and you end treatment on a positive note.

Some communities offer outstanding programs that provide a transition out of treatment. If you live where martial arts, horseback riding, or swimming programs are available, you may be able to move your child from therapy directly into an activity that is appropriate to his sensory needs. Small group activities are also excellent for promoting social participation. Your therapist can help you sort through programs and choose the ones best suited to your child's specific needs. Remembering your child's strengths at this juncture will help you find transitional activities that will further your goal of helping him feel good about himself.

If intervention was based on a sound diagnosis of your child's sensory issues, was relevant to the priorities you set with the therapist, utilized appropriate therapeutic principles and techniques, was monitored along the way to make sure it generated progress, and ended with you taking home meaningful strategies, you and your child will be well on your way to a higher quality of life.

Now that he has received OT, Jake is a completely different person. Do you remember my little boy who had such issues with any type of sound, especially MUSIC?
WELL.

Today Jake and I spent about ONE HOUR in a MUSIC STORE!

HONEST.

We were there to lease a SNARE DRUM.

THAT'S RIGHT! You didn't read that wrong.

We leased the snare drum, beige sticks, and a book.

We purchased a practice (quiet) drum pad, cool red sticks, and a book with CD.

He was the best-behaved kid in the shop.

SOOOOOOOOOOO proud of himself.

When we arrived home, he literally spent ONE HOUR in his room, banging and playing his new DRUM. Talk about great OT!

It was a beautiful sound. NOISE coming from his bedroom, without tears.

CONTRIBUTED BY LAURIE RENKE AND SON JAKE

PART II

Living with Sensational Kids

In the next five chapters, you will spend one day each with five children ranging in age from four to eight years old:

- Ryan, a typically developing first-grader
- LaTanya, an over-responsive kindergartner
- Tam, an under-responsive second-grader
- Ben, a sensory-seeking preschooler
- Abby, a dyspraxic third-grader

Ryan illustrates how most children process sensation. The four sensational kids illustrate what happens when SPD impairs sensory processing. These children have relatively severe SPD, generally limited to one subtype. In real life, children with SPD can have a range of symptoms from mild to severe and almost always have a combination of symptoms from several subtypes.

The families of the sensational children in Part II would have answered *yes* to two or more of the statements below.

___ My child seemed "different" from other children almost from birth, but our doctor cannot tell me why.

___ My child feels "different" from other children and tends to isolate himself or herself from them.

___ My child seems "behind" in development even though no medical or developmental condition has been identified that would cause a delay.

___ Teachers say my child doesn't respond like the other students in classroom and playground situations.

___ I've noticed that my child doesn't respond to some sensations (touch, sound, smell, taste, movement, or others) the way the rest of the family or other children the same age do.

___ My neighbor/friend/relative who has a child with Sensory Processing Disorder told me I ought to have my child screened for the condition.

___ When I read the "Red Flags" for SPD in Part I of *Sensational Kids,* I recognized my child's behavior in at least one of the subtypes.

___ My child has screened positive for sensory issues at a kindergarten round-up, well-child visit, or in another evaluative situation.

___ I feel something's "wrong" with my child, but I don't know what it is.

___ My child feels like something's "wrong" with him or her, and that's causing low self-confidence and self-esteem.

Ryan Dosa is a friendly first-grader who wants to be a pilot when he grows up. He lives with his mother, Marina, stepfather, Viktor, and toddler half sister, Sarah, in the suburbs of a large city, where he attends public school. Ryan is a "typically developing" child whose sensory and motor abilities are normal for his age. We spend a day with Ryan to provide a comparison with the four children with Sensory Processing Disorder described in the following chapters.

Chapter 5

Ryan, a Typically Developing First-Grader

By seven o'clock on Friday morning, the Dosa household is already in high gear. Like so many of today's parents, Marina and Viktor both work outside the home. Mornings are a highly choreographed dance from home to day care for two-year-old Sarah, first grade for six-year-old Ryan, and work for themselves.

As usual, Ryan is already up and contentedly entertaining himself when Marina checks on him shortly before seven o'clock.

"Watch this!" he cries from the top bunk that serves as an airport for his current fleet of paper airplanes. "This one flies all the way across the room!"

Marina needs to leave for work early this morning, but she pauses to watch Ryan, a smile on her face. There must be at least twenty different paper airplanes parked on her son's mattress airport. She can see the faces of passengers drawn at the windows of the one currently in flight.

"That's great, sweetie," she says once the plane has glided to a soft landing, "but we've got to leave for school a little early today. If you're all ready before I get to the kitchen with your sister, you can watch the flying scenes we taped from *Top Gun* while you eat your breakfast."

"*Top Gun!* Whoopee!" Ryan hoots, abandoning the airport to scramble over the end of the bunk and down the ladder. "I can do that!"

> *As every parent knows, children don't all develop at the same pace. Some hit milestones early and others reach them late yet remain within the range of typical development. Ryan is right on schedule. Notice how he regulates himself in the morning, which is one of the indicators that he is developing typically. He wakes up on his own. He's not overly drowsy or overalert. He doesn't need his parents to coax him awake or calm him down. He can entertain himself when they are busy.*
>
> *Though not every child wakes up and entertains himself in bed, most children Ryan's age can occupy themselves with appropriate activities for a short period of time. If they're feeling unusually sleepy, for example, they might stumble into the kitchen to pour a wake-up glass of orange juice or turn on a peppy music CD. If they're too hyper to go right to sleep at night, they know they'll feel better if they spend a few minutes coloring quietly or reading a book to calm down. Like Ryan, they naturally monitor and regulate their arousal levels.**

* *Arousal* is the clinical term that refers to the internal sense of being activated, energized, or stimulated.

Another sign of Ryan's typical development is that he can weigh and choose between conflicting impulses. When Marina reaches her son's room, he's having fun with his paper airplanes. As an aspiring pilot, he could happily play with these toys for much longer. But Ryan is also looking forward to his day at school, setting up an internal battle: play or school? At six, he knows what's right and is able to make that choice without any fuss. He puts his airplanes away because it will please his mother but also because he's looking forward to his day. He can rationalize that the airplanes will be waiting when he gets home again. The enticement of the Top Gun *scenes helps motivate him to move faster than usual, but his desire to play is overtaken by what is appropriate in the context of his family—getting himself ready for school. He doesn't have to get in trouble to do what he's supposed to do.*

For many children with SPD, this is not the case. They do not have the internal motivation and/or the skills to perform the daily living activities required to get the day started on the right foot.

Ryan listens to his mother with Sarah in the next room. If he can get to the kitchen before Sarah is diapered and dressed, he'll have it made. Effortlessly, he pulls on jeans and buttons the shirt with "Future United Airlines Pilot" stitched over the pocket, then chooses socks from a drawer and ties his high-top sneakers over them. It takes only a few moments to smooth the comforter over the lower bunk before he dashes to the bathroom to use the toilet and comb his hair. He swipes at his face with a wet washcloth and reaches the kitchen with four minutes to spare.

"Hey, ace." Viktor is packing school lunches when his stepson barrels into the room making jet airplane engine sounds. "Did you have a good sleep?"

"Uh-huh," Ryan says, taking a bowl from the cupboard and filling it with cereal. "And look!" He stands at attention. "I got dressed all by myself faster than Mom could dress Sarah."

Only the boy's stubborn cowlick is out of order, prompting Viktor to give his stepson a thumbs-up of approval. Ryan helps himself to a slice of buttered toast from a stack waiting on the counter. "And Mom says I can watch my *Top Gun* tape because I got ready so fast."

"Good for you. Is your backpack ready, too?"

Ryan nods. "I did it last night."

The boy carefully pours milk on his cereal before taking a spoon in one hand and the bowl in the other and heading for the table in the family room. The family cat trails, hopefully eyeing the brimming bowl. Ryan turns on the VCR with the remote control and gives his pet a quick squeeze before sitting down to eat.

"Sorry, Silky," he tells the cat. "You know I never spill. Besides, Mom says you can't have milk. It makes you barf."

Among the chief occupations of childhood are self-care activities such as dressing, bathing, going to the bathroom, and brushing hair and teeth. By four or five years of age, most children have these basics under control. Perhaps they can't part their hair or rinse all the shampoo out, but they can do almost everything else. By six, typically developing children like Ryan also can usually choose and dress in clothes appropriate for the weather and practice personal hygiene with consistency if not with perfection.

Again, there are early learners and later learners, and even children who are developing typically may have isolated areas where they are slow to become accomplished. Battles occur in every family. In Denver, where I live, some parents have to establish a temperature below which shorts are forbidden or their children would wear them even in the snow! But typical children don't get "stuck" on self-care issues. They're not unreasonable. The shorts-lovers learn to read the thermometer and grudgingly pull on long pants on the days when it's freezing. Ryan's face could be a little cleaner and his cowlick would be better behaved if one of his parents had combed it, but he can pull himself together enough that Viktor doesn't need to correct him or send him back to the bathroom to finish getting ready for school.

Ryan's mastery of self-care is fostering his self-confidence and positive self-image. When he gets himself ready for school without help, he distinguishes himself from his "baby" sister Sarah and shows what a "big boy" he's becoming. He likes to present himself to his stepdad for inspection because he enjoys the approval it brings and because it validates his growing sense of competence. He's proud that all his buttons are buttoned and his shoes are on the right feet and his hair is mostly under control.

Ryan also demonstrates the typically developing child's ability to do several things simultaneously without thinking about each step. He can talk to Viktor while pouring cereal and listening for the sound of his mother coming from the other room. He's able to carry the full cereal bowl to the table without spilling even though the cat is weaving in and out between his feet. He multitasks automatically and without apparent effort. Some of the children we'll meet later need considerable help to accomplish this.

Likewise, this typical six-year-old exhibits a good sense of time. He hasn't quite mastered reading the hands on the big round kitchen clock, but it's not hard for him to synchronize his activities to the family's morning rhythm. Any child may wake up grumpy or resistant to expectations once in a while, but typically developing kids are able to do what has to be done even when they're out of sorts or when the routine hits a snag.

Ryan shows his awareness and responsiveness to the family rhythm by the way he monitors his mother's progress with

Sarah in the bedroom next to his. He fits his behaviors into the family's rhythm without melting down, even on a morning like this one when Marina needs to pick up the pace. When we spend a day with the children who have Sensory Processing Disorder, we'll find families who can't establish rhythms because their children's sensory issues lead to behaviors that are unpredictable, making it impossible to keep routines.

Another area where Ryan exhibits typical abilities is in his motor activities. At six, he has acquired all the motor skills he needs for the activities that are normal for his age. He has the gross-motor skills to scramble between the bunks of his bed safely and confidently and the fine-motor skills to make paper airplanes, button his shirt, tie his shoes, and work the buttons on the VCR remote control. Only occasionally does he feel frustrated by his body's inability to perform a task that other kids his age easily handle. He has no unusual sensitivities, either. He doesn't mind the stiffness of denim jeans or the fluffiness of the family cat. He eats a range of foods without giving much thought to them.

A half-hour later, Viktor and Marina drive off in opposite directions. Viktor takes Sarah because her day care center is on the way to the telephone company where he works as an electronic technician. Marina, a nurse, drives Ryan because her route passes closest to the elementary school. In the backseat, Ryan buckles himself into his car seat and mutters to the air traffic controllers as he pilots his favorite 747.

"Where are you flying?" Marina asks, glancing at her son in the rearview mirror.

"Cincinnati," he answers. It's a name he heard recently and he likes the way it sounds. His jets have been flying there for days.

"How's the weather in Cincinnati?" Marina asks.

His answer is lost to the wail of a siren from a fire engine approaching from behind. Marina steers the car to the curb, and Ryan forgets his airplane long enough to watch the hook-and-ladder unit scream past.

"Let's follow, Mom! Let's go see the fire!"

"What? And miss school? You'd be so sad!"

Ryan nods slightly but looks longingly after the fire truck. "Maybe when I get tired of being a pilot, I can be a fireman," he says.

Marina smiles. "Why not? You can be anything."

Whenever we go through a transition such as Ryan's transition from home to car, all of us experience new sensations. We usually feel a temperature difference as we move from indoors to outdoors and other sensations as the environment goes from being sheltered to being in the open. When a car in which we're riding starts, we feel the motion. The street sounds become different, and we may notice new smells.

With these new sensations come new demands on our sensory systems. We usually adjust to such demands without conscious awareness or effort. Have you ever stood on a bus or subway car and been unprepared when it started moving? What happened? You lurched or pitched against the seats or fell into other passengers. Your transition began roughly. But then you automatically adjusted yourself to the movement and didn't lose your balance again.

Typically developing children make the adjustments required during transitions as effortlessly as you and I stabilize ourselves when we're standing on a bus that starts to move. Ryan is able to walk from his house to the garage, enter the car, and ride to school smoothly and without discomfort. If his mother turns on the radio, he can continue playing his airplane game without being disturbed by the background sound. Even when a siren introduces an unexpected and noisy element into his transition to school, he's not upset. In fact, his curiosity is

*aroused and he wants to follow the fire engine. When his
mother says they can't, he does not become distraught.*

*Interaction between Ryan and his mother is easy and natu-
ral. The emotional environment is free of tension. Because her
son moves through the morning routine and makes transitions
without tantrums or meltdowns, Marina is in a good mood
even though she is rushed. When his mother speaks to him,
Ryan listens to her and can answer appropriately and cheerfully
even though he'd rather be left alone with his flight fantasy for
the duration of the drive. His ambitions to be both a pilot and
a fireman reveal that his self-image is positive. Ryan is able to
picture himself as a grown-up in responsible roles requiring
training and skill. He's only six, but he already believes in
himself.*

Reaching the drop-off zone at the school, Ryan unbuckles the
seat belt around his booster seat and leans over the front seat to give
Marina a quick kiss.

"Bye, Mom!"

"Bye, honey. I love you. Have a great day."

"Uh-huh. See you later, alligator."

"After while, crocodile."

Ryan lets himself out of the car. At the beginning of the school
year, Marina parked the car and walked her son to class every day. By
October, he argued that he was big enough to "do it myself." The first
day or two she let her son navigate to his classroom alone, Marina
called the teacher later to make sure he had arrived on time with all
his things. Now she feels comfortable with her son's self-reliance.
Sometimes it seems her firstborn is growing up faster than she imagined possible, but she's not tempted to hold him back because she can
see that the more he does for himself, the more self-confident he feels.

Inside the primary school building, the hall is jammed with children sorting themselves among the classrooms. Ryan threads his way

through the crowd, high-fiving several passing classmates and sticking his tongue out at the back of the red-haired girl who always beats him at four-square. In Mrs. Strong's first-grade room, he hangs his coat on his peg and puts his lunch in his cubby. Before stowing his backpack, Ryan pulls out the books, paper, and markers he knows will be needed between now and lunchtime and slips a small red biplane into his shirt pocket.

He takes his desk next to his best friend, Shawn, who immediately leans over and cups his hands around Ryan's ear. "Mom gave me extra chocolate chip cookies so you could have some," he whispers. Ryan grins and runs his tongue around his lips. Shawn's mom definitely makes the best chocolate chip cookies in the world.

> *Ryan's arrival at school requires him to negotiate a complex series of steps without anyone telling him what to do. He has to exit the car, enter the school building, navigate a crowded hall, take off and hang his coat in the classroom, and prepare himself for the workday by going through his backpack and transferring what he needs to his desk. These steps involve motor planning, which we will explore in detail when we meet Abby, a third-grader with dyspraxia, in Chapter 9. Ryan moves through all the necessary motions smoothly and with a positive attitude. There is no sign of fear, reluctance, or anxiety, and he easily jokes with his friends at the same time he performs other tasks. His dexterity is sufficient for everything required of him, from unbuckling the seat belt to organizing his classroom materials. Although the sensory environment is somewhat chaotic, he's relaxed and enthusiastic about the day ahead.*
>
> *Because Ryan has no sensory issues that get in the way of performing these basic tasks, the first-grader is free to focus his energy on interacting with the kids around him. His progress in this area is evident even in the hallway, where he spots boys he knows and greets them with high fives. He's not isolated.*

Nobody views him as "weird" or "different." He doesn't need to be surrounded by a special social group in order to be social; he feels like part of the crowd and being part of the crowd feels good to him. Even sticking out his tongue at someone he doesn't like is a form of social participation, albeit one his parents and teachers would probably frown upon. Shawn's eagerness to let Ryan know he has brought extra chocolate chip cookies for him is a sign that Ryan is making and sustaining friendships. He is already a success at one of the other primary childhood occupations: social participation.

Ryan's favorite subjects are math—where the children often manipulate beads and blocks to practice their emerging arithmetic skills—and art, which frequently includes wonderfully messy projects like sculpting clay and making face masks. In general, Ryan prefers activities that let him use his hands to shape, form, and build. Even handwriting interests him because he likes trying to duplicate the letters Mrs. Strong draws on the board. His least favorite part of the day is reading, which isn't coming easily. He's in the middle reading group and is having trouble matching some of the letters to their sounds. Still, he pays attention and doesn't give up, which is what typical children do.

Mrs. Strong starts the day as she always does, by reading the school announcements and then talking about the activities she has planned for the day. At his desk, Ryan fingers his red biplane while he listens. Though Mrs. Strong is what his mom calls "strict," the teacher doesn't make the children sit empty-handed. As long as they show they are paying attention by following directions, they can doodle or handle a toy while they listen. This is helpful for Ryan, who is always happiest with something in his hands, especially if the something is an airplane.

"Are there any questions?" the teacher asks when she finishes. One little boy has his head on his desk and doesn't seem to be listening, and two girls are whispering to each other, but the other twenty-four heads wag back and forth. "Then let's start with spelling. Please take out your paper and pencil for our spelling test."

Ryan is ready when Mrs. Strong starts reading the words, his full name lettered in the upper right-hand corner of the page. Marina drilled her son on the spelling words last night, and the boy is confident about most of them, reminding himself there's an *h* in *what* even though he can barely hear it. When the teacher has finished dictating the ten words, Ryan hands his paper in, pretty sure he got them all right.

Next comes reading, and for a change Ryan is actually looking forward to it. Today the children are illustrating stories they've been composing during the week. Ryan's story is about a jet that was supposed to fly to Cincinnati but decided to fly to the South Pole to see penguins instead. He has already cut out several airplane shapes and pasted them onto each of the story's eight pages; now he's working on making snowflakes for the South Pole scene. The room hums faintly with the murmur of children at work.

When Mrs. Strong announces recess, Ryan is overdue for a stretch. He swiftly puts *Flight 206 Flies South* into the reading folder and is one of the first children to don his coat and line up. When the teacher opens the outside door, he jets first to the slide and then to the swings, undecided about where to start. Then he spots the teacher carrying the ball bag and signals to the buddies who have been moving around the playground with him in a small noisy swarm.

"Four-square!" he shouts to the others. "Let's go get a ball!"

One of the characteristics of typical children is an innate sense of drive to master the next step, a quality that is sometimes called "mastery motivation." As infants and toddlers, if they are sitting, they want to crawl; if they are crawling, they want to walk; if walking, they want to run. When kids like Ryan start school, the drive for mastery continues and carries into academic areas, allowing them to meet ever more complex intel-

lectual challenges. Even in subjects that don't come easily, typi-cal children strive to learn, not just to please their teachers but because of this drive for mastery.

Ryan also demonstrates an ability to progress in different contexts. Mrs. Strong runs a relatively tight classroom where there are strict rules about hand-raising and quiet. Ryan's kindergarten teacher taught with a different style—allowing the children to choose their own seats and tolerating more noise and movement—but Ryan operated equally as well in her classroom as in his current one. This is another hallmark of typically developing children: They can adapt and succeed in different settings with different people.

Ryan's healthy age-appropriate development enables him to focus his attention on the academic tasks of first grade. The higher part of his brain needed for conscious "executive func-tions" doesn't have to be called upon just to balance on his chair or figure out how to hold his pencil. He doesn't have to stop and think about where his spelling words belong on the line or how much room to leave between the number and the period. These skills come naturally. As we'll see when we be-come acquainted with the four children in the following chap-ters, this is not always the case.

When it's time for recess, Ryan smoothly makes the transi-tion from work to play. Though he's eager to go outside and run, he is able to delay his gratification and regulate his behav-ior so that he's not pushing and shoving in line. He knows that if he's patient, everyone will get outside faster and have more time to play. He can see the bigger picture and fit himself into it seamlessly.

Back in the classroom with recess long past, Ryan's attention strays to his growling stomach and speculation about how many chocolate chip cookies Shawn's mother sent for him. At Mrs. Strong's signal, he puts away his math manipulatives and joins the jostling at the cubbyholes as kids dig for lunch money or lunch bags. The teacher marches the class to the cafeteria in a reasonably straight line, but at the lunchroom door she frees the children to fan out to their favorite people and spots. Ryan joins Shawn at a tableful of boys, eager to open today's lunch. On the days when his stepdad packs, there are often surprising little flourishes. Today Ryan finds potato chips smashed into his chunky peanut butter and jelly sandwich. There's the usual crisp green apple but there's a little bag of sweet pickles, too. Ryan puckers when he bites into one of the pickles but likes the odd sweet-sour taste. He offers one to Shawn, who responds by holding out an unfamiliar fruit in exchange.

"What's this?" Ryan asks, sniffing and squeezing Shawn's offering.

"Fig," Shawn says, stuffing one into his mouth. "They're really good. My grandma grew them on her own tree. She said that's where Fig Newtons come from."

After another energetic twenty minutes on the playground following lunch, Ryan is ready for the afternoon quiet time. Though he no longer takes naps, the school day feels long to him; he always benefits when Mrs. Strong puts on soothing music and he can play quietly for a few minutes with one of his airplanes while other children read or color. Besides, this is Friday, the day that Marina takes off early and picks up Ryan and his sister for special outings. Today Marina has promised to take the children to a park in another neighborhood where the shell of an old Air Force fighter plane is parked in the sand and Ryan can crawl into the cockpit to practice being a pilot. That's even better than flying paper airplanes off the top bunk, and Ryan wants to be rested and ready to go.

Food is not a big issue with typically developing kids. Generally, their parents pack lunches to accommodate their children's tastes, or the kids go through the cafeteria line and deal with what's on the menu. If it's pizza, they're really happy. If it's mystery meat with runny mashed potatoes, they're not so happy, but they live with it. They know how to use their utensils and they don't make a big mess. They may not put their napkins on their laps, but they'll wipe their faces and even their clothes if they drop something. Occasionally someone spills their milk, but they don't fall apart over the incident. They clean up and go on. In short, food is simply body fuel that is consumed without a lot of thought or effort, a status that can elude kids with SPD.

More important than food itself is the social interaction involved in eating with others in the lunchroom. Children generally don't have assigned seats at lunch, so they sit with whomever they like, usually with a fairly stable group of companions. While they eat, they talk, unchallenged by performing two tasks simultaneously. They interact, they tell silly jokes, they laugh. Maybe they plan what they'll do on the playground once they finish. They're just happy because they're not in class and because, once they're finished, they'll get to go outside and play some more. Like other typically developing kids, Ryan can adjust from the active, social lunch hour and recess to the quiet time that follows, which is another example of normal self-regulation.

At the end of the day, Ryan gathers his things and races to the drop-off zone, where Marina is waiting with Sarah for a trip to the park. A dozen other youngsters are already playing when the Dosas drive up, and the number grows as area schools let out. One frail-looking little girl is rooted at the edge of the playground, loudly protesting to her mother that she can't step onto the sand because it will "hurt." Ryan barely notices her as he zooms to the fighter jet while Marina sets off for the swings with Sarah. When nobody joins him in the airplane shell, Ryan climbs out to search for a playmate.

The first prospect he tries is a bigger boy squatting at the edge of the sandy area that holds the playground equipment. The boy is picking up handful after handful of sand and letting the grains dribble between his fingers into a small mound.

"Whatcha doing?" Ryan asks, bending over to watch. "Is it a game? Can I play?"

The boy doesn't answer, and Ryan's not sure he even heard. He tries again. "How do you play?"

Before Ryan gets an answer, he hears his sister send up a wail of toddler grief. He spots her sprawled in the sand with a shocked look on her face and dashes over to where his mother is lifting the little girl to her feet.

"You're okay, Sarah," Marina soothes. "Look! No owies! You were just surprised, weren't you?" A mother Ryan doesn't know is leaning over his sister, too. Ryan thinks she looks worried the way his mom looks when she's really late to work and can't find her car keys.

"I'm so sorry," the woman says. "I don't know why, but my son just doesn't seem to understand that he can't run into people." Ryan follows the mom's glance to a nearby tree where a small curly-haired boy somewhat younger than himself is hopping from foot to foot, then springing up and down on both feet, then hopping again. Ryan correctly surmises the boy has been put in time-out for knocking Sarah down.

Marina concentrates on her daughter. She doesn't want to be judgmental, but she's annoyed: Sarah is barely half the boy's size and was standing in clear sight when the bigger child barreled into her.

"Some people say he has ADHD," the woman continues, "but I don't want him on medication and his doctor isn't convinced that's the problem anyway." She sighs. "I just don't know what to do."

The youngster is now trying to run up the tree. Ryan watches in fascination as the boy backs up, takes a running start, tries to charge straight up the tree without using his hands, then crashes to the ground with a loud *Ugh* and starts all over again. *Weirdo,* Ryan thinks. *That must hurt!* He's tempted to ask the mom why her son does this, but just then two girls move in the direction of the jet. He sprints after them, calling, "Wait up!" eager for playmates, even if they are girls.

"Wanna play airline pilot?" he says when he catches up. "I fly for United." He points to the logo on his shirt.

The girls consult each other with their eyes and then the taller of the two nods for both. "Sure! What do we do?"

"I'll be the pilot and one of you can be the copilot and the other one can be the engineer and then we can trade. Come on!" He zooms around the tall girl and races up the ladder, the smaller of the two girls at his heels.

"Come on!" the girl calls to her friend. "This will be fun."

"I'm coming!" the first girl replies, though she looks awkward as she crosses the sand toward the jet. "I'll be engineer first. You guys start the engines."

Ryan is explaining the throttle to his copilot when the tall girl reaches the bottom of the ladder. Neither Ryan nor his newfound playmate seem to notice how long it takes the other girl to position her feet on each rung of the ladder in order to climb up. By the time she reaches the top, the two pilots have decided to see how high they can fly on the swings and are scrambling out the other side of the cockpit, leaving the tall girl alone to work her way back to the ground without ever joining the game.

Marina has watched the scene from where she's gathering Sarah's sand toys for the trip home. She looks around and sees a man crossing toward the jet.

"You need a hand, sweetheart?" he asks, watching his daughter labor back down the ladder. The girl shakes her head, but Marina thinks she looks as if she might cry. Marina wonders if something's wrong with the girl, who appears to be quite a bit older than Ryan yet couldn't climb the ladder to join the airplane game.

Even though he's in an exciting environment after a full day at school, Ryan regulates his activity level at the park so that his

*behavior is appropriate, a contrast with the whirlwind of a
boy who first runs into little Sarah and then repeatedly con-
trives to crash by attempting to run up a tree. Ryan also
demonstrates healthy motor development when he zips across
the playground and scrambles in and out of the jet, which sets
him apart from the tall girl who can't move fast enough to join
in the airplane game. When he initiates contact with unfamiliar children, he exudes a self-confidence and social aptitude
that distinguish him from the silent boy who dribbles sand
through his fingers and doesn't reply to Ryan's overtures and
from the slight girl who never even reaches the playground because she's immobilized by her fear of stepping on sand.*

*You've probably guessed by now that the children Ryan en-
counters during the park outing all have sensory problems. The
human whirlwind is a sensory seeker and the tall older girl has
dyspraxia, a problem planning and performing activities that
require a series of movements. The boy who doesn't seem to notice Ryan's attempts to play is an under-responder, and the
wispy girl who's afraid to touch the sand is an over-responder.
Because of his typical development, Ryan arrives at the park
already ahead of these kids in his social, motor, and emotional
development. Then he is enriched further by the positive feedback and practice of successfully regulating his activity level,
moving with ease and dexterity, and effortlessly interacting
with other kids.*

*Although SPD is believed to affect an estimated twenty
million children (and that's a conservative estimate), it's not
likely that one playground would draw so many children with
the disorder on the same afternoon. I brought these kids together to help illustrate how typically developing children differ
from children with Sensory Processing Disorder and to provide
a glimpse at how SPD disrupts children's lives at the sensory,
motor, and emotional levels. Unless kids like the ones Ryan en-*

*counters in the park receive intervention, they are likely to fall
further and further behind typically developing kids.*

At home later that night, the Dosas enjoy Marina's spaghetti with
meat sauce and take turns telling about their day. Even Sarah participates in the nightly table talk, waving the flowers she made out of pipe
cleaners at day care and correctly identifying the color of each. After
dinner, Viktor does the dishes while Marina gives the children their
baths and washes their hair. Both of the youngsters look pleasantly
sleepy as all four family members crowd onto the sofa with Silky the
cat to watch a Disney video, their Friday night tradition.

It's been a long, busy day after the long, busy week. When the
movie is finished, Viktor reads *Goodnight, Moon* only once because it's
already past bedtime. Ryan calls his mom back to the bedroom with
a plea for one last sip of water but falls asleep before she gets there.
Marina sets the water glass on the nightstand in case Ryan wakes up
thirsty, then softly shuts the door and returns to the family room to
spend the rest of the evening relaxing with her husband.

> *The Dosas are a family that functions well. Nothing "big" is
> going on. They don't have to work at being at school or going to
> the park or eating dinner or watching a video or falling asleep.
> It all just happens. On Friday night, they are able to savor
> their family rituals and look forward to a recuperative week-
> end together. They don't need a plan or strategies to get through
> normal routines.*
>
> *The absence of crisis and the relatively seamless transition
> the family makes between activities is as natural for the Dosas
> as it is elusive for families with children who have SPD.
> Granted, children who are developing normally may still be
> finicky eaters, night owls who can't wake up in the morning,
> dreamers who don't hear classroom instructions because they're
> so engrossed in their own fantasies, or "Energizer Bunnies" who*

can't stand still in line. But typical children—even at the extremes of normal development—still feel good about themselves. They have friends and they work, play, and take care of themselves without much struggle. They are able to cope with transitions and unpredictable changes of schedule, adapting and self-regulating in many contexts. Their families are able to function without structuring and scheduling entirely around their children's sensory needs.

The children you'll meet in the next four chapters wake up and eat breakfast, go to school, to day care, or to the park, then return home to family, dinner, and bed—just as Ryan does. However, unlike Ryan, these children—LaTanya, Tam, Ben, and Abby—encounter sensory obstacles that make each step far more difficult.

LaTanya Brown is a slender kindergartner who lives with her parents, Tina and Martin, and her boisterous seven-year-old brother, Trey, in an urban row house. Because they were already veteran parents when LaTanya was born, the Browns spotted the red flags quickly when LaTanya responded hysterically to a wide variety of sensations. They began searching for an explanation while their daughter was still a baby, and at four LaTanya was correctly diagnosed with sensory over-responsivity. She attended six sessions of occupational therapy, the maximum the family's health insurance covered. LaTanya's parents continue to use the strategies they learned in OT with their daughter and occasionally schedule an appointment with the occupational therapist when LaTanya meets new challenges at different developmental stages.

Chapter 6

LaTanya, an Over-Responsive Kindergartner

At shortly after six A.M., the alarm clock that Tina and Martin Brown fondly call their "morning magic" begins its stealthy job of waking LaTanya. The clock's alarm is designed to start with a subtle, dawnlike light that brightens as slowly as a sunrise. Then aromatherapy scents release into the air. Next birds begin to chirp—just one or two at first and then a few more, until an entire chorus is singing cheerily. Finally, music starts to play softly, growing louder as gradually as the light and birdsong did. When the Browns discovered the clock they were almost giddy with relief. *At last!* they thought. *No more wake-up tantrums!* Until then, tears and fears were inevitable unless one parent spent a good ten or fifteen minutes at LaTanya's side, gently easing her from sleep the way the clock now does.

On this particular morning, however, the clock is only halfway through its reliable magic when a loud *BA-BOOM! Rat-a-tat-TAT!* slices through the soft sounds. In the next bedroom, seven-year-old Trey has slammed his door shut and is playing a lively drum roll on the back of it. The thumps bring LaTanya's sleep to an abrupt end. Her eyes fly open and her hands jerk to cover her ears. A wail of terror follows.

The girl's mother dashes into the room. "LaTanya," Tina croons, resisting the urge to brush her daughter's tears away. "It's okay." Tina firmly pulls the wailing girl into the close, hard embrace the occupational therapist recommended for moments when LaTanya's sensory alarms are clanging. "It was just Trey closing his door. Everything's okay." After LaTanya calms a little, Tina releases her daughter and raises her own hands, her palms toward the girl. "Push against my hands, honey. See if you can push Mama." This is an exercise LaTanya has done before. The little girl is still breathing unevenly, but she places her hands against her mother's palms and pushes. "That's right," Tina encourages her. "Push hard."

It takes a few minutes for LaTanya to relax, but she eventually wipes her tears, gulps, "I'm okay now," and drops her hands. Tina resists the temptation to give her daughter a reassuring kiss on the forehead. Experience has taught Tina and Martin that when their daughter is in a state of overarousal, the light touch of lips on her face has just the reverse effect: Instead of calming her, it agitates her. So Tina just gives LaTanya a final quick, firm hug and says, "Then up and at 'em, baby."

Before returning to dressing herself, Tina opens her son's door. "Trey!" she scolds. "You should know better than to make that racket when your sister's waking up. Hush now or we'll all be late and you'll miss the bus again."

LaTanya has a Sensory Modulation Disorder (SMD), which makes it hard for her to match the intensity of her responses to the intensity of the sensations she feels. LaTanya's SMD takes the form of sensory over-responsivity, which causes her to be more alert than most people. Even when she's asleep, LaTanya's "engine" is running too fast, the way a car's engine does when the idle is set too high. This causes sounds and other sensations to seem more intense to her than they would to a typically developing child. Even something as innocent as Trey slamming and drumming on his door jolts her into instant and complete alertness the way a big BOOM coming from the furnace room of the house would alarm you or me.

LaTanya reacts dramatically because she is frightened. Her heart is racing and she's starting to sweat. These physiological manifestations of fear are as old as life itself, defensive reactions that are genetically programmed into our systems to let us know when we are in danger. The trouble with LaTanya's system is that it cannot filter sensations in a way that would allow her to come up with an appropriate response. She alerts to Trey's noise-making even though there is no real danger. Once she discovers the real source—it's just her "bratty" big brother again—she's angry, fearful, and resentful. She hasn't been awake for five minutes, she's in the safest place she can possibly be—her own bed—and her sensory systems and emotions are already under assault.

Tina's strategy of calming her daughter with a firm hug followed by having LaTanya push against her hands demonstrates the use of two of the most effective sensory tools that therapists and parents have for soothing children with over-responsivity: deep pressure and proprioceptive stimulation. These tools utilize mechanical forces that are known to quiet the alarms tripped by over-responsivity.

Here's why they work: Perceived danger activates the parts of the brain responsible for arousal and emotions. Proprioceptive information (from the joints and muscles) and deep pressure (from the skin) travels to these areas, too, and can diminish the activity of the brain, overriding the danger signals. The effect is the one you may have experienced if you've ever taken a bite of ice cream so cold that it made your teeth hurt. The pain was a "danger" signal, but if you pressed your fingers hard against the throbbing area, you probably found the pain went away. That was because the deep pressure trumped the message of pain that the sense of cold was sending. This is the same result Tina is after with her hard hug and her pushing exercise. And it works: LaTanya calms down.

LaTanya swings her feet over the edge of the bed and carefully slips them into the tight ballet slippers that she meticulously positioned at her bedside the night before. Crossing to her closet, she chooses one of the ten well-worn cotton sweatsuits that hang from the rod and then moves to her dresser to select socks. She frowns as she eyes the selection and doesn't see her favorite pair. She tries a green pair but feels a seam on one toe that feels like a pebble against her foot. She pulls off the sock, her frown deepening. Next she tries a red sock and then a purple one, but none feels better than the green did. Giving up, she hurls a sock across the room and stomps back to the closet, her toes curled tight against the bottom of her feet in a protective reaction because she's so mad about the socks that she forgot to put her ballet slippers back on. Deciding she doesn't need stupid socks anyway, she sticks her feet into her sneakers and clomps off to the bathroom.

More trouble awaits here. Trey has already come and gone and the bathroom is a disaster—towels on the floor, the counter covered with nasty, sudsy soap, the top off the icky toothpaste, and the toilet seat wet because Trey didn't raise it. LaTanya tenses at the very sight of the disorder, but then goes to work putting everything in its place. She actually feels better as she cleans up because making the bathroom neat gives her a sense of bringing the crazy morning under control. It also enables her to avoid the personal hygiene chores that are uncomfortable for her—washing and drying her face, brushing her teeth, and running a pick through the tight curls in her hair.

The problem is that cleaning up takes time and now LaTanya is even more behind than she already was. She has heard her dad's car rumble down the driveway and that means she should be eating breakfast by now. Even though she knows her mother will be upset, the girl skips washing her face, gingerly gives her teeth a couple of swipes, doesn't bother with her hair, and heads for the kitchen. Only Trey is there, enthusiastically slurping his Raisin Bran and executing tabletop drumrolls with his spoon when he's not shoveling food into his mouth.

The morning so far has been one sensory assault after another for LaTanya. First, the big bang of Trey's slamming door sent her arousal level skyrocketing and her tolerance for frustration plummeting. Failing to find comfortable socks and inadvertently walking over the carpet with bare feet further depleted her reserves—and that all took place before she found Trey's mess in the bathroom. Although putting the bathroom in order was calming, it also ate up the time she needed for self-care chores. Throw Trey's gleeful drumming at the kitchen table into the mix and now we've got a child who feels the way many parents do after a long afternoon at Chuck E. Cheese—frantic for a minute's peace and quiet. LaTanya is a brave girl, but she's just about run through her daily supply of courage and perseverance. Because stress from sensory bombardment tends to be cumulative, she is already building toward an eventual meltdown.

The rest of the family is under stress, too. Because LaTanya's day has started off-kilter, the household's entire

morning rhythm is upset. Tina is harried and behind schedule,
LaTanya is on edge, and Trey spent several minutes fuming in
his room because he got scolded. Parents of children with sen-
sory over-responsivity tell me they feel they're constantly tiptoe-
ing through a minefield—always braced for the next event that
will trigger a crisis. A family like Ryan's, with its two typically
developing children, can have routines that allow everyone to
move efficiently and predictably through the morning. This
isn't possible for the Browns. Even on the days when no mines
are tripped, everyone is holding their breath in dread of the
one event that will set off an explosion.

"Be quiet!" LaTanya commands her brother. Trey grins and beats
the spoon harder. LaTanya covers her ears, but that means her hands
aren't free to make her breakfast. She uncovers one ear and uses the
freed hand to open the refrigerator. Her nose crinkles as a wave of food
smells assaults her; she closes the door quickly without taking anything
out. Just then Tina rushes into the kitchen, nervously checking
her watch.

"The bus will be at the corner in ten minutes. Did you guys eat
breakfast?" Trey nods enthusiastically and holds his near-empty bowl
above his head. LaTanya avoids her mother's eyes.

"LaTanya?" Tina peers into her daughter's face.

"I'm not hungry," the girl answers.

"But you need to eat." LaTanya's lack of interest in food is a
chronic concern for Tina and Martin. Although her height is in the
thirty-fifth percentile, their daughter's weight is just under the fifth.
The doctor says the fragile-looking girl needs to gain at least five
pounds before she turns six, but LaTanya rejects so many foods the
goal seems hopeless.

"I'm not hungry," LaTanya repeats. Tina wavers. She feels guilty
when she lets LaTanya go to school without eating, but she doesn't
have time for a battle. She's already been late to work eight times since

September after LaTanya had meltdowns that caused the children to miss the bus. Tina can't chance being late in order to drive them to school again, but the bus is due at the corner in moments.

"Okay, then. Trey, bowl to the sink. LaTanya, get your CD player. Time to go."

Watching the Browns get ready for the day, we see several more family dynamics common in homes where a child has SPD. One is the relationship between LaTanya and her brother, Trey, who is two years older. Trey is a typically developing, rough-and-tumble boy. He's physically active and needs to play. His social skills are well developed and he enjoys goofing around with other boys, the more actively and noisily the better. He definitely doesn't care what the bathroom looks like.

As normal and natural as all of this is, it makes Trey a poor match for oversensitive LaTanya. She is bothered by nearly everything her brother does. Because he's older, Trey knows he should be patient and take care of his sister, and he tries. But even if he can contain himself for a little while, it never seems to be enough to make the environment comfortable for LaTanya. Unless he's out of the house or the two siblings are widely separated, LaTanya is either disturbed by Trey's noise and boisterous behavior, or Trey is frustrated because his natural inclinations must be repressed. Sometimes the boy feels that all he ever hears from his mom and dad is "should should should" until the shoulds are coming out his ears. Resentment is setting in. Drumming on the kitchen table, which he knows drives his sister up the wall, is one of the subtle ways he's beginning to get back at her for the "shoulds" he hears and all the attention she gets. These sibling dynamics need to be addressed or the children are likely to grow up estranged and possibly even hostile to each other.

Another family dynamic is Tina's ever-ready sense of guilt. Tina is aware of the nutritional and social importance of

*mealtimes, especially for LaTanya, but she also needs to get the
kids to the bus and get herself to work. She doesn't push the
breakfast issue because everyone is already running late, yet she
feels guilty for not doing so. Self-doubt and guilt surrounding
food are common among parents of over-responsive children, in
whom nutritional deficiencies are widespread because food
aversions eliminate so many healthy options from their diets. In
severe cases, "Failure to Thrive" can develop as the child does
not take in enough nutrition to gain weight and grow. LaTanya
has not been diagnosed with "Failure to Thrive," but she is desperately thin and growing far more slowly than most children
her age, making food a chronic focus of attention and worry
for her parents.*

*Aside from the nutritional issues that her food aversions
create, her diminutive size and waif-like frailty make the little
girl look different from her peers. This only worsens the problems of social acceptance she's already having because her sensitivities cause her to seem odd to the other children. Aware as she
is of the ramifications of LaTanya's eating issues, Tina's sense of
guilt grows and grows. In fact, Tina always feels guilt about
something, including the sad truth that no matter how hard
they try, she and Martin can't save up enough money to pay for
more private OT sessions they know would make things better.*

At the bus stop, Trey gives his mother a kiss on the run and
plunges into the crowd, looking for his favorite seatmate. LaTanya
hovers at Tina's side, keeping a wary distance from the clump of talking and laughing children on the street corner. Tina helps her daughter secure headphones over her ears and finds the beginning of "My
Brain Is a Working Machine," her current favorite from the Wiggly
Scarecrow CD for kids with SPD.*

* See "Music" in Appendix A: Resources for Parents, Teachers, and Therapists.

As the bus rolls to a stop, the mom lifts one earphone to say, "Bye, baby. Have a great day," which prompts LaTanya to latch on to Tina's arm with a sudden ferocity. Tina gently extricates herself. "Uh-uh, LaTanya. We've both got jobs to do. I have to go to the bank, and you have to go to kindergarten and day care. I'll see you this afternoon."

LaTanya starts to sniffle but then stops herself, pressing her lips together in a visible show of determination. After all the other children have mounted the steps and moved far enough down the aisle that she can keep her distance, she waves a long good-bye to Tina and gets on the bus for the ride to school.

Transitions are difficult for many children with SPD, but they are especially difficult for children with over-responsivity because these children depend on predictability to hold their little worlds together. For a child like LaTanya, who is already experiencing sensation too intensely, the loss of predictability during times of change is problematic, even traumatic. She resists—an act of self-defense like the tight little ball the roly-poly bug rolls into when it's touched. If additional stress is present, her protective response grows stronger. LaTanya has learned to handle the daily shift to school fairly well, but because she has had a stressful morning, the transition of leaving her mother and entering the scary, unpredictable school bus is harder today. Other transitions this morning are likely to be more problematic as well.

This is another example of the cumulative effect seen in some children with SPD and especially in those with over-responsivity. A typically developing child gets a sensory message such as the big bang of Trey slamming his door, figures out the cause, and lets it go. In children with sensory-processing problems, this ability to let go of past messages sometimes appears to be impaired, leading to a "backlog" of sensation that accumulates until it overwhelms the child's coping skills. Think of a child like LaTanya as a busy office worker who has an in-

basket but no out-basket. She finishes an assignment but, even after it's done, the assignment sheet stays in the in-basket. Every time she completes another assignment, the in-basket gets fuller. Eventually she grows frustrated and finds it harder to complete new work because the pile of old work is growing precarious and she has to spend a lot of energy just making sure it doesn't spill. At last, there's one assignment too many. It doesn't even have to be an important assignment; it's just the proverbial "last straw" that brings down the whole mountain. It is believed that the cumulative effect of undisposed sensory messages is what causes children with SPD to eventually fall apart over triggering events that are minor.

LaTanya's CD player is one of the tools suggested to her parents during occupational therapy. By muffling sound and replacing the chaos of unpredictable outside noise with the comfort of familiar music, the headphones and CD soothe the girl's oversensitive auditory system and make noisy situations more tolerable. CD players are frequently found in the "toolboxes" of over-responsive children.

LaTanya has a long list of school activities she hates. Along with announcements on the horrid loudspeaker, deviations from the everyday schedule, and surprises like fire drills, riding the bus is near the top. As far as the oversensitive little girl is concerned, the bus contains too many kids making too much noise in too small a space, and she feels trapped. Tina has arranged her hours so she can pick up the children from day care and sometimes Martin drives them to school, but the parents haven't been able to eliminate the bus ordeal entirely.

This morning's ride is especially harrowing. LaTanya always tries to sit at the front of the bus because it minimizes her physical contact with the other kids, but today all the front seats are filled. As she makes her way down the aisle, she holds her arms tight against her body, trying to make her tiny self even smaller to avoid grazing any-

one. She almost succeeds, but just as she spots an open seat, an older
boy interferes. He's learned he can make LaTanya cry just by touching her, and he reaches out to run his fingers, spiderlike, down
her arm.

"*Don't!*" LaTanya yelps, stumbling as she pulls away.

"*Don't!*" the boy mimics, twiddling his fingers near her face.
"*Baby!*" He hisses, reaching out to touch her again.

"*Don't!*" LaTanya wails, pitching down the aisle toward an available seat, her stoicism fast evaporating. Feeling shaky, she carefully
seats herself as far from her seatmate as possible. When the bus finally
rocks away from the curb and heads down the street, she closes her
eyes, concentrates on the music in her headphones, and tries to block
out all other sensation.

But her trials aren't over. The scream of an approaching fire engine suddenly punctures her fragile cocoon. LaTanya makes a frantic
effort to shut out the noise by clamping her hands over the headphones and pushing the pads hard against her ears, but the cumulative effect of the morning's sensory battering has finally caught up with
her. She crumples against the seat, sobbing.

The driver has pulled the bus to the curb to let the fire truck pass,
and he recognizes the cries even before he checks his mirror to locate
the source. When he spots LaTanya, he sighs. All the other drivers
agree that LaTanya Brown makes this route one of the most difficult
because the girl gets almost hysterical over things the other children
don't even notice. The driver turns to a quiet older boy sitting immediately behind him.

"Duwayne, would you do me a favor and go tell LaTanya she can
have your seat? She seems to be having another one of her days."

Shifting to the front seat where she sees only the driver in front
of her and knows she will be able to escape as soon as the bus comes
to a stop helps LaTanya pull herself together sufficiently to get through
the rest of the ride. All the same, she reaches school feeling as if she's
been under attack from the minute Trey woke her up. She quickly de-

scends the steps and heads straight for the library, her head bowed low so she can shut out the sight of all the random movement going on around her.

La Tanya's ordeal on the bus ride to school illustrates the potential for using A SECRET. La Tanya is able to ride to school peacefully in the family car with one of her parents, but the bus environment introduces sounds and physical contact that alarm her sensitivities and make it hard for her to function. Changing the environment to create a better fit with La Tanya's sensory issues would make getting to school less problematic for her and would set up her school day for success.

Arranging to drive their daughter to school every day would be a dramatic environmental change the Browns could make to help La Tanya, but such modifications are not always feasible. Less dramatic but still significant would be joining a car pool that allowed La Tanya to ride to school with fewer children. However, even relatively minor environmental changes could help. For example, if the bus driver saved the front seat for La Tanya every day, the sensory input the girl had to process on the bus ride would be reduced and she would reach school feeling less bombarded. Everyone would win: The driver would make the trip with fewer distracting outbursts, and the bully who makes La Tanya cry would lose a victim. Let's face it: There will always be at least one child in the crowd who enjoys making another child cry. Reducing the opportunity would be good for both the bully and La Tanya.

If La Tanya needed a wheelchair or had another physical limitation that made it hard for her to function on the bus, transportation accommodations like an assigned seat would have been made for her long ago. However, because her handicap is invisible, accommodations are made on a spot basis and only after she falls apart, which just confirms everyone's opin-

ion that this is a kid with big problems. Changing the bus environment would eliminate one of the situations most likely to feed that stereotype.

Manipulating other SECRET elements could help, too. The Browns have already adjusted LaTanya's attention by supplying her with earphones and CDs. Giving her a task to perform during the ride (e.g., drawing on an Etch-A-Sketch) or supplying a relationship (e.g., an assigned seatmate who was also a quiet child) are other possibilities.

One aspect of riding to school that would remain problematic is the element of the unexpected—the screaming siren today, a backfire tomorrow, a screech of car brakes the next day. Because LaTanya is over-responsive to sound, chances are good that the siren would still bother her even if everything else in the environment was ideal. However, if other stressful aspects of the environment were reduced, she would probably cope with surprises better and calm herself more effectively.

The library is LaTanya's safe place, a refuge negotiated with the school by her OT and her parents. Earlier in the year, when LaTanya was forced to spend the minutes before class on the chaotic playground, her overstimulated sensory systems never calmed sufficiently before school started for her to focus on classroom activities. Now she goes directly from the bus to the library, where she colors or looks at picture books until the halls are nearly empty. At the last possible moment, the librarian sends her to class, always loaded with a heavy stack of books for the girl's teacher. LaTanya likes being the last one to class every day and she likes the librarian. When she thinks about her future, she thinks she might like to work in a library someday.

In the classroom, the other children are already seated on their bright-colored carpet squares when she reaches the room. This eliminates the likelihood of being jostled in the rush to sit down and minimizes the other unpredictable sensations that arise when LaTanya is in a crowd. Better yet, bringing the library books to the teacher feels like an important job and makes the girl feel good in ways she can't describe.

> LaTanya arrives at school exhausted but is able to function somewhat because she is smart and has loving and supportive parents who are working diligently to make the world more tolerable for her.
>
> One of Tina and Martin's most significant efforts has been working with school officials to implement strategies to improve their daughter's school success. LaTanya would not qualify for services in every school system, but the Browns moved into their current district because of its excellent record for providing services for "at risk" children. The school worked with them to develop an Individualized Educational Plan (IEP) stating that LaTanya has sensory problems causing her to have behavioral issues that hurt her academic performance. The plan contains specific objectives ("IEP goals"), and one of these is to calm her overreactivity so she can pay attention in class.
>
> The daily before-school time in the library is part of the plan and another illustration of how adjusting the elements of context can help kids with SPD. The library is a predictable, quiet environment—a perfect place for lowering the level of arousal LaTanya feels by the time she reaches school. The minutes she spends there are pivotal for calming her overalert sensory systems and recharging her batteries for the big challenge of the classroom. The librarian, who participated in the meeting to create LaTanya's educational plan, provides a welcoming and supportive relationship, which has made her the girl's favorite adult on campus.
>
> LaTanya's assignment to carry a stack of books to class is

an example of how a task can be used to change behavior. In occupational therapy, this kind of job is known as "heavy work," a term applied to any activity that engages the muscles and joints of the proprioceptive system. As explained earlier, stimulating proprioception can generate calming messages to the brain.* Tasks that engage more or bigger muscles generally create greater proprioceptive stimulation and have the biggest effect on behavior.

Giving LaTanya more books to carry—or having her walk farther with them or carry them upstairs—would soothe her even more than the current assignment. However, carrying even one heavy stack of books down a short hall engages LaTanya's muscles and puts pressure on her skin, replicating the soothing activity Tina provided earlier with a hard hug and the pushing game. In therapy, children are taught to recognize when they need heavy work and to generate it for themselves with activities such as pushing against a wall or another resistant surface, pulling a heavy load like a wagon with another child as a passenger, or walking up flights of stairs.

Heavy work tends to lower arousal levels and reduce cumulative effect so that the child is prepared for the next sensory surprise. If someone brushed against her while LaTanya was carrying the books to her classroom, she would react less violently than if she hadn't enjoyed the quiet time in the library and received the proprioceptive benefits of carrying the books. Heavy work for LaTanya is the equivalent of finding the volume button on the background noise that is always buzzing in her sensory systems and turning it down.

---

* Proprioception can also be alerting, depending upon how it's used.

"Heavy Work" for Modern Children

Interjecting heavy work into the lives of today's children can be a challenge. In "the olden days," heavy work just happened. Children living in rural areas often worked alongside adults at physically demanding chores. In the city, they played long and hard in their neighborhoods and walked or biked to school.

Today, it is often necessary to "invent" heavy work the way the book-carrying chore was invented for LaTanya. We are no longer an agrarian society; few children pitch hay or milk cows. Even in relatively safe neighborhoods such as LaTanya's, children don't ride bikes or play street games because of safety concerns or because their parents work and the children are at day care or in organized activities after school. At school, much of the playground equipment and many of the games that once offered heavy work opportunities—jungle gyms, monkey bars, merry-go-rounds that were started with a running push—are gone for a host of reasons. Physical education classes are popular targets of school budget cuts. Even children who play sports are likely to be driven to and from the sports activity and then spend much of practice waiting their turn and much of the games sitting on the bench. Not much heavy work there!

As a result, children today work hard cognitively and socially but aren't working physically. When they are developing typically like Ryan, they are motivated to seek a variety of sensory experiences that includes proprioceptive and vestibular stimulation. Ryan frequently proposes wrestling matches with his stepdad and feels relaxed when they're done. That's because when he leans all his weight into Viktor's trunk or tries his best to collapse Viktor's legs or puts all his strength into pulling his stepdad to the ground, he's doing heavy work. Heavy work is one of the most important components of a complete and healthy sensory diet. By wrestling with

Viktor, Ryan is successfully satisfying his proprioceptive appetite just the way you or I do if we take a jog around the neighborhood or spend a long day working in the garden.

Everyone needs a complete sensory diet. Proprioception is the hardest "daily dietary requirement" for any child to get in an increasingly sedentary world and is especially hard for children with SPD. Those who have sensory over-responsivity tend to avoid heavy work because their sensitivities make proprioceptive activity uncomfortable. This deprives them of a natural means of soothing themselves. All children benefit from their parents and other adults creating heavy work opportunities for them; for children like LaTanya, such invention is essential.

By mid-morning, LaTanya has almost recovered from the unpleasant surprises the early morning held. She is a bright girl and there are stretches of the school day that she enjoys. A precocious reader, she excels at alphabet games and loves the quiet story time when everyone sits very still and listens to the soft, steady voice of the teacher reading a tale. As long as nothing unexpected happens to set off her sensory alarms, she sometimes feels quite content.

Today's unexpected event is a special guest—a local sculptor with long gray hair tied in a ponytail bearing a boxful of clay balls that two children are assigned to pass out to the students. When Miss Sorensen introduces the visitor and explains that he'll be teaching them to shape clay into mugs for their moms and dads, LaTanya tentatively raises her hand.

"LaTanya?"

"But what about *Stuart Little*?" the girl asks. "This is when you read *Stuart Little*."

"Yes, it is, LaTanya. But today Mr. Washington is our very special guest so we're going to save Stuart for tomorrow."

LaTanya sticks out her lower lip. "But I don't *want* to save Stuart for tomorrow!" she grumbles. "This is when we're *supposed* to read *Stuart Little*!" The other children stare and Miss Sorensen is embarrassed.

"This is not a choice," the teacher says in a slightly annoyed voice. "This is what we're doing today."

Something unexpected is always happening at school. Field trips, substitute teachers, fire drills, assemblies, room mothers, birthday parties, special events, and other deviations from routine are common. For most children, these are special times. For LaTanya, the lack of routine is always a threat because she knows that some unknown sensory challenge might be lurking in it.

One of the strategies that would help LaTanya cope with surprises would be informing her ahead of time about upcoming changes in her routine. For example, if Miss Sorensen had warned her at the end of the previous school day about the guest sculptor, his appearance would no longer have been unexpected. LaTanya could have called upon her cognitive powers to overcome the discomfort she felt at finding the familiar story period replaced by a stranger.

Miss Sorensen has been briefed on LaTanya's disorder and she helped to develop the child's educational plan. Nonetheless, the teacher is beginning to view LaTanya as a disciplinary problem because of behaviors provoked by her sensitivities. Miss Sorensen is a fine teacher, but teachers have individual styles and temperaments. Miss Sorensen tends to be inflexible, which makes her less than a perfect fit for LaTanya. The relationship between children and their teachers is one of those SECRET elements that can significantly influence a child's context and success within it. LaTanya is doing okay with Miss Sorensen,

but a more empathetic, open teacher might enable her to do
better. Matching sensational children with specific teachers is
one of the functions school OTs often perform.

The special guest ends his presentation just before recess. The
other children carry their freshly sculpted mugs to their cubbyholes
to dry and then line up to go outside, but LaTanya continues sitting
at her table, the ball of clay untouched in front of her.

"LaTanya," Miss Sorensen calls. "It's time for recess. Put the clay
in your cubby and come line up."

When the teacher isn't looking, LaTanya uses a paper towel to gingerly pick up the clay—which she didn't shape because it felt so icky—
and deposit it in the wastebasket. She knows she'll be in trouble if Miss
Sorensen sees what she's done, but there's no way she's letting that
awful stuff in her nice clean cubby.

As she did at the bus stop, LaTanya hangs back while her classmates elbow for position in line. LaTanya hates the transition to recess because it forces her out of the relatively predictable classroom and
onto the playground, where balls pop into the air without warning,
children bump into each other with squeals and shouts, and the sand
gets into her shoes or on her clothes, where it will irritate her for the
rest of the day. As far as LaTanya is concerned, kindergarten would
be much better if it didn't have recess at all.

When Miss Sorensen opens the door, the other children burst
outside, relieved and impatient to spend their pent-up energy. LaTanya
drifts to the farthest edge of the play area, where a sprawling tree
stands. While the other children organize themselves into games or
play on the equipment, she slips behind the trunk and pretends to examine the tree bark. This is how she spends nearly every recess. Miss
Sorensen has told the Browns about LaTanya's withdrawal, but so far
they haven't come up with a way to entice her away from her hide-
away. Tina and Martin fret that their daughter will never have friends.
Miss Sorensen doesn't say so, but she thinks the real problem with the

girl is that her parents aren't strict enough and fail to make LaTanya do what she should.

> LaTanya's behavior at recess is an adaptive "flight" reaction. "Fight/freeze" responses are protective behaviors familiar from the animal kingdom. Black bears generally run away when surprised (flight), while grizzly bears attack (fight). When faced with an enemy, opossums play dead (freeze), while cats arch and hiss (fight). These are ancient teleological reflexes that developed as a defense against danger.
>
> Humans typically use reason to override reflexive behavior—thinking through situations in order to avoid getting to the "fight/flight" mode unnecessarily. The problem for LaTanya is that her "flight" response occurs so fast that she doesn't have time to cancel it out with reason. As a result, she flees situations that aren't really dangerous. Withdrawing on the playground is an example of this over-responsive flight reaction, but flight can take more subtle forms. Aloofness or shrugging away from touch can be forms of flight, as can reluctance to try new activities, crying, and whining in response to sensory stimulation.
>
> "Fight," too, can manifest in behaviors that range from dramatic to subtle. A parent once told me about her over-responsive son turning on his best friend and biting him because the buddy gave him an unexpected hug. When she asked her son why he did it, the boy said, "I don't know, Mom. It just came out." A more subtle form of fight would be calling a classmate a name.
>
> Most children with sensory over-responsivity have a dominant protective style. LaTanya's style is to flee; she does it reflexively, the way you or I pull our hands away from scalding water. In the same situations, another over-responsive child might become aggressive, or simply freeze.

With the dreaded bus ride and recess finally behind her, the second half of the morning is usually the best part of LaTanya's school day, a time when she can relax her sensory vigilance and focus better on classroom activities. She is typically the first to finish each day's arithmetic worksheets, and she always looks forward to reading.

Although sounds from inside and outside the classroom pose a constant risk to her sense of calm, nothing happens to puncture it today. Better yet, the second half of the morning means that day care begins soon—something LaTanya genuinely looks forward to. When the bell rings to signal the end of school, she is impatient for the other children to finish gathering their things so she can get hers and leave.

LaTanya's day care provider, Sue, is waiting at the curb when LaTanya emerges from the school building. Sue waves and LaTanya happily scampers to join her. The Browns spent many weeks interviewing day care providers willing to work with their daughter's sensory issues and they consider Sue to be a real find.

> *LaTanya's day care arrangement is another illustration of the effective use of A SECRET. Once LaTanya had been assessed and diagnosed with sensory over-responsivity, the Browns understood why the environments of the extended day care centers and family day care homes they had tried were so traumatic for their daughter. They resolved to find a caregiver willing to limit the environment to two children—LaTanya and Trey.*
>
> *The Browns interviewed twenty-five people before meeting Sue, and they pay a premium for the relationship she provides their children. A new mom who stays at home with her six-month-old daughter, Sue is eager to learn about LaTanya's disorder and try strategies suggested by LaTanya's OT. She doesn't mind taking extra time to prepare and serve foods that won't set off LaTanya's sensory alarms, and she understands LaTanya's need to chill out and organize herself with quiet activities like watching TV when she arrives after school.*

Within walking distance of Sue's house is a park with climbable animal-shaped statues but none of the movable equipment the youngster finds so upsetting. Sue takes the children there nearly every day, making sure LaTanya gets some heavy work on the way by helping to push the stroller. The new mom is delighted that her baby has a "big sister," and the baby wriggles with delight when LaTanya shows up. The interaction with the baby pays dividends for LaTanya, who feels good about being the competent "big girl" for a change. What's more, when the baby sends sensory signals that otherwise might be problematic for LaTanya—shrieking or spitting up, for example—the kindergartner is able to call on her emotional attachment to the infant and her reasoning abilities to override her sensory alarms. This is good practice for her.

It's already dark by the time Tina gets off work and reaches Sue's house, where Trey joined his sister once his after-school soccer program was over. Though he enjoys Sue's almost as much as LaTanya does, both children are ready to go home.

"Okay, kids," Tina says as she noses the car into a parking space at the supermarket on the way home. "I bet we can do this in ten minutes. Trey, you be the official timer. LaTanya, you be my assistant and remind me where to find the things on the list." Trey loves the timing game that Tina uses to make errands endurable. He punches the button on his seat belt, eager to get started, but LaTanya has shrunk into her seat and is cupping her hands over her nose.

"*No!*" she wails. "I *won't* go in. It *stinks* in there!"

"No, it doesn't, baby. Grocery stores have giant odor eaters to make sure they don't smell."

"Their odor eaters don't *work!* Grocery stores make me *sick!*"

Tina checks her watch. With enough time, she could use A SECRET to work through LaTanya's resistance, but it's getting late. There are still dinner, baths, and bedtime to get through, and it's already nearly six o'clock. She tries another strategy. "You'll be a very sad little girl if we don't have vanilla yogurt for your breakfast tomorrow," she says, "and we're all out. Trey's Raisin Bran is gone, too."

"*I . . . don't . . . care . . . about . . . vanilla . . . yogurt . . . or . . . Raisin . . . Bran!*" Each word erupts from LaTanya in a short, loud burst. In the next parking space, a woman unlocking her door peers into Tina's car. "Okay." Tina surrenders with a sigh. "We'll go home and Daddy can run out for food later."

"But I want to go in the store and play the game!" Trey protests as his mother turns the key in the ignition.

"Sorry, sweetie," Tina says, feeling the familiar surge of guilt that comes whenever she lets LaTanya's complicated aversions override Trey's simple desires. "Mommy can't leave you guys alone in the car. We all go or nobody goes." LaTanya sinks farther into her seat, a tense frown on her face. Trey glares at her.

Sensory over-responsivity can manifest in one or more sensory systems. The ones in which LaTanya is primarily affected are sound (auditory), touch (tactile), taste (gustatory), and smell (olfactory).

Olfaction, the sense of smell, is the oldest and most primitive sensory system humans have, the one our ancestors used first as an early warning system for danger. Unlike sight, sound, and other sensory messages that are processed and modified with multiple connections on their way to the brain's highest level, smells reach a primitive part of the brain's cortex directly through a system that is closely linked to emotion. When an odor is detected, we reflexively evaluate whether the smell is positive or negative based on previous experience and respond both emotionally and behaviorally to that evaluation. The aroma of baking cookies, for instance, registers positively and unconsciously as "smells good" and draws us to the kitchen.

A whiff of rotten eggs registers as "smells bad" and triggers withdrawal.

LaTanya's resistance to entering the supermarket is another example of her flight reaction. Her overly sensitive olfactory senses cause smells that other people find inoffensive or even pleasing—wintergreen, citrus, and mint are typical examples— to set off alarms. When we monitor children with olfactory over-responsivity in our research laboratory, we see this reaction on a physiological level. Something as benign as milk can trigger sweating, an increase in heart rate, shallow breathing, and other physiological reactions that are normally seen in the presence of a real danger, such as a snarling dog.

As automatic as her response may be, it is nonetheless hurting LaTanya's relationships and limiting her daily life. A potentially harmonious family outing becomes a moment of frustration, calculation, and manipulation that interferes with Tina's legitimate need to buy food and adds fuel to the fire of Trey's resentment.

At home an hour later, Martin rushes into the house just in time to take over the nightly task of coaxing LaTanya to the table. When she was a newborn, LaTanya nursed happily but later resisted the move to solid foods and often gagged on them. By the time she was two, her oversensitive gag reflex made vomiting at the dinner table a common, if unpredictable, mealtime event. The dinner hour became one more minefield where LaTanya might erupt at any time in anger, despair, or frustration. Mealtime issues were one of the red flags that drove the Browns to seek an explanation for their daughter's behaviors.

The occupational therapist was helpful in providing techniques for banishing the dinnertime blues, and Tina has found additional ones in an online support group for families of children with SPD. She called Martin before he left the office to recruit his help in trying out a new tactic she had read about in the chat room.

"Hey, kids," he calls. "You want a treat?"

Trey races to the kitchen and throws his arms around his dad's waist, but LaTanya edges into the room, sniffing suspiciously. When she finds that her mom has turned on the fan to disperse the cooking odors, she relaxes enough to look around. "What treat?" she asks.

Martin holds up a jar and a pair of straws. "Applesauce appetizers," he says. "But you only get one if you can eat it through a straw."

"I can do that!" Trey shouts.

LaTanya scrunches her nose. "Nobody eats applesauce through a straw."

"I bet you can. In fact, if you can eat half of this through the straw, maybe your mom will let you try it another night with vanilla pudding."

"Pudding? *Before* dinner?"

He glances toward Tina, who nods.

LaTanya stirs the applesauce with the straw. It's the smooth kind, one of the few foods she genuinely likes. She puts the straw between her lips and takes a tentative pull, followed by a harder one. Her eyes cross as she watches the sauce rise through the straw, and so do Trey's. They all laugh.

> *The dinner hour is a time when the stresses of each family member's individual daytime experiences collide with hunger to create one of the toughest times of the day for any family. Common struggles are compounded for LaTanya and her family by issues directly related to the smell, taste, and texture of food. Although LaTanya has benefited from her six sessions of OT, the touch of an ordinary item like ground meat still feels repulsive to her and is interpreted as a threat. Spices are intolerable—even a sprinkle of pepper will end her meal. Food temperature is another issue. LaTanya frequently complains*

*that her food is either "too hot" or "too cold," even when the
rest of the family finds it perfectly acceptable. New foods are especially suspect, triggering unconscious fears that they will
"hurt" her. LaTanya would never look forward to surprises like
the sweet pickles and figs that delighted Ryan, the typically developing boy.*

*When the weather is good, Martin often takes LaTanya
outside to rake leaves or work in the garden with him after he
gets home because these heavy work activities calm some of his
daughter's food sensitivities. Sucking applesauce through a
straw is an indoor variation on the same heavy work theme.*

Tina is filling the plates. On LaTanya's, she places chicken breast
cut into small, manageable bites, a handful of green beans, and a large
serving of mashed potatoes. Because LaTanya refuses to eat different
foods if they're touching, Tina uses a picnic plate with compartments.
She doesn't bother putting salad on the plate because the girl absolutely refuses to touch it. *"Too messy!"* she says.

Once the family is seated, Trey digs in with his usual gusto, clown-
ing around as he alternates bites between his fork in one hand and the
spoon in the other. In her booster seat next to him, LaTanya uses her
fork to arrange the green beans in a perfect row down the center of
one compartment, taking care not to touch them with her fingers. She
takes a few bites of chicken but works her way steadily through the
potatoes. As she swallows each bite, she tips her chair onto its back
legs, a common dinnertime habit. Martin and Tina exchange glances
but don't order their daughter to stop.

*LaTanya's organization of the green beans and insistence that
her foods don't touch are ritualistic behaviors common among
children with eating sensitivities. Unable to screen or filter sensory information from her environment, LaTanya feels threat-
ened at a primal level. Organizing her world in a compulsive*

*and reliable manner—by lining up green beans, for exam-
ple—is her way of fighting back. Parents sometimes see perfectionist behaviors and worry that their children suffer from a
serious psychiatric condition such as Obsessive-Compulsive
Disorder. In LaTanya's case, these worries are unwarranted.
Her sensory over-responsivity entirely accounts for her irra-
tional food rituals.*

*Tipping and banging her chair is another coping mecha-
nism, and it makes LaTanya feel better for the same reason
pressing against her mother's hands and carrying the library
books did that morning. Although she's not generating sufficient proprioceptive stimulation to override her oral sensitivities, she's on the right track. That's why Tina and Martin don't
interfere, even though the thumping is mildly annoying. Tina
introduced a new food tonight—real mashed potatoes—and
knows this may have heightened the anxiety LaTanya always
feels around food. The impact of the chair hitting the floor obviously comforts the girl, and her parents have decided the noise
is a small price to pay for a relatively peaceful meal.*

*It is easy for families to let dinner table tensions set the tone
for meals, but this is another area where occupational therapy
helped the Browns find strategies to address LaTanya's sensitivities and to reduce the number of outbursts that once domi-
nated the family meal. The compartmentalized plate and the
allowance for chair-banging are two such examples. LaTanya
still has food issues to resolve, and they will represent a potential trouble spot when she reaches first grade, where she will
have to eat lunch around other children instead of in the safety
of Sue's cozy day care home. Additionally, Tina and Martin
know they shouldn't hover over their daughter, urging her to
eat more or eat better, but their concern for LaTanya's low
weight often undermines their good intentions. This is an area*

the parents will have to work on. Negative associations with food can lead to eating disorders when children with food over-sensitivities move into adolescence.

After dinner, LaTanya carries the dishes to the kitchen, another form of heavy work built into the family routine to help avoid end-of-the-day meltdowns. While Trey helps his dad fill the dishwasher, Tina sets up the small plastic tub she uses to give LaTanya her bath.

Bathing used to be a nightly ordeal. LaTanya found the bathtub too cold and too hard; showers, with their cascading water, were impossible. Night-long battles filled with promises and threats were common, and for one entire year Martin and Tina resigned themselves to bathing LaTanya only once a week—on Saturdays, when everyone had the whole day free to get through it. One bath, one battle.

The occupational therapist was the one who suggested that a plastic tub might sufficiently reduce the sensory stimulation of bathing for LaTanya to wash more comfortably. The Browns came up with further adjustments to the bathing atmosphere to soothe LaTanya's sensory alertness—turning the lights down and playing soothing music—and now she doesn't mind her bath as long as her hair doesn't have to be washed. Hair-washing, with all the accompanying sensations of water on her sensitive scalp and running into her ears and getting on her face, is still problematic.

After LaTanya's bath, Tina carries her daughter to the bathroom and watches while the girl brushes her teeth, another "icky" task. The goal is for LaTanya to brush for the full minute that the electric toothbrush automatically rotates. As usual, she doesn't make it to a minute, but she gets closer than usual. Tina wonders if sucking applesauce is still having an effect on calming her daughter's usually sensitive mouth.

Martin is the family storyteller, and LaTanya considers their bedtime story rituals the very best time of the day. Her dad has an ample lap and she feels warm and safe when she sinks into it, hugging her worn-out stuffed rabbit "Pinky" while wrapped in a tattered old baby blanket she calls "boo-boo." She's yawning after three stories, when her father carries her to bed. The tired girl is burrowing happily under the sheets when she freezes, suddenly alerted that something is terribly wrong. Throwing off the covers, she springs out of bed, only to be further alarmed by the loopy carpet under her bare feet.

"Daddddeeeeeeee!" she wails. "Something's *wrong* with my bed!" Martin is frantically searching for the problem when Tina sticks her head into the bedroom. It's been more than fifteen hours since Tina's day started, and the mother looks tired.

"There's nothing wrong with the bed, Martin," she sighs. "I changed the sheets. I thought she was too tired to notice."

"I *hate* clean sheets!" LaTanya is jumping up and down uncontrollably. *"Take them off!"*

Tina shakes her head. "It's too late to change your bed, Tanya. Besides, you know you have to sleep on clean sheets one night to make them dirty sheets. By tomorrow night, they'll be perfect."

LaTanya is now sobbing and jumping up and down hysterically. Martin picks up his daughter and sits on the bed, folding her into a hard embrace the way Tina did at the beginning of the day. It takes much longer to soothe her than it did in the morning, and she has to be changed into long-sleeved, long-legged winter pajamas that will minimize her contact with the crisp sheets. Eventually, the exhausted little girl drops into a fitful sleep, but not long after Martin and Tina finally get to sleep themselves, she wakes up, howling about the sheets again, which requires her parents to repeat the entire routine of hugging and soothing. The scenario occurs twice more before dawn, and nobody gets much rest.

When their alarm clock goes off too few hours later, Tina groans. "Next time I change the beds, Martin, remind me to skip LaTanya's." He gives her a big hug—nearly everyone can use some deep pressure now and then—and another day begins.

Although LaTanya's day and night were not as smooth as Ryan's, it's important to recognize that the little girl and her family have made notable progress in reducing the size of the minefield since their short course of occupational therapy.

Some routines, like LaTanya waking up peacefully to the "morning magic" clock, are taking root. Although today got off to a rough start because of the unexpected "wake-up call" from Trey, the disruption didn't end with LaTanya getting emotionally "stuck." She didn't disintegrate at the sight of the disorderly bathroom and she admirably squelched the temptation to retaliate when her brother drummed with his spoon during breakfast.

At the bus stop, LaTanya did cling momentarily to her mother, but she didn't fall apart or plunk herself onto the sidewalk and refuse to move, which would have been classic flight reactions. Like Ryan, she did what she had to do, saying goodbye without tears and getting on the bus. The siren was an unforeseeable event that finally punctured her fragile self-control, but there were other unforeseeable sensations she did overcome and routines she kept during the day. She got through the unexpected guest in her classroom without a tantrum, completed her classroom work, and enjoyed her afternoon at Sue's.

Though the grocery store outing was unsuccessful, dinner was a minor triumph. Tina has been trying to introduce a little more texture into her daughter's food in hopes of easing LaTanya toward a more complete, diverse diet. Substituting real mashed potatoes for instant ones is a step in that direction. Before treatment, LaTanya's vigilance would have alerted her to the new food texture instantly, but if she noticed the change tonight, she didn't show any signs of it. Another mine was evaded. And then she brushed her teeth for nearly a full minute, a rare achievement.

There are still significant areas where LaTanya's sensory

*challenges get the best of her. Among the most important is so-
cial participation. If she continues to be isolated, she'll develop
problems with self-esteem and self-confidence. La Tanya's tense
relationship with Trey is another concern.*

*Nonetheless, the whole Brown family could benefit from re-
assurance that they're doing a good job and making progress.
Because eruptions continue in their daily life, it's often hard for
families like this one to notice the successes and celebrate improvements. Reminding themselves of how much progress has
been made—and being reminded by family, friends, teachers,
and others—will give them the energy they need to strive
for more.*

A SECRET for Your Child with Sensory Over-Responsivity*

Sensational strategies that may improve a child's functioning can be
developed by any parent. Strategies emerge when each element of A
SECRET is examined and one or more elements is modified to improve the "fit" between the over-responsive child's personal characteristics and the world around him. The following chart illustrates
how to use this flexible approach to examine the last three elements
of A SECRET—Relationships, Environments, and Tasks. These are
the elements most readily modified by parents.

---

* A clinical diagnosis of sensory over-responsivity can be made only with a comprehensive
diagnostic evaluation. Sensational strategies are most effective when developed as part of a
comprehensive intervention program provided by an OT or another professional with training in treating Sensory Processing Disorder.

A SECRET for Your Child with Sensory Over-Responsivity

A SECRET for Relationships

Modify RELATIONSHIPS so your child will be calm enough to participate.

Ask questions such as . . .

- What is it that makes some relationships easier for my child? More difficult?
- How can I maximize the qualities that make relationships easier and avoid the ones that make them harder?
- Does my child have difficulties with any siblings or other family members? How can I minimize those difficulties?
- How can I help others understand and accept the way my child's sensory sensitivities affect relationships?
- What are the barriers to my child's social participation and how can I overcome, minimize, and/or compensate for them?

Devise strategies for home such as . . .

- **Peers**: identify potential playmates who are less tactile, noisy, and physical; be proactive about setting playdates with selected children.
- **Siblings**: teach siblings to respect your child's sensory sensitivities and boundaries.

Strategies for school such as . . .

- **Understanding**: develop a script and use it to explain your child's sensitivities and resulting behaviors to school personnel, including teachers, aides, administrators, bus drivers, and cafeteria workers.

Strategies for community such as . . .

- **Understanding**: develop a script and use it to explain your child's sensitivities to extended family, neighbors, service providers, and parents of playmates (see sample letter in Appendix H).

Sensory Over-Responsivity—Relationships (*continued*)

Devise strategies for home such as . . .	Strategies for school such as . . .	Strategies for community such as . . .
• **Tactile**: express and encourage others to express affection to your child in ways that are not alarming, e.g., verbally rather than physically; avoid crowding or jostling. • **Auditory**: use and encourage others to use quiet voices and to avoid loud and unexpected sounds around your child; provide devices to filter out background noise, e.g., headphones, white noise machines. • **Visual**: avoid and encourage others to avoid "surprising" your child visually, e.g., by turning lights on and off unexpectedly or using flash photography; allow your child to wear light-cutting visors, hats, or sunglasses, even indoors. • **Olfactory**: avoid and encourage others to avoid wearing perfumes, strong aftershave, body lotions, or other scents around your child. • **Gustatory**: don't allow others to pressure your child into eating foods that make her uncomfortable.	• **Support network**: identify supportive personnel at the school whom your child can seek out in times of stress. • **Curriculum**: seek to minimize the number of teachers your child sees each day; if possible, seek a two-year assignment to the same teacher. • **Teacher assignment**: request teachers who are more predictable than spontaneous and who relate with language instead of touch.	• **Preparation**: prepare extended family members, friends, and others for the symptoms and management of your child's sensory overload at birthday parties, holiday events, extended family gatherings, and on other special occasions. • **Services**: identify and patronize barbers/hairdressers, dentists/physicians, coaches/instructors, and other service providers willing to learn about and accommodate your child's sensory sensitivities. • **Support**: arrange for your child to be accompanied by an understanding companion to any activity that takes place in an unfamiliar or unpredictable environment.

Sensory Over-Responsivity—Environment

A SECRET for Environment

Modify the ENVIRONMENT to produce calm, safe, and predictable surroundings with minimal sensory stimulation.

Ask questions such as . . .

- What sensory messages in my child's environment are distracting, alarming, or uncomfortable?
- How can I modify the environment to make those surroundings more calm, safe, and predictable?

Devise strategies for home such as . . .

- **Tactile:** select textures for bedding, towels, upholstery, and carpet that are not uncomfortable to your child.
- **Proprioceptive:** provide tools for heavy work, e.g., jungle gym, trampoline; provide self-calming devices, e.g., a weighted vest, exercise bands.
- **Vestibular:** provide equipment for slow and rhythmic stimulation (preferably linear) e.g., rocking chair, glider.

Devise strategies for school such as . . .

- **Personal space:** arrange for work space that is not close to other children.
- **Classroom space:** request assignment to classrooms that are not "open" or unstructured.
- **Visual space:** request assignment to classrooms that are visually uncluttered, organized, and calm.

Devise strategies for community such as . . .

- **Special events:** avoid or prepare your child for settings that feature intense sensory stimulation, e.g., Chuck E. Cheese–type restaurants, malls, Fourth of July fireworks displays, birthday parties, sports stadiums, theme parks.
- **Service locations:** choose shops and professional offices that are small, quiet, and predictable for visits with your child.

Sensory Over-Responsivity—Environment (*continued*)

Devise strategies for home such as . . .	Devise strategies for school such as . . .	Devise strategies for community such as . . .
• **Visual**: use soft lighting, muted room colors, simple and uncluttered decor. • **Auditory**: provide a background of "white noise," especially during bedtime hours; play TV and radio at low volumes; avoid auditory "surprises," e.g., turning on a blender, garbage disposal, or vacuum cleaner without preparing the child. • **Olfactory**: use scent-free household products; use strong fans to disperse cooking odors. • **General**: create a refuge at home where your child can retreat when overwhelmed, e.g., a tent with pillows, weights, calming activities such as coloring books or puzzles.	• **Noise**: request assignment to classrooms where relative quiet is enforced, e.g., children are required to raise their hands before speaking; seek seating assignments in the least noisy location in each classroom; make arrangements for your child to wear noise-muffling earphones in the classroom, especially during individual work times. • **Self-calming**: encourage creation of a separate area in the classroom for times of overstimulation; equip the retreat with toys to stretch, pull, chew, or push against to provide heavy work; provide a rocking chair or another source of slow vestibular input.	• **Travel and transportation**: minimize; if you must travel, choose hours when public transit is least used, e.g., if you must fly, fly overnight when your child can sleep.

Sensory Over-Responsivity—Tasks

A SECRET for Tasks

Modify TASKS to minimize adverse sensory aspects that might interfere with your child's ability to perform successfully.

Ask questions such as . . .

- What types of tasks increase my child's attention span and generate satisfaction? What types of tasks most often distract my child and trigger a negative emotional reaction?
- How can I alter tasks so my child is more likely to be attentive, satisfied, undistracted, and positive about them?

Devise strategies for home such as . . .

- **Sensitivities**: work around sensitivities that get in the way of task completion, e.g., close a window that admits noise (auditory stimulation) or a breeze (tactile stimulation) so she can concentrate on her homework.
- **Simplification**: design tasks so they have a single, clear goal, e.g., "Go put your toys in the toy box" instead of "Go clean your room."

Devise strategies for school such as . . .

- **Transitions**: make sure your child has a readily available schedule of her entire school day broken down by time and activity; make special note of any deviations from the schedule, such as a guest speaker, an assembly, or a field trip.

Devise strategies for community such as . . .

- **Sensory preparation**: prepare your child for activities away from home with calming sensory input, e.g., if she's going to a birthday party, give her deep pressure and proprioceptive stimulation before leaving home.

Sensory Over-Responsivity—Tasks (*continued*)

Devise strategies for home such as . . .	Devise strategies for school such as . . .	Devise strategies for community such as . . .
• **Transitions**: create predictable transitions between tasks, e.g., when getting ready for bed at night, always complete routines in the same order (bath, toothbrushing, toilet) and use charts and stickers to keep track. • **Aversions**: don't assign tasks known to alarm your child's sensory systems, e.g., if she has tactile sensitivities, don't ask her to finger paint; if she has auditory sensitivities, don't take her to loud public events.	• **Curriculum**: request modification for specific school activities that are particularly alarming to your child, e.g., when fire drills are scheduled, your child is told in advance and placed next to the teacher before it begins. • **Performance**: suggest alternative methods for your child to complete tasks if she is aversive to their sensory aspects, e.g., she draws a picture of a jack-o'-lantern on paper instead of pasting facial features onto a pumpkin.	• **Cognitive preparation**: prepare your child for highly stimulating venues by providing information that will help her function, e.g., have her cut pictures out of a magazine and make a book of all the things that may happen at a birthday party before she goes. • **Exiting**: develop two exit plans for every extended family gathering, birthday party, holiday celebration, or other group event/outing that may cause sensory overload in your child; one exit plan assumes a smooth planned departure, while the alternative assumes your child becomes overstimulated and needs to leave before the event's end. • **Activities**: identify extracurricular activities suited to the child's sensitivities, e.g., concerts, swim programs, well-organized library events, yoga or other controlled activities, weight lifting at older ages.

After seven-year-old Tam was born, his mother, Lee, was relieved to have such a good baby. A working single mom, Lee felt lucky that her son rarely cried and quickly learned to sleep through the night. But as Tam grew older, his mother began to worry that maybe her sweet little boy was too good. Even though he didn't wake up at night, he also had trouble waking up in the morning, no matter how long he slept. In fact, Tam had trouble starting anything, much less finishing, and nothing seemed to interest him. At the school he attends in a small resort community, Tam's teachers say he seems to float through class in a fog. He is already behind in many subjects and other children tend to overlook or exclude him. He may not be a "handful" like LaTanya, but he is already "failing" on measures of childhood success such as school achievement and social participation. Lee is afraid her son will grow up feeling incompetent, rejected, and alone.

Chapter 7

Tam, an Under-Responsive Second-Grader

The alarm clock goes off in Tam's apartment bedroom, but as usual the sleeping boy doesn't stir. In the bathroom where she's fixing her hair, Lee listens for signs that her seven-year-old son is up and moving. When she hears nothing but the insistent clamor of the clock, she lays down her brush and covers the few short steps to where he sleeps.

The boy is on his back, his head turned to one side, his lips slightly parted. His breathing is deep and steady. Lee perches on the edge of the bed and strokes her son's silky black hair. Even though it's time to get ready for work and school, she often lingers over Tam's last moments of sleep, savoring the beauty of her quiet little boy. Then she sighs. If only the rest of the day could be this easy.

"Tam," she finally says, mussing his hair. "It's time to get up. Come on, Tam. Wake up!"

The boy's lips move slightly, but he shows no other sign of hearing. "Tam!" she repeats, louder now. "Wake up! It's time to get dressed for school."

No luck. Lee pulls back Tam's covers so that his warm sleeping cocoon disappears, and gives his body a little shake. When his eyes remain shut, she rolls him back and forth on the mattress, cooing his name, then turns on the radio and the bedside lamp. The boy's eyelids rise and flutter briefly but drop again.

"Tam!" Lee snaps, growing impatient. "Wake UP!" Making the radio louder, she slides an arm under the child's back, lifts him into a sitting position, and swings his legs off the side of the bed. Finally, the little boy's eyes open again and he blinks awake.

"Good morning, sleepyhead," Lee says, relieved. "Up and at 'em. We don't want to be late."

What a contrast Tam is to LaTanya, the over-responsive child. In the last chapter, we saw that the sound of a slamming door down the hall was enough to launch LaTanya into a state of fright that required her mother's active intervention to overcome. But Tam sleeps through the alarm, sleeps through his mother's voice, and awakens slowly even when Lee props him into a sitting position.

Like LaTanya, Tam's Sensory Processing Disorder affects his ability to turn sensory messages into appropriate daily behaviors. Although LaTanya's behaviors are over-responsive and Tam's are under-responsive, scientists suspect that both sensory modulation patterns originate in the filtering system of the brain. In the simplest terms, LaTanya's over-responsive system activates too quickly to sensory information of relatively slight intensity or duration, whereas Tam needs sensory messages of great intensity or duration to become aware of them.

Because of how slowly they do everything, under-responsive children like Tam are at risk of being labeled lazy, unmotivated, stubborn, or just plain "bad." The truth is, Tam can't respond any faster. His brain is not getting the stimulation it needs in order to get started.

Understanding the Filtering System of the Brain

Research to identify the specific neurotransmitter systems responsible for sensory modulation problems such as LaTanya's and Tam's has not yet been done in children with Sensory Processing Disorder. However, studies have made it possible for scientists to develop some educated guesses about the neurological, physiological, and/or biochemical mechanisms that make it so hard for children like Tam to get started in the morning and to function at ideal levels during the day.

The operation of the reticular formation—a weblike portion of the brain that runs through the brain stem—is believed to be involved in a key way. This system serves a "gate-keeping" function in the brain, with incoming information from every sensory pathway in the body passing through on its way to the cortex, where thinking takes place. As the gatekeeper, this system helps the brain maintain alertness in a just-right state of wakefulness known as the "optimal level of arousal"* at which a child can pay attention without being overstimulated.

In children with Sensory Modulation Disorder, it is suspected that these so-called "gates" in the reticular formation do not perform exactly as they should. In an over-responsive child, the gates

* Hebb, D. O. "Drives and the CNS (conceptual nervous system)," *Psychological Review* 62 (2005): 243–54.

spring open with relatively mild, brief, or infrequent stimulation, which allows even benign sensory signals that most people filter out to flood the child. LaTanya, who is so overalert that she wakes up in terror at the sound of a noise from the next room, is a good example of this condition. In an under-responsive child, the gates need more than typical stimulation in order to open. Tam, who is so under-alert that he wakes up only after his mother generates sensory messages of several kinds for an extended time, follows this pattern.

What Tam needs to reach an "optimal level of arousal" is sensory stimulation that is stronger, lasts longer, and is more frequent than the input a typically developing child like Ryan requires to reach the same level. Lee is intuitively addressing this need when she essentially "turns up the volume" of sensation with more noise, brighter light, and more movement for her son, and eventually these efforts succeed in waking him up. The filtering gates in his brain begin to let messages through and Tam can finally respond.

When Tam finally stumbles to his feet, Lee checks the sheets. Thank goodness! They're dry. Toileting is one area where her son has definitely made progress. Tam was four years old before he was entirely toilet trained by day and six before he was mostly reliable at night. Now he is usually able to sense when he needs to go in the night and gets himself to the bathroom, but there are still times when he doesn't wake up, followed by mornings when Lee has to strip the bed and start the washing machine in addition to the rest of the morning chores. She's glad this isn't one of those days.

Tam's late toilet training was the first red flag that made Lee think that her son might have some kind of problem. With only one child of her own and little contact with other children, the fact that he hardly ever cried as a baby was unremarkable to Lee. And, understandably, his failure to beg for trips to McDonald's or for candy in the supermarket checkout line or for a hundred presents for his birthday was fine with the single mom. She couldn't afford many extras anyway.

But when her son turned four without being toilet trained even during the day, Lee started to worry. She brought the problem up at a well-child checkup, but the nurse at the county health center said the delay was a result of Lee "babying" her only child. Lee was willing to accept the blame, but then she began noticing that Tam was different from other children in other ways. She'd assumed he was quiet at home because she was basically pretty quiet herself, but she began to see that he didn't talk as much as the other kids at day care. He didn't appear to be making friends, either. Nobody rushed up to greet him when he arrived, and he didn't seek out any of the other children. In fact, he rarely showed interest in playing with other children at all. She continues to ask questions at his checkups, but she has yet to receive any real answers.

Tam's difficulties with toilet training and bed-wetting are extremely common among children with sensory under-responsivity. In a typically developing child, the need to urinate is a sensation that reaches the sensory filtering system and is passed through to the parts of the brain that organize the appropriate responses of waking up, getting out of bed, and going to the toilet. For an under-responsive child like Tam, the sensation of a full bladder doesn't make it through his sensory filter or "gate." As a result, he doesn't get a "Wake up!" message so that he can get himself to the bathroom. In some children, the same problems can occur with defecation, leading to bowel accidents that are even more awkward and worrisome. Lee tackled the toilet issues with a program of scheduled bathroom trips and regular reminders, but it was slow going.

Although it would have been ideal if Tam's sensory issues had been thoroughly evaluated and treated when the toilet-

*training issues first alarmed Lee, the reality is that under-
responsivity often goes unnoticed or undiagnosed until children
reach the primary grades. Children who are under-responsive
don't draw attention to themselves as do children like LaTanya
who have more dramatic symptoms of SPD. Under-responders
don't get in trouble and they don't rock the boat. Although they
exhibit many atypical behaviors—such as not crying as infants—these are often viewed as personality traits and possibly
even welcomed by their parents and society. The child who falls
down and doesn't cry is often rewarded with words of praise:
"What a brave boy you are!" When children like this reach
school, their sensory under-responsivity may lead teachers and
others to conclude they are cognitively impaired, further delay-
ing diagnosis and intervention.*

Now that she's got him out of bed, Lee opens Tam's bottom dresser
drawer and tells her son to put on his underwear and socks while she
finishes getting ready for work. But when she returns ten minutes
later, he's sitting exactly where she left him, monotonously running his
favorite Matchbox mail truck back and forth over the top of the
drawer. Not a single article of clothing has been touched.

"Tam!" Lee moans. "I told you to start getting dressed."

"Okay, Mom," he agrees.

"But you're not getting dressed."

"Okay. I will."

"Tam!" she cries. "You're seven years old! You should know how
to get dressed!" Lee regrets losing her patience, but the boy appears
totally unperturbed.

"Okay," he repeats, unruffled.

The clock is beginning to run out. Lee takes the Matchbox truck
away and pulls Tam to his feet so she can get him out of his pajamas
and into his school clothes, fighting familiar tears of frustration and
self-reproach. Dressing Tam isn't hard and doesn't take that much

time, but Lee can't help feeling bothered by doing things for her son that other children his age have been doing for years. At the same time, she feels guilty. Other kids his age can do these things for themselves, but other kids have other mothers. It's probably all her fault.

Lee keeps up a steady patter of talk as she dresses her son, but he doesn't say much in return. His mother is used to this, too. When Tam was a toddler, Lee had his hearing tested because he was so slow to talk that she worried he couldn't hear. There was no hearing problem, and the clinic assured her that Tam was just quiet—the same way people kept saying he was just a "good baby." Still, she's troubled that he has so little to say even when she actively tries to get a conversation going.

In the bathroom, Lee combs her son's thick hair and washes his face. He could do the tasks himself, she knows, but he would take four times as long. Finally ready for school, Tam heads for the kitchen, where Lee has a plate of hot pop-up pancakes waiting. He eats methodically, oblivious to the syrup that he transfers to his fingers and face in the process. The countertop TV is tuned to *Good Morning America* and he instantly fixates on the show, his eyes never leaving the screen even though there's nothing on it but two grown-ups talking. As he watches, he eats more and more slowly, and when Lee gets to the kitchen, she's exasperated all over again.

"Tam, look at you," she sighs, switching off the TV and reaching for a wet cloth to wipe his face and hands. "You're a mess."

Typically developing children want to please their parents. As we saw in Chapter 5, Ryan goes out of his way to show his stepdad how well he's groomed himself. Even LaTanya worries about upsetting her mom when she skips self-care routines she finds "icky." Tam's relative indifference to his mother's frustration, anger, scolding, and other negative feedback is another symptom of his sensory under-responsivity.

Besides filtering sensory messages, the brain has special centers that interpret whether information is positive or negative

*and then pass this interpretation along so appropriate action
can occur. A typically developing child like Ryan would hear
his mother scolding, interpret this as a negative message, and
organize a response to get himself out of trouble. For instance,
if he was playing instead of getting dressed, he would stop
playing and start putting on his clothes. He might even feel
bad about making his mom unhappy. Tam vaguely recognizes
that his mother isn't happy, but this early in the morning,
when his internal engine has barely turned over, her displeasure
is like the alarm clock—too little stimulation to overcome his
underlying sensory under-responsivity. What Lee intends as a
rebuke registers only mildly. Tam hears his mom, but he doesn't
correctly interpret her displeasure. As a result, he doesn't change
his behavior to adapt to the message. When children like Tam
move into the outside world, where other people are less forgiv-
ing than their parents, this failure to respond to negative feedback often leads to disapproval that in the long term
undermines their self-esteem and self-confidence.*

Lee and Tam finally reach the car for the ride to the before-school
day care program. Lee keeps a special supply of Matchbox vehicles in
the car, and Tam contents himself running one of them in big circles
on the seat beside him. Matchbox vehicles are Tam's favorite toy, and
he can play with them for hours. When a fire engine siren forces Lee
to pull the car to the curb until it passes, her son is so absorbed in his
play that he doesn't look up.

It's a short drive to the busy day care center near the elementary
school. Upon arrival, Lee parks and walks her son inside. After sign-
ing him in, she stoops at Tam's side. "All set," Lee says. "Why don't
you go find a friend to play with?"

"Okay, Mom," he agrees. His mother gives the boy a big hug and
he gives her a half-hug back.

"I love you, honey," she says.

"You, too, Mom," he replies, and, with a small wave her way, ambles toward the coatroom to store his gear.

The hour that follows is uneventful. The center is chronically understaffed, which makes an undemanding child like Tam particularly welcome. While the other kids chatter and scramble on the playground equipment with all the inevitable noise, squabbling, and tumbles that young children typically generate, Tam sits quietly by himself with his back to a wall. Sometimes one of the supervisors makes a special point to urge Tam into the games, and once he's involved he often perks up. But with the staff so shorthanded, this doesn't happen often, so Tam usually sits on the sidelines. He doesn't seem to mind.

Children with under-responsivity generally do not have the transition problems that children with over-responsivity do because they are not as sensitive to changes in their environment. Even as a baby, Tam rarely cried when Lee left him at day care or with a babysitter, instead moving smoothly from one setting or activity to the next, often with even less complaint or resistance than a typically developing child would exhibit. Though his response to his mother's affection is pretty nonchalant, this is not unusual in a seven-year-old boy, so it doesn't send up any red flags. The shift from home to day care contains no dramatic episodes to alert Lee or any of the other adults in Tam's sphere that this child's life is being disrupted by sensory problems.

What taxes families with an under-responsive child is navigating to the transition point. Children like Tam move in such a slow and labored manner that it can be hard for their families to get anywhere on time. The soothing and efficient household rhythms that Ryan's family enjoys don't occur. Parental patience wears thin because it can seem that the child is intentionally slowing everything down. Though the child doesn't melt down, the parent may! In a quiet two-person family like Tam's, Lee is able to exercise patience most of the time. In a

larger or more complex family or in one with a fuller schedule,
the sensory issues that produce Tam's sluggishness might result in
tensions such as the ones we saw in LaTanya's home.

School is more stimulating than Tam's quiet home and the day care center, where he is mostly forgotten, and Tam becomes a little more responsive once he arrives. He likes his teacher, Mr. Anderson, and greets him cheerfully.

Still, there are problems. Tam consistently gets low grades because he has trouble paying attention in class and spaces out when Mr. Anderson asks the class to read silently. He is rarely prepared for tests and hardly ever completes the relatively minimal homework that his second-grade class is given.

Tam's chronic lethargy in school led his previous teachers to conclude he was a "slow learner." In first grade, his teacher assigned him to the low reading group and often modified classroom activities to make things less challenging for him. Tam's second-grade teacher saw the evaluations of his predecessors and initially took the same approach of making things easier for the boy. But shortly into the first semester, Mr. Anderson introduced a science unit on insects, and something unexpected happened. Tam showed an active interest and aptitude in the subject, even going to the school library during lunch hour to do extra reading and to use the Internet for research. The result was an ambitious grasshopper project that revealed grade-level reading and writing skills and an inner drive to explore the topic. Intrigued, Mr. Anderson asked Tam to explain the difference between a grasshopper and a cricket. It was clear that the boy could grasp and talk about ideas and information when he was interested, which made the teacher rethink Tam's intellectual capacity.

Children with sensory under-responsivity are often classified as
"slow" or "delayed" by their teachers, a perception that doubles
the burden these kids already face in school. In the classic study

of how labeling affects school performance (known as the "expectancy effect"), children in eighteen elementary school classes were given an intelligence test at the beginning of the school year. Twenty percent of the students were randomly chosen to be labeled "likely to make surprising gains" that year. At the end of the school year, the children were re-administered the same intelligence test. Even though the label had been applied arbitrarily and without any basis, the children who had been labeled "likely to make surprising gains" had higher IQ scores than at the beginning of the year. The researchers concluded that teacher expectations created by positive labeling resulted in changes in the school environment, which led to significant improvement in IQ scores.*

For kids like Tam, the expectancy effect can produce the opposite outcome. Once pigeonholed as intellectually impaired, their learning _____ nment tends to reinforce the label. They _____ lower-functioning children and are given _____ o challenge them. Lower performance is _____ These children "live down" to the low- _____ 's previous teachers considered the boy to _____ use they associated behaviors like his _____ lligence. In reality, school performance is _____ Tam's need for more stimulation so that his filtering system lets ideas through to his brain, where they can say, "Look at me—I'm important to you." Once he's engaged with material that really grabs him—the intellectual equivalent of "turning up the volume"—he is able to concentrate and perform at or even above grade level. He can finally "get into" school and demonstrate that he's not cognitively delayed.

Tam's enthusiasm about grasshoppers is strong enough that

---

* Rosenthal, R., and L. Jacobson. *Pygmalion in the Classroom.* New York: Holt, Rinehart and Winston, 1968.

his curiosity sends a "wake-up" call to his under-aroused system.
He's finally able to apply the grade-level thinking skills he pos-
sesses. He shows glimmers of potential and, luckily, he has a
teacher who notices. But quiet children like Tam don't demand
much attention and often disappear into the background of a
busy classroom. Eventually academic demands get more com-
plex, and they fall behind because they missed so much when
they were "tuned out" earlier. Unnoticed, they slide into the
lowest reading, math, and spelling groups, where a lack of
challenge only compounds their under-responsivity, and they
begin to see themselves as "dumb." Until Tam's underlying sen-
sory impairment is addressed, he is likely to struggle in school,
as well as in other parts of his life.

Although Mr. Anderson is encouraged about Tam's academic abilities, the teacher has another area of concern. At their latest conference, he told Lee, "Children this age usually show a pretty active
interest in interacting with other children. I just don't see this with
Tam. For example, he always takes his lunch to an empty table. If
other kids join him, he doesn't complain and he'll answer if they ask
something, but he doesn't initiate contact. He just keeps eating, and
he's quite slow at it. The other children generally finish and leave long
before he's done, so he's alone again. Then he goes to the library,
alone, or he goes to the playground and just sits off to the side, alone.
He strikes me as very isolated."

"What happens if the other children invite him to play?" Lee asked.

"Well, I'd have to say that most of the children seem aware of his
disinterest, so they don't often ask him to join them. Sometimes they
need another player for a game and approach him, and he does join
in then. He seems able to play with them, just not in a very interested
manner, and that's a little worrisome. At Tam's age, even shy children
usually have one or two special people they want to play with. Do you
see the same pattern away from school?"

Lee nodded and looked down at her hands, which are rough and dry from her housekeeping job. "It's probably because I work so much and can't arrange playdates for him."

Mr. Anderson shook his head. "I don't think so. Most of the kids in this school have parents who work long hours, and they don't have these issues. Have you tried organized sports?"

Lee sighed. "Soccer and softball at the rec center. He hated them, so I tried an after-school art program and then drama. He'd go, but he didn't really seem to enjoy any of it so I sort of gave up."

Mr. Anderson nodded. "I see the same lack of interest in class. That's why I'd like to have him evaluated by our learning disabilities team. I was pleasantly surprised and encouraged by Tam's work during the insect unit. I think he has the ability to do more and better work than he's doing, but something is getting in his way. There's got to be an explanation and I'd like to find it."

The most serious problem for an under-responder is social engagement. Because Tam is inactive and uncommunicative and seems disinterested in everything happening around him, he is generally ignored by children who are eager to run around and joke and play. This makes him feel "different" and less inclined to reach out to others. A sort of self-fulfilling prophecy sets in: Tam does not play with other children because they do not play with him, and they do not play with him because he shows no interest in playing with them. His self-confidence suffers and this causes him to withdraw even more, which in turn makes the other children less likely to approach him. Until Tam's underlying problem of sensory under-responsivity is addressed, this cycle can be expected to continue spiraling downward, with Tam becoming more and more isolated and feeling worse and worse about himself.

Another of Tam's ongoing challenges is that his mother is in no position to obtain the diagnostic services and intervention

*he needs for the cycle to be broken. Lee is a single mom and
Tam's father is not in the picture. She works at a low-wage
hourly job with inadequate medical coverage, and she has no
personal savings to pay for private services. Mr. Anderson's
awareness of Tam's challenges could become a turning point.
The few resources that the underfunded school district has for
special-needs kids are generally allocated to those who have
clear-cut medically diagnosable conditions. However, with Mr.
Anderson's advocacy and Lee's collaboration, Tam will be evaluated and may receive services. If the evaluation team includes
an occupational therapist or another member skilled in the diagnosis of sensory-based problems, it is very likely that his underlying sensory problem will be identified.*

"There's something else," the teacher added, looking thoughtful.
"Last week we had field day, where all the children participate in track
and field games. Tam fell down and cut his knee on the asphalt. I
would have been jumping around and howling if I'd hit the ground
as hard as he did, but it was as if he didn't feel the pain. He just got
up and kept running. Do you ever see anything like this at home?"

Lee pondered the question a moment. "Tam is quiet at home, so
it's rare for him to do anything where he could get hurt. But, now that
you ask, I remember he didn't cry when he had bad diaper rashes as
a baby. And when I comb his hair and catch a tangle, he doesn't seem
to notice. In fact, I still have to run his bath water for him or he'll run
it too hot or too cold. Lee paused. "Yes." She nodded. "I know what
you're talking about."

*Tam's under-reaction to pain and other sensory information in-
troduces us to the autonomic nervous system where the fight-or-
flight response is believed to originate. Scientists believe the
autonomic nervous system produces our automatic responses to
new or challenging sensory messages. Within this system, two*

*divisions are constantly working together to help us stay calm
yet alert enough that we can deal with potential threats. The
sympathetic nervous system is the division that alerts us to danger. It's the system suspected of over-reacting, which results in
LaTanya's perceptions of danger even when there is no danger.
The parasympathetic nervous system is the division that generates "calm down" signals. Tam appears to be getting too many of
these messages, which may explain why he doesn't perceive pain,
danger, and other sensory warnings that should register automatically. (A more detailed explanation of how these systems
function can be found in Chapter 11, "The Science of SPD.")*

*Impaired sensory awareness can be dangerous for children
with under-responsivity. Remember Jordan, the little boy in
Part I who held on to the lightbulb so long that he ended up in
the emergency room with second-degree burns? This is a real-
life story illustrating one of the requirements for parents, teachers, and caregivers of under-responders: constant vigilance.
Under-responsive children can hurt themselves without knowing it. They can have infections and other illnesses and not
complain because they don't "feel" pain as much as other children do. You rarely hear, "Mom, my throat hurts really bad!"
This is why Tam didn't cry over his diaper rashes and why he
doesn't complain when Lee catches his hair while combing it.
Any child with a pattern of not reporting pain, injuries, or
sensory extremes such as hot and cold should be evaluated for
sensory under-responsiveness (see "Two Patterns of Under-
Responsivity").*

Two Patterns of Under-Responsivity

Children with sensory under-responsivity generally exhibit one
of two patterns: lethargic/withdrawn or dreaming/self-absorbed.

Tam exhibits many symptoms of the lethargic/withdrawn child. Though he may initiate activities, his range of interests and emotional reactions seems relatively limited, and he rarely exhibits the internal drive that typically developing Ryan routinely demonstrates. Though he is only seven years old, this lack of drive is already a consistent pattern. As a baby, he did not take an active interest in exploring his body and environment. As he has grown older, he hasn't sought out or participated in new experiences the way other children do. He is never the child waving his hand in class and crying, "Pick me! Pick me!" Particularly noteworthy is his lack of interest in motor challenges. He rarely moves fast and has no innate interest in rolling down a slope or learning to skateboard or Rollerblade. If encouraged by his mother, he'll slowly climb the jungle gym at the park, but he doesn't want to go higher for the sheer fun of it the way Ryan would.

When Tam does find an activity that interests him, he tends to get stuck on it. At school, he can spin on the tire swing for long stretches of time without ever getting dizzy, further evidence that he doesn't feel stimulation the way typically developing children do. Ryan is interested in his paper airplanes, but he's also enthusiastic about a dozen other activities. Tam likes playing with his Matchbox cars but not much else. Sometimes underresponsive children who are lethargic/withdrawn also appear tired or depressed.

Not all under-responsive children are lethargic or withdrawn, however, and even the lethargic/withdrawn child may not exhibit this pattern all the time. Some exceptionally bright youngsters with under-responsivity create fantasy worlds so complete that they get lost in them, a pattern sometimes called "dreaming/self-absorbed." Dreaming/self-absorbed under-responders often spend far more time on the computer or reading than is typical for their age, and become so engrossed in their own thoughts that others may have trouble breaking through. Creating a dinosaur kingdom in his bedroom, this child would not smell dinner cooking in the kitchen or hear his parent calling him to eat or notice that the day had grown dark. Of course, typically developing children sometimes appear oblivious, too, but in children with sensory under-responsivity, the pattern is chronic and interferes with daily routines and activities.

Many children who are autistic also have sensory under-responsivity. Behaviors such as Tam's repetitive play with Matchbox cars could be symptomatic of autism if they occurred in combination with other features of the disorder. However, SPD and autism are distinct conditions, and a thorough diagnostic evaluation would find that Tam is not autistic (see Chapter 12, "Beyond the Types").

Lee's day has been shorter than usual—the resort was nearly empty last night—so she picks up Tam early from day care. "I thought we'd go to the park," she says. "How does that sound?"

The two are in the car, where Tam is running his Matchbox car over the course in the backseat. "Okay," he agrees.

"Just okay? Not *terrific*?"

He doesn't answer. Lee's bright mood dims a little, but she still offers to help her son make a race course in the sand for his cars. She has learned from experience that Tam then plays more actively when she plays with him. He nods. "Okay."

At the park, the mom and son scoop sand and carve an intricate roadway system that Tam plays with for an hour while Lee reads a magazine. A boy about Tam's age approaches and asks, "Can I play?"

"Sure," Tam says, obligingly holding out one of the cars. The two silently drive the vehicles over the sand for several minutes before the other boy's mother calls him to go home. When the playmate jumps up and races off, Tam just picks up the abandoned car and begins running both vehicles himself again.

Tam retrieves his cars without protest when Lee says it's time to leave the park. They ride home in companionable silence, and Lee asks Tam to join her in the kitchen while she cooks. He obliges but brings his Game Boy and, when she tries to start a conversation, is too absorbed with his game to respond. Finally, Lee gives up and the apartment is quiet except for the sounds of her footsteps as she moves around preparing the meal. Sometimes Lee feels a little lonely, but she's used to this and doesn't let herself think too much about it.

As Lee sets their plates on the kitchen table, Tam makes his usual plea for TV during the meal despite the no-TV rule at dinner. Instead, Lee turns on some soothing music so the meal doesn't pass in complete silence. She continues asking Tam questions but, when she gets only one- or two-word replies, she finally falls quiet.

The domestic picture in Lee and Tam's home vividly illustrates how A SECRET elements affect the "fit" of children with Sensory Processing Disorder.

Tam's environment is a small apartment that offers little space for sensory-motor activities such as the running and jumping that would raise his sluggish arousal level. His mother is a quiet person and the sensory stimulation that appeals to her tends to be quiet and monotonous—the drone of TV news, soft music playing at a low volume. There's no play area outside the apartment, so Tam's recreational time is nearly always spent indoors doing something sedentary like playing Game Boy. In effect, Tam's innate under-responsivity is made worse by specific elements in his external environment.

If Tam's culture were within a big family in a noisy household or even in a smaller family with another child like LaTanya's rambunctious big brother, the built-in level of sensory stimulation would be higher and might activate the boy's lethargic sensory system. Culture is often the most fixed element in a child's context, and that's certainly the case with Tam's family size and resources.

In family-centered occupational therapy, Lee would learn A SECRET way of thinking to improve Tam's functioning within the context of his own home culture. Strategies would be developed to increase sensory input; adjust his environment, relationships, and tasks; and arouse his attention and emotions. A cool wake-up shower followed by a vigorous rubdown with a textured towel and spicy foods at breakfast, for example, are sensory strategies that would probably raise Tam's state of arousal to a more ideal level and jump-start his whole day. With his engine revved up, he would be better able to move quickly and responsively through the routines at home and be more wakeful and attentive when he reached school, which should improve his school performance and make him more open to social interaction.

TV at breakfast would be strongly discouraged because it further lowers his arousal level. Lee might be encouraged to find room in the apartment for a mini-trampoline on which Tam could bounce while she cooked dinner or at other idle times during the day. He could be given a therapy ball to sit on while doing his homework or watching videos, which would raise his overall arousal level by requiring his sensory system to "wake up" in order to balance on the ball. This input would improve his general alertness for other activities, such as the reading and writing required by homework. Even adding a small dog to the family could make a big difference because the pet would provide noise, movement, activity, a friend, positive emotional feedback, and so many other things that this quiet little boy needs.

Many techniques are available to help parents build stimulation into the natural flow of a child's day in order to increase

*alertness. For children like Tam, the ultimate goal is to turn up
the sensory volume of life. Tam and children like him need
bright lights and vivid colors, loud sounds and zesty foods,
novel sensations and lots of movement, heavy work and tactile
(touch) stimulation. The more sensory messages Tam receives,
the more his under-responsive system will begin to wake up, enabling him to perform important childhood occupations more
successfully.*

*Many of the SECRET strategies that would improve Tam's
life are simple, easy, and cost-free. With an understanding of
her son's disorder, Lee could devise and implement them with
success. The hurdle she faces right now is the absence of a diagnosis of Tam's sensory issues and the guidance of a professional
skilled in treating SPD.*

After dinner, the two watch a video together. This is one of the
most satisfying activities Lee shares with her son. Although Tam rarely
initiates a cuddle, he doesn't mind when Lee does. She wraps the two
of them up in a soft old comforter to watch *Finding Nemo*, one of the
many videos in the collection she has assembled from garage sales and
library events. She keeps a big supply on hand because she doesn't like
watching one tape over and over again, even though Tam would rather
see the same few tapes repeatedly.

After the video is finished, Lee runs a bath, and Tam spends nearly
half an hour playing with his extensive collection of bathtub cars. He
seems happy and content, oblivious to the cooling water. His mother
gets no objections when she washes his hair nor does he protest when
she combs it. But when they reach his room, he unexpectedly objects
to going to bed.

"I'm not tired, Mom. I want to watch TV."

"Tam, it's nine o'clock. You need to go to sleep, and there's nothing on TV for children now anyway."

"Then I can watch a video."

"We already watched a video."

He's getting angry. "I can watch another!"

"No," Lee says firmly.

"Yes!" he insists, stamping one foot. "I want another video!"

A battle of wills ensues. It's as if the little boy saved up all the energy he didn't use in the activities where other children were wearing themselves out, and now when the day should be over, he has to spend it in order to go to sleep. Lee feels a surge of desperation. (This, by the way, is the effect of new and alarming information reaching her autonomic nervous system.) *Not again!* she thinks. It doesn't happen routinely, but when Tam gets wired like this at bedtime, it can be midnight before he gets to sleep.

She takes a deep breath. "Tam, it is bedtime and you are going to bed. I want you to take a deep breath the way I'm doing." She takes another deep breath because the activity calms her and she knows it will calm Tam, too.

At first the boy refuses, sticking out his lower lip and folding his arms across his chest, but he's not a stubborn child and he soon gives in and joins her. Once they've both taken a few deep draws of air and Lee, too, is feeling better, she says, "I'll tell you what I'll do. Let's go in the kitchen and heat some milk. We'll both have a cup and then I'll rock you and sing the long version of "Hush, Little Baby." How's that?" she says.

She holds out her hand. Tam hesitates briefly before surrendering. Lee gives his hand a hard squeeze. "That's my good boy."

Tam has not had an opportunity to use his muscles all day, and now his sensory system is finally craving some input. Bedtime problems are not inevitable with under-responders, but they can occur because the children's sensory diets are so limited. Again, Lee is showing good instincts in dealing with her son.

*The deep breathing calms him. Hot milk is calming, too.
"Hush, Little Baby" is a long and highly repetitive song that
will have a soothing effect.*

*Lee is a good example of a dedicated parent who is getting
by on fierce mother love, sound instinct, and strong local support. Teachers, neighbors, and friends in their small town are
tolerant of her son's differences and willing to make accommodations for him. As we saw with the first-grade teacher who
gave him easier assignments, this can sometimes be counterpro-
ductive: Easing up rather than challenging Tam only further
slowed down his under-responsive system. Nonetheless, the
small community provides vital support to this struggling single mom and insulates Tam somewhat from stereotyping
and rejection.*

*At the same time, Tam needs more if he is to enjoy a well-
rounded childhood and develop into a healthy, self-confident
adult. If professional services continue to be inaccessible, tap-
ping whatever resources the school district offers, finding a
health care provider willing to look for the underlying cause of
Tam's placidity, and doing research on her own are Lee's best
chances for helping her son. Books, online support groups and
educational sites, websites she can access on library computers,
local parent support groups, and information workshops in
nearby cities are resources she might tap.*

*Because Lee is somewhat isolated and economically disad-
vantaged, these resources will not be easy for her to access. But
the rewards of persisting until she finds an explanation for her
son's behavior and acquires successful strategies for altering it
will be worth the effort.*

A SECRET for Your Child with Sensory Under-Responsivity*

Sensational strategies that may improve a child's functioning can be developed by any parent. Strategies emerge when each element of A SECRET is examined and one or more elements is modified to improve the "fit" between the under-responsive child's personal characteristics and the world around him. The following chart illustrates how to use this flexible approach to examine the last three elements of A SECRET—Relationships, Environment, and Tasks. These are the elements most readily modified by parents.

---

* A clinical diagnosis of sensory under-responsivity can be made only with a comprehensive diagnostic evaluation. Sensational strategies are most effective when developed as part of a comprehensive intervention program provided by an OT or another professional with training in treating Sensory Processing Disorder.

A SECRET for Your Child with Sensory Under-Responsivity

A SECRET for Relationships

Modify RELATIONSHIPS to foster interaction that excites your child to participate socially.

Ask questions such as . . .

- What types of people encourage my child to be more social? Less social?
- How can the relationships most likely to maximize my child's social participation be encouraged?
- If my child withdraws more than usual in the company of siblings or other family members, how can those relationships be made more engaging?
- How can I help others to understand that my child needs extra encouragement in order to be social?

Devise strategies for home such as . . .

- **Peers:** find playmates who don't mind taking the lead and/or making the effort to include your child; avoid playmates who will not respond well to the high level of stimulation your child needs; actively arrange playdates with identified children.

Devise strategies for school such as . . .

- **Understanding:** develop a script and use it to explain your child's seeming apathy and lethargy to school personnel.

Devise strategies for community such as . . .

- **Understanding:** develop a script and use it to explain your child's need for extra stimulation to extended family, neighbors, service providers, and parents of playmates.

Sensory Under-Responsivity—Relationships (continued)

Devise strategies for home such as . . .	Devise strategies for school such as . . .	Devise strategies for community such as . . .
• **Siblings and other family**: teach siblings to make the extra effort to engage your child; caution siblings and other family not to take offense if he doesn't respond immediately. • **Tactile**: use and encourage others to use touch to get your child's attention before speaking to him. • **Visual**: seek and encourage others to seek eye contact before trying to talk, play, or otherwise interact with your child.	• **Support network**: identify one or more members of the school staff who can be available to engage your child in vigorous movement (e.g., a brisk walk around the playground) before the academic day begins and ideally between academic activities. • **Teacher assignment**: seek assignment to teachers who are tactile as well as verbal and who are vivacious rather than quiet; request teachers who are flexible enough to encourage your child to perform alerting activities in the classroom such as chewing gum, sucking through a straw, or playing music through loud headphones during quiet time. • **Classmates**: ask the teacher to facilitate social interaction by assigning buddy projects and other group activities.	• **Group activities**: volunteer to lead or assist in extracurricular activities (e.g., sports, drama class, Scouts) so you can make sure that your child does not get left out.

Sensory Under-Responsivity—Environment

A SECRET for Environment

Modify the ENVIRONMENT to create interesting, stimulating, complex, unpredictable surroundings that generate maximum stimulation.

Ask questions such as . . .

- What is present in my child's environment that stimulates his active interest?
- How can I modify the environment to make my child's surroundings more fun, engaging, and enticing?

Devise strategies for home such as . . .

- **Vestibular:** provide equipment that permits fast and/or rotary movement, e.g., self-spinning devices, swings, mini-trampoline.
- **Tactile:** integrate the use of direct tactile stimulation into daily routines, e.g., dry your child vigorously after bath with towels of different textures, provide a variety in seating textures, choose clothing with noticeable textures.

Devise strategies for school such as . . .

- **Visual space:** request a classroom that is colorful, filled with objects, and visually interesting; attach an individual light to your child's desk if general lighting is not bright.
- **Classroom space:** seek "open" classrooms or classes that move between classrooms or within the room.

Devise strategies for community such as . . .

- **Special events and outings:** plan outings to settings that feature intense sensory stimulation and vary them, e.g., Chuck E. Cheese–type restaurants, malls, parks, spectator sports arenas, theme parks.

Sensory Under-Responsivity—Environment (*continued*)

Devise strategies for home such as . . .	Devise strategies for school such as . . .	Devise strategies for community such as . . .
• **Proprioceptive**: provide equipment for heavy work, such as a jungle gym, jumping device, or exercise bands; provide a weighted vest to wear during physical activities. • **Visual**: use bright room colors, many and bright lights, colorful and "busy" wallpaper patterns, interesting mobiles. • **Auditory**: provide constantly changing background sounds, e.g., CDs with a mix of fast and slow music; avoid monotonous background sounds, e.g., quiet radio, TV, fans. • **Olfactory**: expose your child to sharp smells, e.g., have him join you in the kitchen when handling pungent foods or in the bathroom when cleaning.	• **Noise**: request a classroom assignment that is more spontaneous and chaotic; seek seating assignments near extremely social children and other sources of sound. • **Self-alerting**: arrange for gum chewing, eating sour candy, constant access to a water bottle with straw, a therapy ball instead of a chair, and other forms of sensory input.	• **Extracurricular activities**: seek activities that take place in highly stimulating settings, e.g., a hip-hop movement class, drumming lessons, skateboarding.

Sensory Under-Responsivity—Tasks

A SECRET for Tasks

Modify TASKS so they increase your child's level of arousal and ability to become engaged.

Ask questions such as . . .

- What are the sensations that most effectively stimulate my child's interest and energy? What are the sensations most likely to dull my child's awareness of what's going on around him?
- How can I assure that my child receives the sensory stimulation he needs to become alert for tasks he performs at home and elsewhere?

Devise strategies for home such as . . .

- **Sensory diet:** increase sensory input before starting tasks, e.g., precede a task such as homework with two to five minutes of intense movement or other stimulation; if your child gets stuck in the middle of a task, stop and provide intense sensory stimulation; at the end of task refresh him with proprioceptive, tactile, and vestibular stimulation.

Devise strategies for school such as . . .

- **Movement:** develop natural or artificial tasks to get your child moving at least once an hour during the school day, e.g., request assignment to carry the attendance slip to the office, return books to the library, open and close the door at recess, arrange for a mini-trampoline for jumping.

Devise strategies for community such as . . .

- **Extracurricular sports:** seek individual sports that require your child to be constantly alert and on the move, e.g., a small gymnastics class, horseback riding, swimming, kayaking at older ages; avoid sports with a large standing-around element.

Sensory Under-Responsivity—Tasks (continued)

Devise strategies for home such as . . .	Devise strategies for school such as . . .	Devise strategies for community such as . . .
• **Tactile**: provide frequent, varied, and extended opportunities for tactile stimulation, e.g., make a game of getting dressed that involves tickling your child's body. • **Gustatory**: have your child eat alerting foods upon wake-up and when sluggish, e.g., grapefruit juice, spicy crackers, peppers, wasabi, spicy sauce.	• **Stimulation**: teach your child to prepare himself for any block of time when he will need to concentrate, e.g., have him eat or drink an alerting food before taking a spelling test.	• **Extracurricular activities**: seek individual activities that are noisy or active, e.g., some music lessons, art classes involving construction (sculpting, woodworking), animal husbandry. • **Perseverance**: persevere in trying activities until you find one or more that engages your child even if he resists; don't surrender to the TV, radio, or computer!

Another Classic Pattern of SPD:
Sensory Discrimination Disorder

Children like Tam who do not feel their bodies will often have co-occurring symptoms of another classic pattern of SPD—Sensory Discrimination Disorder (SDD).

Sensory discrimination is the process of understanding and/or interpreting incoming sensory messages. It is what we use when we distinguish a baby's whimper from a cat's meow (auditory discrimination) or terrycloth from velour (tactile discrimination) or fit pieces into a jigsaw puzzle (visual discrimination). In fact, sensory discrimination takes place in the central nervous system and affects all seven of our senses.

When we interpret sensory messages correctly, we are exhibiting normal discrimination abilities. Children with good discrimination abilities are able to accurately identify sights, sounds, smells, tastes, and other sensations in order to perform the countless activities that are part of learning, playing, developing, and living.

When the ability to discriminate is impaired, a Sensory Discrimination Disorder may be present. If Tam's visual or auditory discrimination were impaired, he might not be able to see or hear the difference between his *b*'s and his *d*'s or hear the difference between *cap* and *cab*. If he had a problem with tactile discrimination, he might have trouble buckling his belt because his fingers wouldn't feel the tongue and the hole so he could fit them into each other. If a vestibular discrimination problem were present, he might have trouble feeling where he was in space. He'd be like the boy whose mother told me her son couldn't tell when he was upside down. Trying to hang by his knees from a trapeze swing on a backyard swing set, the child had once fallen on his head without taking any protective action because he had no idea he was falling until he hit the ground.

Sensory Discrimination Disorder is treated differently and by different professionals depending on which sensory system is affected. Typically, tutors, speech/language therapists, optometrists, some psychologists, and learning specialists work with Sensory Discrimination Disorder if it is auditory or visual in nature. Occupational therapists who are specially trained in treating SPD work with children who have discrimination problems in the vestibular, proprioceptive, and tactile areas, and may also work with visual discrimination issues, e.g., matching shapes or picking figures out of a busy picture like the ones in *Where's Waldo?* The charts below summarize the sensory systems in which SDD is seen* and provide examples of some of the symptoms commonly found in different sensory systems. The diagnostic information listed in the charts represents the most common procedures and diagnosticians involved in evaluating discrimination difficulties seen in children with SPD. However, any professional with specialized training, supervision, and experience can administer standardized tests.

---

* A visual or auditory discrimination problem may occur in the absence of other sensory problems. Sensory discrimination disorder (SDD) otherwise usually occurs with one of the other patterns of SPD (see Chapter 12, "Beyond the Types").

Sensory Discrimination Disorder Symptoms and Diagnosis

Visual Discrimination Disorder

An impairment in the ability to interpret what is seen. A visual discrimination disorder may affect the ability to correctly identify shapes and forms; match visual elements; remember visual information; or recognize objects that are partially concealed.

Sample Difficulties	Common Diagnostic Procedures
• telling the difference between a stop sign and a speed sign by shape • putting silverware in the correct slots in a drawer • remembering how to get to the school nurse's office • recognizing a shoe if part of it is covered up with clothing	Standardized test(s) given by: • occupational therapist • optometrist • neuropsychologist (for older children)

Auditory Discrimination Disorder

An impairment in the ability to process or interpret sounds. An auditory discrimination disorder may affect the ability to correctly discern the source or location of sound; distinguish selected sounds from background noise; distinguish between similar sounds; identify sounds; or remember sounds when they are incomplete.

Sample Difficulties	Common Diagnostic Procedures
• telling the direction from which a moving car is approaching • hearing a teacher's instructions if other children are talking • telling the difference between similar words • remembering all the steps in complex verbal instructions	Standardized test(s) given by: • speech/language therapist • neuropsychologist (for older children)

Tactile Discrimination Disorder

An impairment in the ability to feel light touch, pressure, temperature, pain, and vibration. A tactile discrimination disorder may affect the ability to correctly identify familiar items by touch alone; to identify where a tactile message is coming from; or to distinguish temperature.

Sample Difficulties	Common Diagnostic Procedures
• finding a coin in a pocket if other items are in the pocket with it • knowing where to swat at a mosquito that is biting • feeling whether a cup of liquid is hot or cold	Standardized test(s) given by: • occupational therapist • physical therapists

Vestibular Discrimination Disorder

An impairment in the ability to feel movement of the head and body in relation to the earth's gravity

Sample Difficulties	Common Diagnostic Procedures
• knowing whether you are standing upright when you're in the dark and can't see yourself • intolerance or excessive tolerance of spinning or movement, e.g., elevators, carnival rides • insecurity about being high or having feet off the ground, e.g., fear of heights, discomfort sitting on a swing	• Standardized Sensory Integration and Praxis Scale (SIPT) (given by certified occupational therapists) • Clinical observations during non-standardized sensory motor activity evaluation

Proprioceptive Discrimination Disorder

An impairment in the ability to feel the amount of sensory input to joints and muscles

Sample Difficulties	Common Diagnostic Procedures
• knowing how hard to push a door in order to shut it • exerting the right amount of pressure to lift an object • correctly acting out choreographed movements like a line dance	Standardized tests and clinical observation by: • occupational therapists • physical therapists • others trained in testing sensory and motor skills

Olfactory Discrimination Disorder

An impairment in the ability to differentiate between smells

Sample Difficulties	Common Diagnostic Procedures
• recognizing foods and beverages by smell • recognizing something burning by smell alone	• Parent report supplemented by screening during an OT evaluation

Gustatory Discrimination Disorder

An impairment in the ability to differentiate between tastes

Sample Difficulties	Common Diagnostic Procedures
• tasting the difference between juices of different fruits • distinguishing between various flavors of corn chips	• Parent report supplemented by screening during an OT evaluation

Ben's luminous brown eyes and luxurious chestnut-colored hair make him appear irresistibly huggable—until he starts to move. Then the challenge becomes getting your arms around a cyclone. From the moment he opens his eyes, Ben's day is a headlong quest for stimulation. He wolfs his food, intentionally collides with people and objects, and touches, pokes, and crowds everyone who crosses his path. Anything that requires this boy to be passive is torture for him and he responds by disrupting the activity as swiftly as possible. At his former preschool, teachers said he was a "danger to other children," and he was expelled. Family, friends, and other people have suggested he be treated for Attention Deficit Disorder. Though she's worried about her son, Ben's mother, Nancy, is unconvinced he has ADHD. His father, Mike, says he was like Ben and it's "just a boy thing." Ben has not been evaluated professionally to determine what might be causing his behavior.

Chapter 8

Ben, a Sensory-Seeking Preschooler

During the short days of January, the bedroom is barely light on the weekday mornings when the Rileys wake up to the alarm clock. Today it's still dark when a familiar and unwelcome sound jolts Nancy Riley from her dreams.

"*Eeeeeeee!*" A shriek that's meant to sound like screeching car brakes reaches the mother's darkened bedroom, followed by the thunder of small running feet and the frantic barks of Zeke, the family's Jack Russell terrier. "*Zooooooom!*" The racket means that Ben is up early again and racing the dog through the house.

Nancy turns her head to see if the noise has disturbed her husband, but as usual Mike's still fast asleep. *Not that he would care*, she thinks with a resigned sigh before throwing off the covers and groping her way out of the bedroom and down the hall toward the sounds.

"Ben!" she calls, reaching the living room and switching on a light. "Ben, wherever you are, stop right now!"

The noise grows closer, and an instant later four-year-old Ben runs into the room at full speed, Zeke panting and barking at his heels. Nancy steps in her son's path and kneels to grab him, bracing for the impact. She gets lucky, catching him around the waist and bringing him to a stop before he can plow into her. Nancy nearly always sports a bruise or two from the occasions when she's not so nimble.

"Ben," she repeats, giving the sweating boy a little shake. "It's not even six o'clock! Daddy and your sister are still asleep and you're supposed to be asleep, too. You know better than to run through the house at this time of day. This is our sleeping time, not our playing time."

Ben has been trying to twist out of his mother's grip, but at her words he stops and throws his arms around her, nearly knocking her over. "I'm *sor-ry!*" he shouts, squeezing so hard that Nancy reaches up to work his arms loose. "Sorry, sorry, *sor-ry!* I love you, *Mom*-my! *So* much!" He's chanting at a volume normally reserved for cheering the Denver Broncos, and Nancy can't help smiling. Her son may be a human tornado, but at least he's never short on enthusiasm or love.

"All right, then. If you can't go back to sleep, at least go to your room and play quietly while the rest of us sleep."

"*O-kay! O-kay! O-kay!*" he shouts, and starts a floor-shaking march toward his room.

"Quietly, Ben. Quietly." The boy grows still with obvious effort and tiptoes to his room. Nancy knows this quiet won't last. No matter what she says or Ben promises, experience has proven that he will forget what she's told him within minutes and the supersonic activity will start all over again.

Ben is the third and last child with the SPD pattern of Sensory Modulation Disorder (SMD) we'll visit. Like LaTanya and Tam, Ben has difficulty detecting and turning sensory information into appropriate behavior. But in Ben's case, this difficulty results in craving and aggressively seeking sensory input, a pattern of SMD called "sensory seeking."

Comparing the predawn minutes in the Riley household with what we've seen in the homes of LaTanya and Tam highlights the themes that are common to children with SMD and the behaviors that are specific to sensory seeking. Like LaTanya and Tam, Ben cannot self-regulate. He wakes up too early and can't put himself back to sleep. He knows in his heart that he should be quiet so everyone else can sleep, but his hunger for sensation is so overpowering that he cannot stop himself—he has to get up and start moving. And action alone doesn't satisfy Ben's hunger. He also craves the noise of the yipping dog and the sensation of his feet pounding the floor. If Nancy hadn't stopped him, he would have run into her full-tilt, not because he wants to hurt his mother or doesn't love her, but because it feels so good to make hard contact.

Unlike Tam, whose engine is chronically running too slow, Ben's engine is running too fast. In fact, it's running so fast that he's flying downhill at ninety miles per hour without brakes. Instead of being terrified, as LaTanya would be, this little boy is thrilled! He wants more, more, more.

When Nancy finally gets her son's attention, Ben is able to slow down. Whereas Tam did not detect his mother's displeasure, Ben is sensitive to Nancy's disapproval. He shows the same active desire to respond to her displeasure that Ryan, the typically developing child, demonstrates. In fact, Ben wants and will try to please Nancy and many other people over the course of the day. He even succeeds for the short periods of time dur-

*ing which he is totally focused on the assignment of being still
or being quiet or following rules. This capacity is what allows
him to tiptoe out of the living room and stay hushed all the
way down the hall to his room.*

*But as soon as Ben stops thinking actively about being
quiet, his innate quest for sensation clicks back into gear and
the search resumes. In his room, he starts playing a make-
believe football game with his plastic Denver Bronco figures
and is soon shouting out play calls, sprinting full-speed across
the rug to catch imaginary passes, and delivering key blocks by
crashing into the walls.*

*In short, another typical day in the action-packed life of
Ben Riley is under way, and it will unfold quite differently
from LaTanya's and Tam's. The underlying neurological mechanisms that produce the strikingly dissimilar behavioral patterns
in these children are not yet known, but one thing is certain
about all three: their sensory impairments are already seriously
disrupting their young lives.*

An hour later, the rest of the household is up and moving. Mike,
a contractor with a thriving homebuilding business, is already off to
work. Beatrice, Ben's younger sibling by a tight fifteen months, is
dressed and eating her breakfast while singing to one of her dolls and
looking forward to preschool, which both children attend three mornings a week.

Meanwhile, in Ben's bedroom, Nancy is trying to get her son
dressed. She sometimes jokes with friends that dressing Ben is like trying to dress a boxer in the middle of a fifteen-round fight, but that's
just her way of putting a happy face on a daily struggle. The frustrating truth is that Ben simply will not stand still to get dressed. If he's
not twirling or punching the air or hopping up and down, he's reaching for a toy or trying to run his fingers through his mother's hair or
playing with her buttons or singing a song so loud it gives her a

headache. Nancy dresses Beatrice in about three minutes flat. Ben can take fifteen. On the days he doesn't have preschool, she insists he dress himself, but this sometimes means he's in his pajamas, half-dressed, or undressed for hours. One morning, she barely caught him before he sprinted out of the house in nothing but his Harry Potter cape. He'd gotten as far as taking off his pj's but skipped the rest.

When she finally has Ben dressed, Nancy leads her son to the bathroom for what she knows will be further frustration. Before she can stop him, he turns the faucet on so hard that water splashes all over the counter and mirror; then he grabs the toothpaste and squeezes so hard that two inches of paste squirt onto the floor. Ben finds this uproariously funny and begins laughing in imitation of a hyena he saw in a cartoon movie, an ear-splitting sound that makes Nancy cringe. She gets most of the kinks out of his morning hair but gives up on the rest because he's so fidgety.

Fidgeting is common in sensory-seeking children. That's because touching, feeling, stroking, poking, pulling, and all the other forms of fidgeting generate sensations and feed their hunger for sensory input. The drive for constant activity that shows up as fidgeting in children Ben's age is usually apparent from infancy. Often these children are restless and do not sleep or nap well. They may have trouble with self-soothing activities such as getting their fingers into their mouth or curling up into a fetal position. As soon as they're mobile, they move constantly— creeping, crawling, pulling themselves up on the furniture, moving, moving, moving. More sedentary activities that typical babies love—pop-up toys, building blocks, puzzles—don't interest them unless the activities also produce intense sounds, lights, or other excitement.

Ben's fidgeting affects Nancy's ability to dress and groom her son at home and it shapes his interaction with others away from home. At school, for example, he has a great deal of trou-

ble obeying one of the golden rules of childhood—"Keep your hands to yourself"—and this causes both social and disciplinary problems for him, as we will soon see.

Children who are sensory seeking also have difficulty organizing their behavior. This is what happened when Ben almost ran outside wearing nothing but his cape. The need for sensory input is so consuming that he is unable to organize his activity in an efficient and appropriate order. Thus, in the sequence of "dress + put on cape + go outside to rescue Zeke from marauding Slytherins," he moved to steps 2 and 3 without noticing he'd missed step 1. He's a little like the genius entrepreneur who can imagine entire new universes but needs a second-in-command to run them.

However, Ben is not a genius entrepreneur. He's a little boy whose backpack is always a disaster, whose room is inevitably a wreck, who demonstrates a chronic inability to keep track of his things at home and at preschool, and who occasionally gets very basic sequences—like dressing before going outside to play—out of order. Ben's quest for sensation interferes with every aspect of his life and impairs his ability to succeed in many everyday tasks.

In the kitchen, Beatrice has finished her breakfast and is spooning make-believe cereal into her doll's mouth when Ben plops down at the table and lunges for the toy.

"Look!" he shrieks as he pitches the doll across the room, watching her hit the opposite wall and crash to the floor. "Molly can fly!"

Beatrice bursts into tears and rushes to her doll, wailing, and Ben is immediately remorseful. He races his sister across the room, scoops Molly into his arms, and pretends to check for injuries while Beatrice sniffles at his elbow.

"Don't worry, Bea," he says as he gently hands the doll back. "Molly's okay. She really can fly."

Beatrice takes the doll and gives her a fierce hug. "It's okay, baby," she whispers. "Benji didn't hurt you. Benji loves you, too."

Back at the table, Ben dumps a small mountain of spicy salsa over his toaster waffles. Hot salsa is the boy's current favorite topping for any food that is the least bit bland. He's even tried it on vanilla ice cream.

The incident with Beatrice's doll reflects another side of children who crave sensation. Ben is not a "mean" or "bad" boy, but people sometimes apply these labels because such children behave in ways that distress those around them. In reality, just as Ben is brimming with action, he is brimming with affection, sympathy, or support. All his emotions are close to the surface and his remorse about throwing Bea's doll is as strong and genuine as was his impulse to throw her. At school, Ben is usually the first child to race to the rescue when a classmate falls down and cries. If you had Down syndrome or another disability, Ben might very well be your favorite classmate because he'd always be eager to help when you struggle.

This dichotomy between Ben's aggressive and upsetting sensation seeking and his equally energetic and endearing affection creates conflict in the people around him. Sensory seekers are often responsive, creative, and fun to be around. They can be immensely enjoyable. But when their drive for sensory stimulation is running their lives and running the lives of those around them, they can be overwhelming, too.

The quest for sensation in a sensory seeker may involve one or more sensory areas. In Ben's case, nearly every realm is involved. His predawn footrace with the dog illustrates his craving for sensation in the muscles and joints (proprioceptive sensation), movement through space (vestibular sensation), and sound (auditory sensation). The same hungers were being fed when he shouted and ran and crashed into the walls while

playing with his football figures in his room. The habit of spic-
ing up food is a symptom of Ben's quest for sensation in the
realm of taste (gustatory sensation). He also likes strong smells
(olfactory sensation), and sometimes fixates on objects such as a
bright light or a reflection in the car's side-view mirror and
watches them so long that anyone else's eyes would be tired and
watering (visual sensation). As we follow Ben through his day,
remembering this innate drive for all kinds of sensation will
make his behaviors more understandable and even predictable.

The drive to preschool is another fifteen minutes of what Nancy thinks of as night-and-day motherhood. Three-year-old Beatrice is the sunshine, nestled happily in her car seat and babbling to her doll. Ben, on the other hand, is the night. When Nancy tries to buckle him into his seat in the car, he struggles to get away. This morning, he un-buckles the seat belt and begins springing around in the backseat as soon as she's turned into the street from the driveway.

"Ben! Put your seat belt back on immediately," Nancy orders. In her rearview mirror, she can see him bouncing so high that his head nearly hits the ceiling. "Ben!"

"I can't, Mommy," he pants. "I'm a jack-in-the-box. See how high I can bounce!"

Nancy signals and pulls to the curb to strap her son back in. This time, he stays put but begins to sing "99 Bottles of Beer on the Wall"—a song Nancy suspects her husband taught him, though Mike hasn't yet confessed—at the top of his lungs. The noise is enough to bother even perennially good-natured Beatrice.

"Mommy, make Ben stop," she whines. "He's hurting our ears." She holds up her doll to indicate she's not alone in her suffering. Ben responds by crowing even louder.

Before Nancy finds a way to quiet the boy, a siren sounds and she spots a speeding fire truck coming up fast behind them. For the sec-ond time on the drive, she pulls to the curb. Ben instantly unbuckles his seat belt and leaps to his knees to look out the back window. Pounding the seat with glee, he starts to howl like a siren himself. When the engine streaks past, he plunges headlong into the front seat and starts tugging on his mother's arm.

"Mom, let's follow!" he urges. "Hurry! They're getting away."

Nancy peels Ben's hands off her arm and pushes her son firmly onto the passenger seat. "Ben!" she cries. "Keep your hands to yourself and sit still. *Now!*" She doesn't even attempt to return him to the backseat where he should ride, instead fastening him into the front seat with trembling fingers. Nancy adores her firstborn and feels bad about losing her temper, but she is beginning to feel frantic about getting this boy to school so she can have a break. Abashed again, Ben laces his fingers and makes a concerted effort to obey his mother's command. Before long, however, his feet have somehow found their way to the dashboard and the boy is using them to drum in time with the music on the radio.

Any setting that requires Ben to be confined is excruciating for him, which makes the simple necessity of riding in a car problematic. As a baby, Ben screamed from the instant he was buckled into his infant seat until he was set free. Once he was strong and coordinated enough to let himself out—a milestone the athletically gifted boy hit early—the screaming stopped and the escapes began. Carpooling to preschool is out of the question: The other mothers aren't willing to put up with his antics.

Ben's aversion to car rides is the main reason Nancy's parents always make the trip to visit the Rileys. Even Mike, who generally doesn't mind Ben's rowdiness, can't bear being in the car with his son for the hours it takes to drive across the state to his in-laws' home, and the notion of getting onto an airplane with him is unimaginable. In this regard, Ben's sensory seeking is not only disrupting this boy's life, it is disrupting the entire family's life by making family trips and outings impossible.

Ben's response to the fire truck illustrates again how Sensory Modulation Disorder can affect children in different ways. For LaTanya, a sensory over-responder, the siren was distressing. For Tam, an under-responder, it went unnoticed. But Ben is in a constant search for sensation. The excessive noise of the siren and the sight of the fast-moving, bright red truck are exciting and arousing. He wants more.

At last, the Rileys reach the preschool. Ben lets himself out of the car and darts to the playground without a good-bye or his backpack. Nancy unbuckles Beatrice and gathers both children's things.

"Ben!" she calls, reaching the play area. "Come get your stuff."

Her son doesn't seem to hear. He's just finished one trip down the slide and is racing at top speed to beat three other children back to the ladder for another ride down. He sideswipes a smaller girl, who tumbles over with an angry yelp that fails to slow him down. Reaching the ladder, he squeezes past a boy who'd already set foot on the first rung and scrambles up until he runs into the end of the line.

"Go!" he shouts, butting against the girl in front of him. "Come on! *Go!*"

"Stop it!" the girl shrieks. He pushes her again and she flings her foot in his direction, barely missing his face. A teacher spots the squabble.

"Megan!" she scolds. "No kicking."

"But Ben was pushing me!" the girl calls from the ladder. "Ben always pushes. Make him stop, Mrs. Newman. Please make him stop."

Nancy watched the scene unfold as she made her way from the car with Beatrice and the backpacks. Reaching the slide, she calls to Ben, "Do not push Megan again or I will tell Mrs. Newman you may not slide for the rest of the week. And after this turn, I want you to find something else to play on until school starts."

"I'm sorry," Nancy says, turning to the teacher, who has joined her to watch Ben jiggle and wiggle his way to the top of the ladder. "He just doesn't seem to understand that other kids need personal space and he needs to stay out of it."

Mrs. Newman sighs. "I know. I see it with him all the time. I'm sure you must be trying but Ben really does need to learn some self-control. He just doesn't seem able to discipline himself."

Nancy feels a familiar wave of panic. Ben was expelled from a preschool closer to home because other parents complained about how aggressive he was. Nancy considers the longer drive to the church school he now attends a small price to pay for the three mornings a week when she gets a break from her son's go-go-go mode. The school was willing to take him because the Rileys are active members of the congregation, but the director was clear from the start that physical aggression, explosive tantrums, and behaviors that endanger or disturb the other children would not be tolerated. If Ben gets expelled here, Nancy doubts she'll find another program that will take him.

During Ben's infant and toddler years, the inappropriate be-haviors that grew from his headlong quest for sensation were less alarming to others, outweighed by the endearing ones. As he has grown older and bigger, however, the scale has begun to tip, and Ben is increasingly seen as a "problem child" by many people around him—teachers, neighbors, family friends, and other children. Although his remorse still wins him a lot of for-giveness, there are a growing number of children and adults in his life who aren't sufficiently charmed by his endearing quali-ties to tolerate his disruptive ones.

Expulsion from preschool is a common event for sensory-seeking children, and provides another illustration of the role of context in the lives of children with Sensory Processing Disorder. In the context of the school environment, the sensory craver's extreme need for sensation is on a constant collision course with behavioral expectations. The headlong rush to sensation not only appears willful but can and does lead to injuries and property damage. It is not uncommon for children like Ben to be characterized as budding juvenile delinquents or labeled with Oppositional Defiant Disorder, a recognized mental health diagnosis characterized by negative, hostile, and disobedient behaviors.

Interestingly, at times in our history when children literally pulled their weight on the family farm or in the family business instead of going to school all day for nine months of the year, Ben would have been a superstar! In that context, his physical stamina, agility, and coordination would have been prized and he would have functioned better because his sensory needs would have been met naturally by the routine of his daily life. It is in part because those times are gone and Ben's environmental context is one that puts a premium on sitting still that he needs help in order to succeed.

The behaviors that lead schools to expel children like Ben frequently have an unhealthy secondary effect as well: The children come to see themselves in the negative and self-destructive terms that are applied to them. Some days Nancy asks Ben in frustration, "Why did you do that?" after her son has broken still another object, spilled still another drink, or knocked Beatrice over one more time, and he answers, "Because I'm bad." Too often, this is the first stage in another sad self-fulfilling prophesy. Over the years, I have heard many sensory seekers say, "Everyone thinks I'm bad so I might as well be bad." As they move into adolescence, some of these children seek out other "bad" kids because this is the only peer group in which they feel socially accepted. A downward cycle sets in: The sensory-seeking child is labeled "bad," sees himself as "bad," begins to act "bad," and eventually becomes "bad." This is a terrible fate for any child; it is a completely avoidable tragedy for a child whose behaviors are a result of underlying sensory-processing issues that could be addressed.

All of the children we've met so far would benefit from pro-

*fessional intervention, but Ben's need is urgent. Without help,
he will be at high risk for the social, emotional, and societal
consequences of being rejected and labeled not just "different,"
like LaTanya and Tam, but "dangerous" or "antisocial."*

After kissing both children good-bye, Nancy drives to the nearby
coffeehouse to rendezvous with her old friend Jessica. Because of the
playground problem, she's late and rushes into the café to find her pal
already halfway through a nonfat double latte.

"Sorry," Nancy says, dropping into an empty chair and gratefully
accepting the drink Jessica has waiting for her.

"You look beat, Nance, and it's only nine-thirty in the morning.
Let me guess: drop-off problems with Ben."

"What am I going to do? Mrs. Newman was muttering again
about Ben's self-control and discipline. I know he needs to simmer
down but I just don't know how to make him do it, and I honestly
think I'll die if I don't get these three hours off every other day."

"I suppose Mike is still being his usual helpful self."

Nancy grimaces. Only Jessica knows how frustrating Nancy finds
Mike's attitude toward Ben's behavior. She doesn't even bother sharing with him little problems like the ones on the playground this
morning because he blows them off with trite comments like, "Boys
will be boys" or even "That's my guy," as if their son's overactivity is
a badge of masculine honor. "He just doesn't get it," she says.

Jessica stirs her latte. "Well, you know what I think."

Nancy nods glumly. "ADHD."

"Why are you fighting this, Nance? It's so obvious that Ben is hyperactive. They have meds for this, you know."

Nancy and Jessica have been around this track together many
times. "Jesse, Ben is four years old. I don't want him on medication.
Besides, I've read some stuff about ADHD and I'm not convinced he
has it. Sure, he's active, but there are lots of other parts of ADHD that
just don't fit."

Jessica presses her lips together. "Okay. So he doesn't have ADHD. Then you tell me: What *does* he have?"

Poor Nancy! She has one person in whom she can confide her troubles and even this most supportive friend doesn't provide much support when it comes to Ben.

The mothers we've met so far in Part II are all running out of gas, but Nancy's supply is perilously low. Because the behaviors of sensory-seeking children are often perceived as willful, their parents are frequently blamed for not setting limits that onlookers erroneously believe would solve their problems. This perception can produce a sort of mirror effect in the parents: They, too, become socially and emotionally isolated by their child's behavior and eventually come to feel like "bad" moms and dads. One mother of an over-responder told me about picking up her son from a summer day camp when a counselor bellowed over a bullhorn, "Will the mother of Rick Roberts please stay afterward!" *Her son is a successful young adult today, but she says that moment perfectly summed up the uncomfortable spotlight she constantly felt herself in as the parent of a sensational kid. It was as if she had misbehaved, too.*

Jessica's conviction that Ben has ADHD is a common judgment passed on children with sensory-seeking issues. Just as Tam's under-responsive behaviors might be mistaken for signs of autism, Ben's sensory-seeking behaviors resemble some symptoms of ADHD (see "Is It SPD or ADHD?"). Preliminary research indicates that although the disorders co-occur in some children, they actually are separate diagnostic conditions* (see Chapter 12, "Beyond the Types") .

---

* Ahn, R., L. J. Miller, S. Milberger, and D. N. McIntosh. "Prevalence of parents' perceptions of sensory processing disorders among kindergarten children," *American Journal of Occupational Therapy* 58.3 (2004): 287–302.

Is It SPD or ADHD?

Only small studies of the behavioral similarities and differences in children with SPD and ADHD have been performed so far. The following is a summation of preliminary study data and the observations of clinicians.

Sensory Seeking *vs.* Hyperactive/Impulsive ADHD

Common behavior in both disorders	SPD behavior: sensory-seeking subtype	ADHD behavior: hyperactive/ impulsive subtype
Acts impulsively	Can stop impulsive behavior if sensory input is sufficient	Cannot stop impulsive behavior regardless of the sensory input
Extraordinarily active	Craves activity that is specifically related to sensation (usually vestibular and sometimes proprioceptive)	Craves novelty and activity that is not necessarily related to specific sensations
Seems disorganized	Looks more organized after receiving intense sensory input	Does not become more organized after receiving intense sensory input
Impatient and demanding	More patient if given appropriate frequency, intensity, and duration of sensory input while waiting	Has difficulty waiting or taking turns; waits or takes turns better with cognitive input than with sensory input
Lacks self-control	Touches, pulls, and/or pokes people or objects; frequently seems to need more tactile input than most children	Tends to talk all the time, impulsively interrupting; has trouble waiting turn in a conversation

Sensory Under-Responsivity *vs.* Inattentive/ADHD

Common behavior in both disorders	SPD behavior: under-responsive subtype	ADHD behavior: inattentive subtype
Does not follow through and finish up activities	Does not want to initiate activities but can stick with activities when prompted	Can start activities but not stick with them
Has difficulty with focusing attention	Often in a daze; seems not interested in material enough to focus on it	Interested but makes careless mistakes; focus gets diverted easily
Appears disinterested and uncooperative	Often fatigued and appears lazy, bored, or unmotivated	Often daydreams and seems far away
Does not follow directions well	Unaware of directions being given; has trouble discriminating sounds or has difficulty with motor planning and thus appears to be not following directions	Gets started but has difficulty remembering or following through on a long list of verbal directions; no motor component contributes to difficulty with directions
Does not perform daily routines in a timely manner	Knows the routines but is impossibly slow	Often forgets or gets lost in the middle of a routine but completes at a normal pace when focused

Back at the preschool, Ben is in the thick of a typical day with all the problems that his days typically hold. After Nancy's reprimand on the playground, he got through the rest of playtime without incident, but as soon as Mrs. Newman called the children to line up, there were new upsets. He shoved one boy out of line and then stepped on the feet of another child. The teacher finally pulled Ben aside and held him firmly by the hand until all the other children had filed into the classroom. Ben tried hard to be orderly, but by the time he reached the classroom his face was red and he looked ready to explode.

Now it's circle time, when the children are supposed to sit quietly on the classroom's big, primary-colored rug to hear what their day will hold, and Ben is fiddling with the braids of the girl sitting next to him. She tries to wave him off, but when he keeps it up, she raises her hand and asks Mrs. Newman to make him stop. The teacher orders Ben to leave the carpet area so that none of the other children are within his reach. He obligingly leapfrogs to the edge of the rug, but instead of sitting still and listening, stretches out full length and begins rolling around like a log. Mrs. Newman largely ignores this latest burst of activity because the other children don't seem disturbed, but her patience is wearing thin and the day has barely started.

Taking in the scene is a visitor standing quietly at the back of the room. Elaine Goldberg is an occupational therapist from the local school district, in class to observe another child. Ben's behaviors are nearly always attention-getting and Elaine can't help noticing them, but her attention is interested rather than disapproving. She has seen enough children who behave just like Ben to think the boy is a good candidate for a full evaluation to find out what's causing him to act the way he does.

The first task of the day is an alphabet activity. The children are instructed to use checkers from communal stacks to form the shapes of the letters A through H. Ben's fine-motor skills are not nearly as advanced as the gross-motor skills he shows on the playground, but he is a bright boy who learned his alphabet at home before he reached preschool and the checkers are big enough for him to manipulate without trouble. With a single structured assignment before him, he is able to work diligently and successfully for several minutes until— uh-oh!—he's done.

Finishing ahead of other kids leaves Ben with idle time that requires self-regulation, which is always a challenge for the busy boy. First he starts picking at the sleeve of the classmate sitting next to him. When the boy swats Ben's hand away, Ben starts chewing on his own shirt, a habit that has left ragged little holes in many of his tops. Tiring of this, he stands up on his chair and tries balancing on one foot until Mrs. Newman orders him to sit down and be still. He sits down, but moments later he can't resist rolling his extra checkers at the letters his tablemates are making.

"Ben messed up my C!" a girl in a fuzzy sweater howls when he scores a particularly devastating hit. The classroom assistant looks up from the next table and sees the girl's broken C. Ben is making silly faces at the boy across the table.

"Ben," the aide admonishes. He looks at her and crosses his eyes. All the children twitter, except the girl with the ruined C . The assistant frowns and moves to Ben's chair. "You have to go to time-out."

Ben immediately calms down. "I'll be good," he pleads, sitting on his hands. "Really I will. Don't put me in time-out. Please."

The aide pulls Ben's hands out from under him and tugs the boy to his feet. "I don't want you to be in time-out, either," she says, "but you are not following the rules and you are disturbing the other children." She draws him toward the corner.

If the morning assignment had been to handwrite *the alphabet, Ben would not have finished first. Because he is always on the move, Ben has had ample opportunity to develop his gross-motor skills but little chance to develop the fine-motor ones that require small muscle movement. Ben crawled and walked early but was delayed in developing the dexterity needed to put small objects like Cheerios in his mouth. At four, he knows his letters and can make them with the big checkers, but he has not yet mastered even the simple block printing of most preschoolers. Activities such as puzzles, Legos, drawing, and art projects that require tools like scissors and glue are highly frustrating because he hasn't been able to sit still long enough to practice and achieve competence.*

These difficulties illustrate another way that Ben's sensory seeking is disrupting his development and foreshadow future problems. Fine-motor skills are essential for many activities central to academic success. As long as Ben's sensory issues interfere with his development of those skills, his academic future is at risk.

Ben wants to be a "good boy," but he can't. Reaching the corner, he plants his feet and lets out a roof-raising scream that seems to go on and on and on. All activity in the classroom stops. The children farthest away stand up to get a better look and all of the kids gawk. Ben raises his hands like claws over his head and stamps his feet with rage while he screams, "I'm trying to be good! I'm trying! I'm trying!" But to the others, it doesn't look as if he's trying.

Disruptive as Ben's behavior is, the class has been through his outbursts before; Mrs. Newman has learned there is a predictable pattern to them. The aide stays at the boy's side to make sure he doesn't hurt himself or anyone else, and eventually the screaming subsides. Ben drops to the floor, sobbing, and begins to rock forward and back, forward and back. The other children gradually return to their work, and after a few minutes, Ben dries his tears. He starts chewing on his shirt again, resigned to enduring his time-out. The visiting OT crosses to Mrs. Newman.

"Could I ask you something about the little boy in the corner?" the OT asks.

"Sure," says Mrs. Newman with a tired sigh, "but I can't guarantee any answers."

"Well, I couldn't help wondering if his parents have had him evaluated, either by the school district or privately," she says. "For example, has anyone like me ever come into the classroom to observe him?"

The teacher shakes her head. "Not as far as I know. I've suggested to his mother that he be evaluated for ADHD, but I don't think she's followed through."

Recovered from his tantrum, Ben has drawn his knees against his chest, wrapped his arms around them, and begun spinning in place like a little top. The speed at which he whirls is always astonishing, and Mrs. Newman signals to the aide to monitor the boy from where she is circulating among the tables of working children. Even though Ben never shows any signs of growing dizzy, the teacher always worries he'll hurt himself whenever he gets going this way.

Elaine continues, "Well, without a thorough evaluation, I don't have any answers, either. But since you say this is a recurrent pattern, I suspect the behavior you're seeing could have a physiological basis. If that's the case, there are some fairly simple activities that are calming for most children and might be especially helpful for this little guy. If you're interested, I'd be happy to jot them down for you."

"Please," Mrs. Newman says. "I'd welcome anything."

Ben looks angry and even frightening as he roars and makes claw hands and stamps, but he's not. Ben is frustrated. He has been trying to get his quota of sensory stimulation since he woke up hours ago, and he has not succeeded. Now it is mid-morning and his sensory hunger has been building like steam in a pressure cooker without a valve. His unsatisfied needs have to find an outlet and the outlet is his tantrum.

One strategy for satisfying sensory craving is to provide stimulation that will have a calming effect on one or more of the non-movement sensory systems. Ben seeks movement (vestibular stimulation) and sensation in his muscles and joints (proprioception). Calming his other senses with sound (with soft rhythmic music), sight (with low lights), and/or smell (with vanilla or another sweet scent) very likely would lower his overall level of arousal and subdue his vestibular and proprioceptive cravings. Non-rhythmic vestibular stimulation could also help Ben at times when he is seeking sensory input. Non-repetitive activities such as twisting himself in one direction on a swing and then reversing to untwist would be good.

The Role of the Vestibular System

Ben's spinning in the corner following his tantrum illustrates his quest for stimulation in another system often implicated in Sensory Processing Disorder: the vestibular system.

The vestibular system is comprised of several structures in the inner ear. When the head tilts in any direction, fluid moves small hairs within the structures and their movement lets us know our position in relation to the earth's gravity. This is how we know when we are in motion.

Humans need vestibular stimulation and use it for both calming and arousing. If you've ever relaxed by moving back and forth in a glider or a porch swing, you know what it feels like to calm yourself with this system. It is the same effect Ben is after when he rocks in the corner. Likewise, if you've ever found yourself itching to get up and move around during a long meeting or on an airplane flight, you know how it feels to hunger for the arousing effects of vestibular stimulation. This is what Ben is seeking when he begins to spin.

Children generally need and want more vestibular stimulation than adults do, which explains why many babies and toddlers thrill at being lifted or even tossed in the air and why spinning and whirling toys and rides are so popular with kids. The difference between a sensory-seeking child like Ben and typically developing children like Ryan is that Ben seeks more of this type of stimulation. Inside, he constantly feels the way you or I would on a cross-country flight where the "Fasten seat belt" sign never goes off.

Among the proposed explanations for this pattern is that the threshold for detecting movement is higher in sensory seekers, requiring movement that is stronger, lasts longer, or occurs more frequently in order to trigger their sense of movement.* Whatever research eventually finds, there is little question that children like Ben respond well and function more successfully when they are given activities that calm their sensory cravings.

As LaTanya did, Ben would also benefit from engagement in tasks requiring heavy work, which would provide direct input to his proprioceptive system. If Ben were given the responsibility every morning for removing all the chairs from the tabletops and setting them in place before preschool starts, he would gain a constructive source of sensory stimulation and would spare everyone the collisions that currently occur on the playground. Pushing and pulling activities would help, as would having Ben sit on a therapy ball instead of a chair. Access to "fidget toys," such as a curly telephone cord attached under the tabletop where he sits, could give Ben an "acceptable" means of fidget-

---

* Some researchers believe the behavior of children who are sensory seeking stems from sensory under-responsivity such as we saw in Tam. Although this subject has not been well researched, my view is that the same underlying neurological mechanism is unlikely to produce such dramatically different behaviors and that, with time and study, we will find two different pathologies.

ing or getting extra sensory input. Oral-motor activities such as chewing gum or sucking water—better yet, sucking something thick like yogurt—through a straw might provide the same soothing effects and would be a lot less expensive and destructive than his current method of self-calming: shirt chewing.

In fact, the entire class could benefit from many of the activities that Ben needs, eliminating Ben's being repeatedly singled out for attention. Getting children into the "just-right state" of arousal promotes concentration. If Mrs. Newman integrated activity songs like "Head, Shoulders, Knees and Toes" *before work time, the entire class would be more ready to focus. All children get overexcited from time to time, especially around holidays and other special events. Teachers who understand self-regulation needs can incorporate therapeutic activities into the schedule that will help all the children better manage their level of arousal.*

Creating a quiet corner in the classroom where any child can retreat to take a break from the classroom routine may also help maintain order and help overaroused children self-regulate. If the quiet corner (a tent or a loft is nice) contains heavy pillows for children to move, a weighted blanket, or other materials that provide soothing effects, the benefits will be even greater. If these were available for Ben to calm himself, everyone in the classroom would be better off.

Nancy returns to the school to pick up the children before lunch. Most of the other four-year-olds stay all day, but getting through lunch and quiet time have proven too much for busy Ben. The Rileys and Mrs. Newman agreed that a half-day schedule would be in everyone's best interests for the time being.

Nancy's mood in the afternoon is often linked to the expression on Mrs. Newman's face at the end of Ben's half-day. Today she takes Mrs. Newman's smile and wave to be positive signs.

"Did Ben have a good day?" Nancy asks hopefully.

Mrs. Newman's smile dims slightly. "Well, not exactly, but I may have something promising." The teacher describes her conversation with the visiting OT and hands Nancy a copy of Elaine's strategies. The teacher has already made copies for everyone who works with Ben at the preschool.

"Some of her suggestions are so easy, it seems hard to believe they'd really work. But I already tried one and it seemed to help. We keep all the balls and other portable playground equipment in a box in the classroom. Usually I have the children each carry one plaything outside. Today I asked Ben to push the entire box out of the room and onto the playground. I was a little worried because it's pretty heavy, but you know how strong and coordinated he is. He was absolutely determined to do the job himself, and he managed it without any help. I can't say he became an entirely new child, but he did seem a little better during that break. He seemed somewhat more self-disciplined."

The occupational therapist's conversation with Mrs. Newman illustrates another key concept in helping sensational children: "reframing." Anyone who has ever put a familiar picture in a new frame and been startled by the difference in how it looked knows about reframing.

As long as Ben's behaviors are blamed on his personality or on Nancy's parenting style, people will see the way he acts as something he and/or his mother can control. If his behaviors are "reframed" as symptoms of an underlying neurophysiological disorder, people are likely to view him differently. With reframing, Ben could cease to be seen as a "bad" child and begin to be seen as a child with a disability. His disruptive and inappropriate behavior at school could be approached as symptoms of the disorder and activities such as the heavy work of pushing the toy box could be built into the day to modify those symptoms.

At home after school and lunch, it's nap time. Ben falls asleep almost instantly, thanks to the rigors of his morning in preschool, and Nancy takes advantage of the quiet time to read the occupational therapist's suggestions. She doesn't understand why things like having her son chew gum could possibly help, but the OT has stapled her business card to the list, and Nancy makes a note of the telephone number. She knows Mike probably won't go along with anything incorporating the word "therapy," but if the problems with preschool continue, even Mike will have to admit that Ben needs some help. Besides, the therapist wrote on the back of her card that Ben might qualify for a free evaluation from the public school district even though he's only a preschooler.

Nancy knows Ben's nap has ended when she hears him jumping on his bed, signaling that it's time to bundle the refreshed children into the car for the short drive to the park. Both children thoroughly love park outings, but Nancy has mixed feelings about them. If there are too many other kids on the equipment, Ben tends to get into the same kinds of run-ins he has at preschool, except Nancy ends up having to deal directly with alarmed or outraged parents. This is always embarrassing and sometimes humiliating.

Today turns out to be one of the good days. Only a handful of children are at the park and all of them are already involved in their own activities. At first Ben races frenetically from one piece of equipment to another. He pushes the merry-go-round and jumps on when it's going so fast that Nancy barely can make out his face as it whirls past. Then he jumps off before it stops and races to the slide and then the jungle gym. There's a pole within the jungle gym that other children use to slide down from the top platform, but Ben scrambles up it, agile as a little monkey. A few bystanders pause to watch him climb and Nancy feels a rare surge of pride. One thing is for sure: Ben has *athlete* written all over him, just like his dad.

After the first half-hour or so, Ben's pace gradually slows and he stops racing from one piece of equipment to another. Eventually he settles on top of the jungle gym, where he calls reports to his mother.

"Look, Mommy! I'm the captain of a pirate ship and I'm sailing all the way around the world." He makes tooting boat and crashing wave sounds but focuses mostly on steering his make-believe craft through heavy seas, rocking with the waves as he goes. He's so content that Nancy lingers for nearly two hours, until Beatrice grows cranky and dinnertime looms. She's a little tired herself and barely notices that her son slides into his car seat without a protest and stays put all the way home.

Back at the house, Ben plays a short game of Candyland with Beatrice and Molly the doll and then wanders into the kitchen to snack on fresh carrots his mom has put out. The evening is unfolding so smoothly that Nancy decides to bring up the problems she saw on the playground at the beginning of preschool.

"Why did you keep butting into that girl in front of you on the ladder this morning, Ben?" she asks.

The boy shrugs and chomps on a carrot. "I don't mean to do things like that, Mommy. They just happen. Things come out all by themselves. It's like there's a good Ben inside me that wants to do everything he should, but the bad Ben inside won't let the good Ben out."

When the Rileys first arrive at the park, Ben behaves the same way he does upon arriving at preschool: speeding randomly from one piece of equipment to the next—trying this, trying that. If there had been more children around, he almost certainly would have clashed with them in his desperate, unfocused rush to meet his sensory needs.

But something wonderful begins to happen the harder Ben plays. He starts to calm down and his play becomes more organized. Instead of merely moving around, he is able to coordinate his movements with the inventions of his well-developed imagination. If another child approached him while he was captaining his jungle-gym pirate ship, it is much more likely he would have been able to play cooperatively and appropriately.

This is because the little boy is finally getting a complete sensory diet through activity. Ben is like a starving man who's been fed exactly what he fantasized about when he was hungry, which enables him to stop thinking about food and start thinking about how to escape the desert island. What's more, the boy's innate strengths of physical agility and coordination have been showcased, and both he and his mom have enjoyed the relatively rare experience of general approval.

It's too bad that Nancy doesn't notice how comfortably Ben travels home from the long park visit and how successfully he plays with Beatrice back at home. She loses an opportunity to praise her son for his appropriate behavior and congratulate herself for meeting his sensory needs. However, by the time he joins her in the kitchen, she recognizes that Ben is having one of his better days. The fresh carrot snack was an idea from the OT's list. In therapy, she would learn that the proprioceptive stimulation of biting down on the hard and resistant food provides the same calming influence LaTanya derived from sucking applesauce through a straw.

Minutes later, the door from the garage bursts open and Mike Riley bangs into the house. "Hello-O-o!" he hollers. "Where's my gang? Daddy's home!"

Her husband's nonchalance about Ben's behavior may leave Nancy feeling all alone with her son's problems, but she's the first to give him credit for being a great dad. He always arrives home with a big happy holler and bear hugs all around. After giving Beatrice a giddy tickle and throwing Ben over his big shoulder where the boy can hang and harmlessly pound on his dad's back, he hunts Nancy down in the kitchen and gives her a sloppy kiss.

"Hey, baby. How was your day?"

"Good," she says. For a change, it actually has been. "How about yours?"

"Great," he says. He lowers Ben to the floor headfirst and then springs into a boxer's crouch for an exchange of playful punches as soon as the boy rights himself. Nancy squeezes herself into a corner while the two punch it out until Mike raises his hand for a halt. "Hey, big guy. Daddy's going for a quick run. Wanna ride your bike along-side? Maybe Zeke wants to come, too."

"Sure!" Ben cries, his brown eyes dancing.

"Then go get Zeke and your helmet. I'll meet you in the garage."

"But, honey . . ." Nancy says. The men in her life watch as she scans the pot-covered stovetop. Dinner is nearly ready. Nancy sighs good-naturedly. "Okay, but make it quick, would you? I don't want everything to get cold."

Here's another example of the power of a good "fit" in the lives of sensational children.

In Ben's life, any task that requires him to be quiet or still—riding in the car, sitting through circle time, waiting his turn—is a poor fit because it gets in the way of his quest for sensation. Any task that delivers extra helpings of propriocep-tion and vestibular stimulation to his sensory diet is a better fit. This is why Ben is more successful at athletics than at hand-writing assignments.

Fit applies to relationships—the big R in A SECRET—as well. People who operate at Ben's high level of activity are a good fit for the sensory-seeking boy, and his big, noisy, athletic dad is one of those people. When Mike returns home from work and boxes with his physically gifted son or takes him along on a jog with the racing, barking dog, the dad is filling his son's sensory need for movement just by being himself. In fact, it is quite possible that Mike has some of the same under-

lying sensory issues Ben does and that he's instinctively meeting his own sensory needs as well as unconsciously satisfying his son's. This is only an educated guess; the causes of Sensory Processing Disorder are not well known and a thorough evaluation would be necessary to diagnose Mike. However, heredity is strongly believed to play a role in SPD, and the similarity between this father and son could be related to an undiagnosed sensory-seeking condition in Mike (see Chapter 13, "Causes and Prevalence").

Although Nancy doesn't share the sensory appetites of her husband and son, she helps foster their special relationship. By routinely planning active outings like the trip to the park, she provides Ben with precisely the sensory stimulation he craves. As a result, the boy is often in the best shape he's been in all day at just about the time Mike arrives home. When Mike greets his son with further vigorous activity—wrestling, roughhousing, jogging, doing heavy yard work together—Ben's sensory appetite is at last sated. No wonder Mike seems oblivious to Ben's problems and Nancy feels discouraged about her mothering! Mike gets the happy little boy whose sensory appetites are satisfied and Nancy gets the disruptive, angry one who is hungry. What's more, Mike is rarely the parent who has to field the complaints, criticisms, and blame that Ben provokes, which makes his parenting experience quite different and more rewarding than Nancy's.

Both parents are providing Ben with vital support. Mike's perspective as a sensory-hungry parent gives Ben a reliable emotional oasis where the boy's activity level and physical acumen are applauded and where his behavioral lapses are accepted. Nancy's perspective as the parent who doesn't crave sensation enables her to see the bigger picture of how Ben's behavior is disrupting his total childhood experience.

Crucial as each parent's individual support is, the entire

Riley family would be better off if Mike and Nancy could
work more as a team. Mike's acceptance of his son's behavior
prevents him from seeing that Ben needs to learn self-regulation
and from supporting Nancy. Nancy's understandable resent-
ment of being left alone to deal with Ben's problems is causing
tension in the couple's marriage. If Mike resists or rejects evalu-
ation and intervention for their son, more tension is likely to
ensue. Marital stress is a common secondary effect of childhood
SPD and is another reason that early diagnosis and interven-
tion are imperative for sensational kids and their families.

Mealtime with Ben can take an eternity because he's up and down from the table so many times—swallowing a bite of food, racing off to his room for a toy, leaving the table to turn a couple of somersaults. Sometimes Nancy thinks her girlfriend Jessica is right and Ben should be on medication for ADHD.

But tonight, the boy keeps his hands to himself and his bottom on his chair. The long visit to the park followed by the carrot snack and the spirited bike ride have worked their magic and now the boy is relatively calm. After all, Ben is only four! He's just a little guy and now he's a little guy whose hunger for sensation has been satisfied. He seems happy as he stumbles with his eyes at half-mast through his bath and bedtime routines, and Nancy doesn't even get through one story before he is fast asleep.

Later, as she's drifting off herself, Nancy counts the good moments of the day as she always does and finds there were more than usual. For a change, she's still smiling when she falls fast asleep herself.

If Nancy follows through and calls the occupational therapist,
Ben will be screened and, if the screening warrants, evaluated.
Given Ben's academic and social problems, it is probable he
will qualify for school services. With OT through the schools

and/or from a private provider, his chances of succeeding in kindergarten and beyond will improve dramatically.

In the meantime, Ben's sensory-seeking behaviors can be reduced by implementing at least two thirty-minute periods of vigorous activity every single day, preferably one before school and one after school. More would be even better. Arranging for an hour or more of focused physical activity (not to be confused with organized sports that involve standing around on an athletic field waiting for a ball to come by) might sound overwhelming to Nancy, but this hour of activity would be an investment in Ben's day that would pay off in all his settings and relationships. Ultimately, making sure Ben spends time feeding his sensory appetite before going to school will be much less time-consuming than dealing with the consequences of his unsatisfied sensory cravings.

It is easy to focus on the deficits of a child with Sensory Processing Disorder, but it is crucial for families also to see the strengths of their children and of themselves. When I interview parents, the first question I ask is always about the gifts that make their child special. With his physical prowess and strength, Ben is a natural for athletics. He is smart and kind. Activities that capitalize on his strengths would develop his self-confidence and give him some positive feedback to offset all the negative feedback he receives because of his inappropriate behaviors.

Another question I ask parents is what activities the family likes most and whether there are valued activities they cannot do because of their child. This helps me design a therapy program targeted at parents' priorities for change. By developing an intervention plan for Ben that fits into his family's lifestyle and focuses on the positive input that each parent can provide, the entire family benefits. Good family-centered care produces successful outcomes for every family member.

A SECRET for Your Sensory-Seeking Child*

Sensational strategies that may improve a child's functioning can be developed by any parent. Strategies emerge when each element of A SECRET is examined and one or more elements is modified to improve the "fit" between the sensory-seeking child's personal characteristics and the world around him. The following chart illustrates how to use this flexible approach to examine the last three elements of A SECRET—Relationships, Environment, and Tasks. These are the elements most readily modified by parents.

---

* A clinical diagnosis of sensory seeking can be made only with a comprehensive diagnostic evaluation. Sensational strategies are most effective when developed as part of a comprehensive intervention program provided by an OT or another professional with training in treating Sensory Processing Disorder.

A SECRET for Your Sensory-Seeking Child

A SECRET for Relationships

Modify RELATIONSHIPS to foster interaction that is characterized by tolerance and appreciation for your child's activity level.

Ask questions such as . . .

- Around what types of people can my child stay focused and behave appropriately? Around what types of people is my child most inattentive and provocative?
- How can I facilitate relationships with people, both children and adults, who are the better fit for my child?
- If some siblings or other family members have greater difficulty tolerating my child's sensory seeking, how can I promote understanding in those people or modify the situations in which they come into contact?

Devise strategies for home such as . . .

- **Peers:** identify potential playmates who are physically active but can channel their activity in structured ways; actively supervise activities with peers to prevent meltdowns and aggression.

Devise strategies for school such as . . .

- **Understanding:** develop a script to explain to all school personnel your child's need for extra sensory stimulation.

Devise strategies for community such as . . .

- **Understanding:** develop and use a script that explains the circumstances most likely to make your child unmanageable; use it to explain your child to extended family, neighbors, service providers, and—especially—the parents of playmates.

Sensory Seeking—Relationships (*continued*)

Devise strategies for home such as . . .	Devise strategies for school such as . . .	Devise strategies for community such as . . .
• **Siblings and other family**: teach your child that others may be uncomfortable with his need for high activity or sound; respect the needs of others to minimize time around your child, e.g., if Grandma has trouble with your son, don't ask her to babysit him. • **Self-regulation**: teach your child to be aware when his engine is running too fast and distance himself from others until he satisfies his sensory needs appropriately. • **Tactile**: use deep pressure to calm your child when he is overaroused. • **Proprioceptive**: prepare for times of intense personal interaction by engaging your child in activities that provide input to his muscles and joints (e.g., pushing, pulling, running, jumping). • **General**: build breaks for yourself into the day; your child needs so much active stimulation that he can wear you out!	• **Support network**: identify one or more members of the school staff who can be available to engage your child in heavy work (e.g., moving furniture, carrying heavy books, helping the janitor sweep) at regular intervals throughout the day or when sensory-seeking behaviors are seen. • **Teacher assignment**: request teachers who can tolerate highly active children and who are flexible enough to assign your child to heavy work activities as needed. • **Classmates**: request that children who can tolerate your child be matched with him for projects.	• **Intervention**: provide concrete suggestions and strategies for use by people who may be in charge of your child at times when he is growing overexcited, agitated, overactive, or disruptive. • **Services**: identify and patronize service providers (barbers/hairdressers, dentists/physicians, coaches/instructors, and others) who will tolerate and accommodate your child's need for heavy work and extra sensation; avoid service providers who routinely make you wait for your appointments. • **Support**: make sure an informed, understanding adult supervises activities outside your home in order to prevent your child from getting out of control.

Sensory Seeking—Environment

A SECRET for Environment

Modify the ENVIRONMENT to create interesting yet organized surroundings that provide novel experiences with intense sensations.

Ask questions such as . . .

- What types of environments help my child pay attention and behave appropriately? What types of surroundings cause him to be disorganized, distracted, and/or overstimulated?
- How can I modify the environment to increase his attention, support appropriate behavior, increase organization, and prevent overstimulation?

Devise strategies for home such as . . .	Devise strategies for school such as . . .	Devise strategies for community such as . . .
• **Proprioceptive**: make tools available for sustained heavy work activities, e.g., a climbing rope, tricycle or bicycle; provide self-calming devices, e.g., fidget toys, heavy rubber bands. • **Tactile**: organize the environment so that things your child uses routinely have textures that provide tactile stimulation, e.g., bath mats, seating materials, stuffed animals, shoes and socks.	• **Personal space**: define personal space in a visible way, e.g., in preschool, draw a square around his desk area with masking tape on the floor. • **Classroom space**: seek a rigidly ordered classroom (e.g., desks in rows) that also contains opportunities for sensory stimulation during free time.	• **Special events and outings**: seek settings that promote vigorous organized movement, preferably outdoors, e.g., parks, water parks, amusement parks, gymnasiums. • **Summer and special programs**: vary activities to minimize sameness. • **Shops and offices**: seek settings with minimal breakable items.

Sensory Seeking—Environment (*continued*)

Devise strategies for home such as . . .	Devise strategies for school such as . . .	Devise strategies for community such as . . .
• **Vestibular**: make equipment available that provides purposeful movement requiring an organized response, e.g., a swing with a target he kicks at the top of each arc. • **Visual**: maintain order and organization, e.g., label drawers and shelves for clothes and toys to minimize clutter; use muted colors and lighting. • **Auditory**: provide a means to listen to loud recordings as needed; supply earphones to minimize impact on others; provide a steady background of quiet sound, e.g., classical music, not heavy metal! • **Gustatory**: provide foods with intense tastes. • **General**: provide constant change, e.g., rearrange the furniture in his room regularly; change seating positions at the dinner table every night.	• **Tactile**: arrange for your child to have constant access to fidget toys and tactilely diverse materials. • **Proprioceptive**: arrange for your child to sit on a therapy ball instead of a chair during class; teach him isometrics and "chair sit-ups" that provide proprioception without requiring him to leave his place. • **Visual**: seek a well-ordered and predictable classroom , e.g., books are always shelved. • **Self-calming**: encourage creation of a separate area in the classroom for times of overarousal; equip the retreat with toys to stretch, pull, chew, or push against to provide heavy work.	• **Travel and transportation**: avoid if possible; when unavoidable, provide extra opportunities for activity beforehand, e.g., jump rope in the gate area before boarding an airplane; carry tools for heavy or structured work and novel activities, e.g., a straw for cotton ball soccer, gum to chew, highly structured activity books.

Sensory Seeking—Tasks

A SECRET for Tasks

Modify TASKS to make them interesting and novel so that your child remains organized and his attention is sustained.

Ask questions such as . . .

- What kinds of activities engage my child for extended periods of time?
- How can I incorporate the engaging aspects of those activities into other tasks that he doesn't like as well?
- What kinds of activities are most problematic for my child?
- How can I modify those activities to help him overcome his difficulties with them?

Devise strategies for home such as . . .

- **Sensory diet:** provide additional sensory stimulation while your child is working on tasks that have low sensory input, e.g., have him sit on a therapy ball while he eats dinner.

Devise strategies for school such as . . .

- **During class:** make sure your child has something to fidget with, such as a curly telephone wire or a stretchy elastic.
- **During tests:** make sure your child is always supplied with something to do if he finishes work early.

Devise strategies for community such as . . .

- **Extracurricular sports:** seek individual or team sports that require sustained, active, organized movement, e.g., water polo, track events; avoid sports with large standing-around element.
- **Extracurricular activities:** choose non-sports activities that involve physical activity, e.g., theater, animal husbandry.

Sensory Seeking—Tasks (*continued*)

Devise strategies for home such as . . .	Devise strategies for school such as . . .	Devise strategies for community such as . . .
• **Intervention**: develop and use reliable techniques for satisfying your child's craving for activity when he is acting out, e.g., if he's becoming agitated while you are on the telephone, assign him to jump all the way up and down the stairs in your house five times while you time him (and talk). • **Chores**: assign household chores that will build extra movement into your child's daily routines, e.g., vacuuming, gardening, moving books, sweeping, raking.	• **Tasks**: seek assignment to teachers who create interesting worksheets, books, and projects and have extra activities for children who finish early. • **Preparation**: whenever possible, have the child prepare for focused tasks by obtaining extra proprioceptive and vestibular input, e.g., running laps around the playground before taking a long test. • **Concentration**: provide a moving surface (therapy ball or seat cushion) for use during demanding tasks.	• **Understanding**: identify for adult leaders, caregivers, and others ways they can modify tasks to make them achievable for your child. • **Sensory preparation**: prepare your child for outside activities with sensory diet, e.g., if he's going to a birthday party, give him deep pressure and proprioceptive stimulation beforehand. • **Sensory satisfaction**: if necessary, provide additional sensory input during taxing events, e.g., take breaks during a sports event for the child to climb the stairs of the arena several times.

If children were born with labels, Abby Hudson believes hers would have been "Klutz!" For as long as the third-grader can remember, things all the other kids could do felt hard to her. For a long time, Abby's parents tried comforting her by pointing out that even though she walked long after other babies the same age, she learned to walk. This only made Abby feel like she'd been behind since birth and would be behind forever. Things finally improved after Abby was evaluated and diagnosed with Sensory-Based Motor Disorder, one of the three classic patterns of Sensory Processing Disorder. After she began occupational therapy, she began to blossom socially and her clumsiness became less important. She started feeling better about herself. Abby's sensory handicap has not been "cured" and probably never will be, but she has improved tremendously by learning to adapt in situations where she still has problems.

Chapter 9

Abby, a Dyspraxic Third-Grader

The clock radio in Abby Hudson's bedroom bursts to life with a raucous popular song and the sleepy third-grader's eyes flutter open. Monday. Beginning of another work week. That's how Abby thinks of school: as her work. Sometimes it's tough, but it's what eight-year-old girls do, and Abby takes pride in the way she does it.

As always, she listens to one complete song before giving up the warm nest of her covers. Her door opens just as the song ends. "Morning, Sunshine," says her dad.

"Morning, Daddy."

"Ready to rise and shine?"

Abby gives herself a last, luxurious stretch and nods cheerfully.

Henry Hudson is surveying the floor of his daughter's room without the dismay a typical parent would feel to find it covered with clothes. Everything Abby will need for the day is spread out so that nothing can be forgotten, and each item is turned with the front facing down so that when she pulls it on, the front will be to the front and the back to the back.

"Good girl," Henry says. "Breakfast in fifteen."

Abby gives her dad a smile that's bright in spite of the gaps where new permanent teeth are still missing. "Any chance of oatmeal with brown sugar and raisins?"

Henry checks his watch. "There might be for any little girl I find in the kitchen fifteen minutes from now."

Abby's smile brightens a few more watts and she throws off her covers. "Toast, too?"

Henry laughs. "Toast, too."

Before Abby was diagnosed with dyspraxia and went into occupational therapy, mornings weren't so sunny around the Hudson home. Long after most kids could dress themselves, Abby had to be dressed by one of her parents or re-dressed after she put her clothes on "wrong"—one sock on backward and one inside out, shirtfront facing backward, shoes on the wrong feet.

When she got to the kitchen to eat, there were more problems. Abby couldn't fix her own breakfast. If she tried, she poured so much milk over the cereal that it overflowed the bowl. She missed the glass with the orange juice. She even had trouble getting the spoon to her mouth without spilling: The proper use of silverware was a puzzle and sometimes it seemed to take forever for her to feed herself a bowl of cereal.

When these and other such failures occurred, Abby grew frustrated with herself and with whatever she was trying to handle. She'd call herself "stupid" and "idiot" and "klutz" and feel angry. Her parents were often angry, too, but mostly with each other. Henry, her dad, usually wanted to give her a helping hand, but Cindy, her mom, said he was just making things worse by babying the girl. Everyone would end up upset about how long little things took to accomplish and how late they always were. The Hudson marriage was already in trouble and these tensions didn't help. It was a tough time for the whole family.

Abby introduces us to another classic pattern of SPD: Sensory-Based Motor Disorder. SBMD symptoms occur in two subtypes:

- Dyspraxia—difficulty translating sensory information into planning and/or sequencing physical movement, especially new or unfamiliar actions
- Postural disorder—difficulty stabilizing the body during movement or at rest to meet the demands of a given motor task (see "Postural Disorder: The 'Other' SBMD")

Many children with dyspraxia also have postural disorder or another form of SPD (see Chapter 12, "Beyond the Types"). Although Abby has some postural problems, her primary diagnosis is dyspraxia—difficulty planning motor activities.

Motor planning is something that most of us do all the time without realizing it. We don't stop and think about sequences such as:

- *putting one arm into a coat or sweater, tossing the garment behind our bodies, and then pushing the other arm into the other sleeve, or*
- *filling a tray in the cafeteria line and then maneuvering around people and other obstacles to a table, or*
- *lining up the numbers in columns to perform a simple arithmetic problem.*

Children like Abby do have to think about these activities, which makes them slow, awkward, and clumsy.

If you've ever attempted a new motor activity as an

adult—skiing, knitting, a new dance step—you've experienced what these children feel all the time. I experienced a memorable "dyspraxic moment" while learning to roll a river kayak. I was supposed to turn my kayak upside down and then "simply" roll it back up. Try as I might, I couldn't get it. Finally, my daughter—all of eleven years old at the time—said, "Mom, you're thinking too hard. Just do it like this!" She flipped over and popped right back up. "Use your body, not your head." I eventually learned how to roll, but it would be fair to say I was "delayed" in learning this skill.

Delays like this are found throughout the development of dyspraxic children. As babies and toddlers, they are frequently slow to roll over, crawl, walk, run, and reach all motor milestones. Tam was delayed in these areas, too, but his delays were caused by the failure of his brain to notice incoming sensory messages unless the messages were intense or longlasting, not because he couldn't organize the messages. Once he got interested in his second-grade grasshopper project, for example, he was capable of arranging his specimens in rows on poster board, matching the right labels to the specimens, and placing labels under each insect. Abby would have difficulty planning and executing all the steps involved in completing this project.

The task of organizing sensory information into appropriate physical motion occasionally challenges all but the most kinesthetically gifted of us, as my experience in the kayak illustrates. For a child such as Abby, however, the challenge is severe and chronic. Without the treatment she's received, she would still be struggling with the most simple of motor-planning activities.

As Abby puts on each item of clothing, she happily awards herself a big peel-off sticker on the chart where all of her self-care chores are listed. If she has enough stickers at the end of the week, she gets to choose the restaurant where she and her dad or mom will go for Friday night supper before she changes houses, and Abby loves choosing the restaurant. Once she's dressed, the cheerful youngster heads for the bathroom to wash her face and brush her teeth and comb her short blond hair. There's a chart on the bathroom wall similar to the one in the bedroom and another set of peel-off stickers in a drawer. Each grooming chore is on the chart; even at eight, Abby consults the list frequently to make sure she is covering all her bases and earning her stickers.

In the kitchen, Henry has the oatmeal waiting when his daughter arrives.

"Look at me! Hair, teeth, clothes, shoes!" With a proud grin, Abby points to her head, mouth, body, and feet. Someday she will take getting herself dressed and groomed for granted, but at her age this still feels like a huge accomplishment—and it is! Henry salutes his daughter with a slice of hot toast.

"And for such good work, how about some apple butter? I'll even spread it."

After Abby was diagnosed and began intervention, her occupational therapist provided the Hudsons with strategies to help their daughter complete the self-care chores that had always been so hard for her. The techniques included breaking sequences of movement into their component steps, giving Abby checklists and rewards for completing each task, and removing obstacles in her environment that could easily be eliminated.

At bedtime, whether she's at her mom's house or her dad's, a parent helps Abby pick the next day's clothing and lays the items on the floor in the exact order and easiest position for her to handle. There are identical charts and stickers in both homes, and clothes at each parent's house are kid-friendly. Pants have elastic waists instead of buttons and zippers, shoes close with Velcro instead of shoelaces. Even Abby's hairstyle—

short and simple—has been chosen to make it easy for her to comb without help. In the morning, the entire household gets up early enough to make sure Abby has plenty of time to get herself dressed and groomed at her own slow pace, thus eliminating the tense race against the clock.

With help, Abby has made similar progress with feeding herself. On mornings when her mom or dad doesn't cook something, everything she needs is set out the night before: cereal, bowl, spoon, napkin. Milk is stored in single-serving containers in the refrigerator so that she doesn't overpour. Before treatment, Abby sometimes drooled when she ate, one of a few postural issues she has. She couldn't spread or cut with a knife and often spilled or dropped food. In addition to treatment in the clinic, her OT gave the family tactile and proprioceptive activities and strength and coordination exercises to help Abby learn to make body movements with better timing and sequencing. Eating still takes Abby longer than it does typically developing children, but she now has the abilities she needs.

Abby chats busily with her dad on the drive to school. Her class is putting on a program of scenes from *Peter Pan* next week, and Abby is director of the show. She has dreamed up elaborate scenery that her classmates have executed, but she's frustrated with her teacher's refusal to rig up a wire that would allow Peter to fly above the stage.

"Maybe you could convince her, Daddy. Or you could come to school and build something yourself! It doesn't even have to be a wire. It could be a rope swing like in OT. That wouldn't be as good as a wire, but people could imagine that he was flying. It's better than having him *jump* around." She rolls her eyes with dramatic exasperation.

"I don't think the problem is rigging something up, Sunshine. The school is probably worried about legal issues."

"Legal issues, beagle issues. That's so dumb!"

Despite her outspoken griping, Abby is excited about the play and generally upbeat about school. Many activities required of third-graders are still challenging for her, which is why she continues to think of school as "work." But there are also many activities at which Abby succeeds, and these have given her mostly a positive attitude. Even on bad days when Abby comes home discouraged, she bounces back with her parents' support and returns to school the next day with renewed determination.

Like the other children with SPD we've visited, Abby was falling into a downward cycle before she reached kindergarten. Every morning was a negative experience filled with struggles and conflicts over dressing, grooming, and eating. The negativity continued when she got to preschool, where she couldn't keep up with the other children either academically or at play.

Abby's pre-kindergarten teacher gets the credit for interrupting the cycle. Having taken several courses in child development, Miss Judy recognized the difference between slow physical functioning and slow mental functioning. Spending one-on-one time with the little girl, she discovered that Abby possessed precocious verbal skills but seldom displayed them at school because she felt so defeated by her failures in other areas. By the second week of pre-K, the teacher was so alarmed by the degree to which Abby's struggles were interfering with her success that she called the Hudsons.

Miss Judy alerted the parents to the federal law requiring public schools to provide a free, appropriate public education for preschool children with qualifying disabilities and urged the Hudsons to see if Abby qualified for an evaluation. The Hudsons followed through immediately, Abby qualified easily for an assessment, and she was soon diagnosed with motor problems (dyspraxia) and adaptive behavior problems (dressing, eating, grooming) by a team that included an occupational therapist, a speech therapist, a physical therapist, and a psy-

chologist. She was placed in a publicly funded preschool for children at risk for school problems because of their developmental delays.

After consulting with the OT on the evaluation team and doing some reading on their own, the Hudsons realized Abby would make faster progress if she had private OT to complement the services she was receiving at preschool. The parents conducted face-to-face interviews with several OTs and selected the one who seemed to be the best match for their family's style and Abby's personality.* The Hudsons finally selected Kevin Benson, an OT who had been practicing for seven years and was certified to give the Sensory Integration and Praxis Test developed by Dr. Ayres. Diagnostic intervention began almost immediately (see "Abby's Diagnostic Intervention").

Because Abby was diagnosed with dyspraxia so young and given special services at school and private treatment away from school, she received the help and accommodations she needed in order to succeed from an early age. Without such intervention, she quite likely would have entered kindergarten and been quickly labeled developmentally delayed or low-functioning the way Tam was, a categorization she would have had trouble escaping because of the "expectancy effect" I described earlier.

Abby's Diagnostic Intervention

When the Hudsons first took Abby to Kevin Benson, the occupational therapist recommended twice-weekly treatment for a

---

* "Fit" issues considered in selecting an occupational therapist may include the therapist's personality, how much the child likes the therapist, convenience of the clinician's hours and office location, and others. In this case, the therapist's ability to deal with dual households for the same child was one of the issues explored.

month while he continued to assess their daughter's problems. The practice of providing treatment while evaluation continues is called "diagnostic intervention," which most children need in order to confirm their initial evaluation and to determine how therapy can best address their functional problems.

Abby attended OT twice a week for four months. During the preliminary period, Kevin observed the girl in multiple situations in order to test and validate the preliminary diagnosis of dyspraxia. As a result of Abby's intensive diagnostic assessment/treatment time, Kevin developed a thorough understanding of her strengths and limitations and the priorities of her dual families. With that information, he was able to help the Hudsons understand which of Abby's delays were due to motor-planning problems and which were behavioral styles that had become Abby's method of dealing with her challenges. For example, Abby's failure to get dressed quickly was due to her motor-planning problems, but her gravitation to the television set was a behavioral style. He taught Abby's parents the clinical reasoning elements of A SECRET to help the Hudsons figure out ways to change undesirable behaviors that resulted from Abby's sensory problems and provided the parents with a toolbox of practical ideas for home.

Kevin also helped the family "reframe" Abby's difficulties for her teachers, caregivers, relatives, and others so the significant people in her life could understand and see the little girl in a more positive and accurate light. One of those who benefited from reframing was Abby's own mother, Cindy. An amateur triathlete and go-getter executive on the fast track, Cindy had been impatient with her slow-moving daughter almost from birth. Her belief that Abby could do more and better if she put her mind to it—just the way Cindy herself did when she was challenged—was radically different from Henry's sense from early on that Abby's struggles were beyond her control and deserving of help from her parents. Once the mom understood that her daughter had no control over her slowness, Cindy was able to transfer her considerable energies from being annoyed with Abby to supporting her daughter's efforts and nurturing her growing self-esteem.

Abby's "legal/beagle" complaints are drowned by the shriek of a racing fire engine. Henry steers sharply to the curb and the father and daughter watch as a hook and ladder truck streaks past their car.

"How long are the ladders on those trucks, Daddy?"

Merging back into traffic, Henry admits, "That's a good question, Abby. I've never thought about it."

"Well, what's the tallest building they can reach? Two stories? A hundred stories?"

Henry shakes his head with a little laugh. "You've got me there. Not a hundred stories but probably more than two. Maybe you can look it up on the computer in the library during lunchtime."

"Uh-uh," Abby replies forcefully. "Brittany and me have big plans for lunchtime."

"Brittany and I."

"Brittany and *I* are going to work on our Pets at School campaign."

"Is that your plan to convince the school to let the kids with disabilities bring their dogs with them to class?"

"Yup. I've already thought up about a million slogans. Brittany's going to make the posters while I give her the words."

Some children with dyspraxia develop dazzling verbal creativity to compensate for their motor deficiencies, and Abby is one of them. Her ability to create and verbalize complicated and engaging schemes and games is one of the strengths that Kevin used in OT to build self-confidence and to show Abby how to make friends in spite of her motor-planning impairment. Now Abby routinely comes up with fun fantasies and ambitious

*projects that other children want to be part of. Additionally,
because she's personable and smart, she's able to charm the
other kids into doing the parts that are difficult or impossible
for her while reserving for herself the roles she can handle.*

*Abby's imaginative and verbal abilities equip her to partic-
ipate in school activities that would otherwise be extremely discouraging. For example, if she had to paint scenery or use a
needle and thread to sew costumes for the Peter Pan program,
she would be in trouble on many levels. She might fail in the
activity, attract derision from the other children, or feel bad
about her participation. By taking the role of director, she is
able to avoid the motor-planning activities that are so difficult
for her while displaying skills at which she excels. Instead of
feeling bad about herself, she ends up feeling good.*

*The substitution of verbal wizardry for physical activity in
children with dyspraxia does have some pitfalls. Dyspraxic children who always invent the games and direct their playmates
sometimes act or are perceived as "bossy." Since few children
want to be the underling in every game, this can complicate social interaction. What's more, teachers generally aren't willing
to assign the same child the coveted leadership role every time
one is available. Although not all children with dyspraxia are
leaders, children like Abby often must be taught to exercise
judgment and find ways to participate without assuming control of every situation.*

*Despite the occasional challenges, the benefits of Abby's
ability to participate socially cannot be underestimated. While
academics are valued in our society, the key to feeling happy
and successful is having friends, being accepted and admired,
and actively participating in social groups. When children are
happy, they are able to feel fulfilled and be successful even if
they have significant sensory and/or motor issues. Because Abby
is not socially isolated the way the three children with Sensory*

Modulation Disorder are isolated, she is at much less risk for future social, emotional, and academic problems than they are.

Notice, too, that because her sensory problems do not involve her ability to modulate incoming sensory messages, Abby reacts to the shriek of the passing fire engine without the behavioral extremes we saw in LaTanya, Tam, and Ben.

Determined and bright as she is, once Abby gets to the classroom, things get tougher.

Any activity with a fine-motor element is problematic for the third-grader, especially writing. Abby's handwriting is so poor that it's almost impossible to read. Even with special instruction, holding a pencil feels awkward to her. Her letters are often too big or too small, and they typically overlap or are too far away from each other. She doesn't close letters like O that are supposed to be closed, and sometimes she gets letters backward. Writing is another one of those mysteries that everyone but she has solved.

For a long time, written tests attached terrible consequences to the mystery of writing. Before the classroom aide started giving Abby spelling tests orally, she nearly always failed them because it took her so long to fill in the answers. By taking the tests verbally, she now scores at or near the top of the class in spelling. However, as soon as she has to start writing something down again, it's back to hard work.

The non-academic "fun" segments of the school day also challenge Abby. Dyspraxia affects the timing and rhythm of motor actions, which makes a special class like music difficult for her. Her sweet little voice enables her to sing well, but she can't keep the beat when the class plays sticks in time to the music, which she finds humiliating. Art is another embarrassment. Unless the class is doing completely unstructured activities—pasting tissue paper in a random manner to make "stained glass windows," for instance—art feels hopeless. She is creative and can "see" the art in her head, but when she tries to execute it, everything goes wrong. When the class made paper

Thanksgiving turkeys this year, she got only three feathers cut out in the time it took the other children to cut out all the feathers they needed. Then she got glue all over her hands, and when she attached her feathers to the turkey, one feather stuck to the turkey's beak and the other two got attached to the wrong places on the bird. She knew how the turkey was supposed to look and she fully understood the instructions, but she couldn't plan and execute the complex sequence of steps necessary to construct a reasonable facsimile on paper. Even her friends couldn't help giggling a little at her turkey. Abby was outwardly good-natured about the episode, but it still hurt.

Abby is a lot like the little boy with dyspraxia who once told me, "It's like my head is separated from my body. I can think things, but I can't do them." When children with dyspraxia are very young, this disconnect may cause them to struggle as Abby did with self-care and other issues but won't automatically lead to a diagnosis of Sensory Processing Disorder. That's because there is a broad band of "normal" development within which any child may simply be "late" or "delayed" in reaching milestones. Once the child reaches school—or even preschool—expectations become more complex and increasingly require precisely the abilities that are a problem for children with Sensory-Based Motor Disorder. Dyspraxia is commonly diagnosed about the time Abby's was—between the ages of four and six—or later in the second or third grade when the demand to write quickly and neatly outstrips their abilities.

"Academic" activities tend to be associated with "thinking" rather than "doing," but the truth is that motor planning is built into the three R's and countless other school activities. As a result, dyspraxic children often "fail" even in subject areas where they possess intellectual mastery. Consider the simple arithmetic assignment. Copying problems from the chalkboard onto paper and then working them requires:

- *getting out paper and a pencil,*
- *locating the correct problem on the blackboard,*
- *finding the right place on the page to place the problem,*
- *remembering the numbers long enough to write them down,*
- *writing the numbers down in the correct columns, and finally,*
- *working the problem.*

A child like Abby has no problem with the cognitive pieces of this puzzle—she can remember the numbers and she knows how to add them—but all the other steps take her a long time and result in errors because of her impaired planning abilities. For instance, she knows where the problem should go on the page, but when she writes it down, she lines the columns of digits up incorrectly and thus gets the wrong answer. Abby can add, but her motor-planning problem makes it impossible for her to demonstrate that she can.

Fortunately, the OT's suggestions for accommodations have helped bridge the gap between what Abby knows and what her motor-planning difficulties allow her to demonstrate. Her oral spelling tests are a good example of how simple accommodations can make a big difference. Being allowed to spell the words aloud enables Abby to demonstrate her mastery even though she cannot write fast enough to pass a timed, written test. Her difficulty with transferring problems from the board to paper was addressed by providing special worksheets. Now Abby's arithmetic problems are pre-written on graph paper, which helps her keep the numbers lined up correctly. If she can't finish the problems as fast as the other kids because of her slow writing, she is allowed to take work home without penalty, which enables her to get good grades. She is also given extra time during any test she cannot take verbally.

Abby would make an excellent candidate for typing instruction and a classroom laptop. Her handwriting will im-

prove with time and practice, but it will always be messy and hard to read. Once she has memorized the repetitive and relatively simple keystrokes required for typing, written work will become easier for her and more legible for her teachers.

Lunch and recess used to be the worst part of Abby's school day—even worse than music and art.

In the lunchroom, she had to slip a tray from the stack, select utensils from the holders, and move down the line to get food. Before she met Kevin and went through OT, this was a daily trial. Because she was so slow, children behind her in line grew impatient and took cuts, often muttering about how stupid she was. Then she had to weave among the other children to a table with the tray. On the way to her friends, she often bumped into tables or even other kids. Occasionally, she dropped her tray and people sometimes called her names or made fun of her. Like Tam, she was usually the last child to finish and leave the lunchroom, which cut down on the important social time that followed outside at recess.

Once Abby reached the playground, the same body awareness and planning problems that caused her to bump into tables and people in the lunchroom resulted in poor ball-handling and other sports skills. This remains true even now, after OT. Sequences of multiple movements are tricky for her. She has enough trouble jumping over a rope that lies motionless at her feet, but if the rope is swinging, synchronizing with its back-and-forth or up-and-over rhythm is simply impossible. Before she found happier ways to spend recess, she routinely felt the sting of being passed over when kids picked teams and the dread of having a ball come her way or taking her turn at any of the games.

In the physical arena, Abby is the polar opposite of Ben, the sensory-seeking boy in the last chapter. All the amazing motor skills that Ben displays are areas in which Abby fails. Dr. Ayres would have said that Abby's physical awkwardness resulted in part from what is called "body scheme"—the internal, unconscious model each of us carries about our bodies in space. It is body scheme that enables us to get up in the middle of the night and find our way to the bathroom in the dark without bumping into the furniture in our bedroom. We are able to do this because our proprioceptive and vestibular senses give us an awareness of where our body is in relation to the objects in the room. Children with dyspraxia have a poorly developed "body scheme," which is what made it hard for Abby to work her way through the line in the cafeteria or to position her hands to meet and return a ball in four-square or to organize any of a thousand other motor activities.

Abby also lacks flexibility in thinking through motor activities. If she hasn't done something already, she can't figure out how to do it. She's like the little boy who once arrived for a therapy session with me wearing his Halloween costume. Since Sammy was dressed as Spider-man, we attached netting to hooks and created a web that was suspended within reach but above his head. Even though the room was full of objects he might have used to boost himself into the net, the boy couldn't plan a way to climb in.

I finally asked, "What could you use to help you get into this net?" and Sammy readily answered, "A ladder." He could conceptualize a solution in the abstract but lacked the mental flexibility to turn the abstract concept into the motor act of pulling a climbing aid under the net and scrambling up. When he finally got into the net with prompting, I asked him to climb into the "ship's lookout" of a higher net to search for pirates, but he couldn't generalize what he'd learned about climbing into the first net in order to climb into the second one.

With effort, children like this little boy and Abby may learn a "splinter skill," such as jumping a rope, but they can't generalize the ability to jump over a rope to performing a long jump, broad jump, or high jump. This dooms those parts of the school day, such as gym class, that revolve around constantly mastering motor abilities and then generalizing them to new activities.

Nonetheless, Kevin was able to provide the Hudsons with strategies to help Abby take more pleasure from the inescapable parts of the day. Now she skips the cafeteria line. Her lunch from home includes only easy-to-eat finger foods: peanut butter sandwiches that don't drip, precut apple slices and mini carrots that can be eaten in a single bite, plastic juice containers that don't require pushing a straw through a tiny hole. Besides sparing her the embarrassing lunch line, the homemade lunches are healthier and quicker to eat so she can join her friends outside.

The Hudsons also followed through on Kevin's suggestion that they avidly seek out other girls in Abby's class who weren't interested in motor activities and then actively foster friendships with them. For months, the family "tried out" potential friends with out-of-school playdates and outings, and eventually a core group of girls who were a good match for their daughter emerged. Now during recess, Abby has Brittany and a handful of other girls who aren't interested in the equipment or four-square or footraces, and she can pass the time happily huddled with them talking, planning, or playing make-believe games. Abby can look forward to lunch and recess, which is a big improvement.

Back at her desk after lunch, Abby is dismayed. Oh, man. What a mess!

Even though she's been taught strategies for keeping her things in order, organization remains a huge hurdle for Abby, especially away from home and the vigilant oversight of her parents. Her desk at school is one of the places where the organizational hurdle is most visible. Because she's always behind in her work, Abby is forever stuffing the last thing she used into the desk and grabbing the next thing she needs without putting anything in its place. As a result, the interior of her lift-top desk gets messier and messier as the day wears on. If her spiral assignment notebook disappears in the process—which it often does—she starts writing her assignments on little scraps of paper. But then she throws the scraps into the desk, too, and can't find them when she needs them.

By the end of the day, she doesn't know which books she needs to take home and can't find the worksheets she's supposed to do for homework. The more she searches, the more frantic she becomes. Sometimes she just slams the desk closed and gives up. Her teacher tries to take a few minutes near the end of every school day to help Abby reorganize her desk, gather the books she needs to take home, and make sure all assignments are written in her daily planner, but some days there's no time for this, and Abby cannot manage the job on her own. On these days, she typically returns the next day unprepared. This is the primary reason her grades are so-so in spite of how bright she is and all the help she gets from her parents, her OT, and the school.

Abby is doing so much better that it is easy to forget she still has to stop and think about what she's doing, which means she needs a huge supply of a limited commodity—time. When it comes to keeping track of her homework assignments, Abby needs time for the laborious task of writing down the assignment and then she needs more time to put her assignment book back where it belongs in her desk. She must consciously go through mental steps such as these: "This is my assignment calendar. I need to write down my math assignment neatly so I can read it later. Then I need to put the calendar in my desk. I should place it near the top of my belongings because I'll need to take it home. It should be under things that are smaller than it is so I can still see the other things, too." That's a lot of planning to record a single homework assignment.

Manipulating the SECRET elements of environment and relationship could increase Abby's organization considerably. The environment of her desk could be modified by fastening shallow boxes or plastic containers inside. Each container would be sized to its assigned contents, and the assignment book would have its own designated place. Abby's smart. She'd have no trouble memorizing the proper locations and it would be easier for her to keep things in order. She would still have to write down every assignment, but she'd be able to find her assignment book more efficiently so she didn't waste any of her limited writing time. The relationship element of Abby's context could be modified by appointing a "homework buddy" to make sure she writes down every assignment in the book, possibly in exchange for Abby being the other child's "proofreading buddy" or "spelling practice buddy"—a win-win situation for two children.

Order is a lifelong issue for people with dyspraxia. Abby is likely to be one of those women whose car is a perpetual mess and whose purse is overflowing. However, if she learns strategies for maintaining order now, the habits should make things easier for her later on.

When Henry picks Abby up from her after-school program, he finds his daughter uncharacteristically quiet. With some prodding, he learns that the teacher assigned her class to write each of this week's twenty spelling words in sentences, a task Abby knows from experience will take every free minute she has between now and bedtime.

"Sounds like you've got your work cut out for you," Henry says sympathetically. "I guess you'll need to get busy as soon as we're home."

Abby's lower lip slides into a pout and she heaves a world-weary sigh. "But I'm so tired, Daddy. I already did twenty multiplication problems and a stupid art project and even PE today. It's too hard. I can't do it."

"Of course you can, Sunshine. And you have to do it."

"Why?" Abby bursts into a wail. "Why do I have to do it? I already know how to spell the stupid words. I haven't missed a spelling word all year. Why do I have to spend all night doing something I don't need to do?"

Henry understands the frustration of his hardworking daughter, but he doesn't relent. "Because you need practice writing, Abby. Because if you don't keep working on the things that are hard for you, they'll never get easier."

"But it's Wednesday!" Abby persists. "Mom never makes me do homework on Wednesdays. She says everyone deserves a day off."

Henry is familiar with this ploy, but he's not about to fall victim to his daughter's divide-and-conquer tactics. "I'll tell you what. You can watch TV while I get dinner, but as soon as we're done you need to go to work with no complaints. I'm willing to bet you can come up with the world's shortest sentences and that won't take so long. After an hour, we'll go to the market together and I'll let you buy some cookies for your lunches this week. That will give you a break before you finish up."

Abby nods without enthusiasm. Lunch cookies are a rare and welcome treat at her dad's—he's more the granola-bar type—but the market trip means she'll have to get back into the car for the ride to the store and then push the cart through the store. Her dad *always* makes her push the cart even though he's perfectly capable of doing it himself. What Abby really wants to do is park in front of the TV from the minute she gets home until bedtime. Since she knows this idea will never fly, she simply mutters a resigned, "Okay."

With Kevin's help, Henry has built on his good native parenting instincts to utilize a number of winning strategies, including the way he handles his daughter's desire to spend the evening vegging. Henry recognizes that Abby has a legitimate need for a break after her hard day's work, and he offers her one. He uses A SECRET to modify and simplify the spelling assignment, and he firmly refuses to take the "Mom never makes me" bait.

Henry also finds a way to increase the sensory component of Abby's evening with some heavy work at the supermarket. Like most dyspraxic children, Abby avoids physical activity because it's hard for her, which can lead to deficiencies in her sensory diet. Given a choice, she would read, watch TV, or talk all evening long. Henry and Cindy both actively combat this tendency in their daughter. When Abby was younger, Henry was the only dad in a "Mommy and me" gym program. As she has grown up, he has become more inventive about working exercise into her day. In the months when the days are longer, he often insists on father-daughter walks after dinner or gardening activities as simple ways of building more exercise into his daughter's routine. He gives her chores—changing bedsheets, taking out the trash, vacuuming—that provide her with proprioceptive stimulation, and he often saves supermarket and mall outings for the days she's with him. His shopping lists are typically contrived to require the duo to work their way through an entire store or shopping center to find everything.

Henry's efforts to get Abby moving are worthwhile for social as well as health reasons. Already Abby is somewhat chubby because of her aversion to activity. With her cheerful and winning personality and her successes in other areas, she is not yet experiencing any weight-related self-image or social problems. But dyspraxic children whose inactivity and eating habits in early childhood have made them overweight may feel bad or become socially isolated in their teens, when appearance becomes more critical to social success and self-image. Sedentary habits also deprive children like Abby of opportunities they need to receive sensory input and to practice motor responses. Just as Ben's mother needed to create opportunities for her sensory-seeking son to get all the movement he craved, Henry and Cindy diligently work to assure that Abby gets a complete sensory diet even when she's not enthusiastic about it.

By the time she and her dad return from the supermarket, Abby's spirits have lifted. Her dad was right. She was able to devise spelling sentences of no more than five words each and the assignment didn't take all night after all. It was even kind of fun to see how short she could make each one. The verbs were especially easy. She used "pursue" and "maintain" in two-word sentences—"I pursue" and "You maintain"—and then modified the approach for the nouns. In the end, she completed all twenty sentences in less than a hundred words.

At the market, she complained briefly when Henry rejected her plea for Oreos, but he agreed to vanilla wafers, and the two returned home satisfied. After a relaxing bubble bath, Henry even helped his daughter get her pajamas on—another treat. Usually he insists Abby dress herself for the same reason he insisted that she complete the spelling assignment—for the practice. But tonight he gave her a helping hand just to speed things up after a particularly trying day.

Nestled under her covers at last, Abby closes her eyes while her father reads another chapter of *Ramona, Age Eight,* their current bedtime favorite. Her dad's a better out-loud reader than her mom and makes up different voices for every character, so she doesn't mind bedtime at his house. Besides, she really is worn out.

"So how do you rate the day?" Henry asks as he closes the book at the end of the chapter. "One to ten."

Abby wrinkles her nose and reviews the day's events in her mind.

On the one hand, any school day when she has both art and PE gets marked down. On the other hand, her teacher agreed to let Henry examine the auditorium ceiling to see if there was a way to dangle a rope so that Peter Pan could swing across the stage in at least one key scene. And now the vanilla wafers are already tucked into tomorrow's lunch.

"An eight-point-five," she finally declares.

"Whoa! Eight-point-five! Yesterday was only a six." Henry kisses his daughter on the forehead and rumples her hair. "Way to go, Tiger. I sure do love you."

Abby's eyes are closed but she smiles. "I sure do love you back."

Abby is really doing well. Her life is not as easy as typically developing Ryan's, but it's a good life and she's happy with it. Sure, she has her ups and downs—don't we all?—and she still struggles with some of her childhood occupations, but she doesn't feel like a loser. She doesn't get down on herself about the things she doesn't do well, and she relishes the activities and relationships she has mastered. She's able to take each day as it comes and put it into perspective. Yesterday may have been a 6, but today was an 8.5. She works hard and she enjoys the rewards of her hard work, whether they come in the form of social acceptance or cookies.

Also noteworthy is that Abby's family—both halves of it—is doing well. Henry and Cindy both understand Abby's needs and limitations and have worked together to develop sound, practical adaptations for them. They have stopped fighting over parenting issues, which enables them to be more effective parents individually and as a team. The home environments in which Abby lives are relatively serene and function well.

Abby Hudson has a good life. She is content and she is assembling the social, academic, organizational, and other abilities she needs for a successful future.

A SECRET for Your Child with Dyspraxia*

Sensational strategies that may improve a child's functioning can be developed by any parent. Strategies emerge when each element of A SECRET is examined and one or more elements is modified to improve the "fit" between the dyspraxic child's personal characteristics and the world around him. The following chart illustrates how to use this flexible approach to examine the last three elements of A SECRET—Relationships, Environment, and Tasks. These are the elements most readily modified by parents.

* A clinical diagnosis of dyspraxia can be made only with a comprehensive diagnostic evaluation. Sensational strategies are most effective when developed as part of a comprehensive intervention program provided by an OT or another professional with training in treating Sensory Processing Disorder.

A SECRET for Your Child with Dyspraxia

A SECRET for Relationships

Modify RELATIONSHIPS to foster interaction that accommodates your child's motor-planning limitations.

Ask questions such as . . .

- Is there anything about my child's motor-planning problem that is interfering with her social life?
- What can I do to facilitate relationships in spite of her motor-planning problems?
- Is she being ridiculed or penalized by her siblings or other family members for her sensory-motor problems?
- How can I eliminate any negative feedback my child receives because of her motor-planning problems?

Devise strategies for home such as . . .

- **Peers:** suggest and encourage play activities your child is good at when playing with friends, e.g., make-believe games instead of art projects requiring fine-motor skills; teach your child to let others be in charge sometimes.

Devise strategies for school such as . . .

- **Understanding:** develop a script and use it to explain your child's motor-planning disorder to school personnel, especially cafeteria workers and art, music, and physical education teachers.

Devise strategies for community such as . . .

- **Understanding:** develop a script and use it to explain your child's lack of motor competence and her need for extra time and help with motor-planning tasks; use the script with extended family, neighbors, service providers, parents of playmates, and others.

Dypraxia—Relationships *(continued)*

Devise strategies for home such as . . .	Devise strategies for school such as . . .	Devise strategies for community such as . . .
• **Siblings and other family**: teach tolerance of your child's lack of speed and accuracy in motor activities; build activities that do not require motor skill into family life.	• **Support network**: arrange for helpers to assist your child in the lunchroom, at recess, with organizing personal space, and with managing take-home materials. • **Teacher assignment**: seek assignment to teachers willing to learn about and accommodate your child's motor problems without punishing or getting impatient.	• **Support**: make sure an informed, understanding adult supervises activities outside your home in order to prevent your child from being teased or from failing due to motor problems. • **Extracurricular activities**: seek non-motor activities in which your child excels and will be praised or acknowledged.

Dypraxia—Environment

A SECRET for Environment

Modify the ENVIRONMENT to create streamlined settings that place a minimum of obstacles in your child's path.

Ask questions such as . . .

- In what environments does my child succeed in planning motor activities? What is present in my child's environment that makes life more complicated for her?
- How can I organize the environment to remove obstacles and make life less frustrating for her?

Devise strategies for home such as . . .

- **Personal organization**: help your child maintain strict organization of all her personal space, e.g., closet, dresser, desk, bookshelf, laundry, bathroom, backpack.
- **Family space**: eliminate furniture and other clutter from rooms so that your child's movement is unobstructed.

Devise strategies for school such as . . .

- **Personal space**: request special help with personal space organization such as desk and backpack.
- **Classroom space**: request assignment to classrooms with ample open space and minimal obstructions to movement.

Devise strategies for community such as . . .

- **Special events and outings**: identify and patronize a small number of community settings that can become familiar, e.g., go to the same park, the same movie theater, the same library, the same grocery store.
- **Summer and special programs**: seek out activities that minimize motor skills, e.g., theater programs, modern art.

Dypraxia—Environment (*continued*)

Devise strategies for home such as . . .	Devise strategies for school such as . . .	Devise strategies for community such as . . .
• **Checklists**: post weekly and daily schedules in a prominent place; post step-by-step checklists in every area of the house where your child routinely does chores and activities. • **Simplicity**: use the simplest household fixtures (faucets, doorknobs, locks, drawer pulls) you can find. • **Novelty**: provide a swing set, jungle gym, ladder, net, or other tools that will give your child new and complex motor activities that consistently push her; make obstacle courses that vary daily.	• **Seating**: request a desk in a location with minimal congestion and with easy access to frequently visited sites in the room such as the teacher's "in" basket, pencil sharpener, or bookshelf. • **Outside the classroom**: arrange extra time for your child to move between classes or areas of the school and through locations that require multiple motor skills, e.g., the cafeteria, assemblies, other special events, and outings.	• **Shops and offices**: avoid stores and other settings filled with breakable items; seek out organized environments that are not overly complex or cluttered. • **Travel and transportation**: remember that your child does not have a good sense of space, easily gets lost, and should never be left unattended; do not require your child to keep track of his own things or to help you keep track of yours; bring activities that do not require dexterity, e.g., audiotapes, books to read.

Dypraxia—Tasks

A SECRET for Tasks

Modify TASKS to minimize motor-planning challenges and make achievement possible.

Ask questions such as . . .

- At what kinds of tasks does my child excel? How can I build more of these into her life?
- What is it about difficult tasks that makes them hard for her? Is it the number of steps, the type of material she has to handle, the motor requirements? How can I change the tasks to make them easier?

Devise strategies for home such as . . .

- **Timing**: expect everything to take more time to do; build in time for that.
- **Simplify**: break complex tasks into their simpler component steps, e.g., lay out the place mats, silverware, and dishes before you tell your child to set the table; avoid implements that will be problematic, e.g., use plastic ware so she doesn't break dishes.

Devise strategies for school such as . . .

- **Organization**: create routines and request special help for your child to keep her personal space, papers, and homework assignments in good order.
- **Time**: make arrangements for your child to have extra time for assigned tasks; eliminate timed tests from her program.

Devise strategies for community such as . . .

- **Understanding**: create a script and use it to explain that it takes your child more time to do routine tasks so people do not have unreasonable expectations.

Dypraxia—Tasks (*continued*)

Devise strategies for home such as . . .	Devise strategies for school such as . . .	Devise strategies for community such as . . .
• **Organization**: create mechanisms for helping your child stay organized, e.g., make sure every space she occupies is orderly with labels, color codes, or diagrams to help her know where things belong.	• **Assignments**: request that your child be able to demonstrate mastery verbally if fine-motor requirements are too great.	• **Extracurricular activities**: choose activities that match your child's motor-planning abilities; she could do modern dance but not tap or ballet; seek talk-based activities, e.g., talking to elderly in nursing homes but not knitting caps for the needy; seek out active options rather than activities that involve only watching and listening; avoid team sports.
• **Activity**: build noncompetitive activities into family routines to keep your child moving, e.g., replace TV and computer time with activities that require her to move around.	• **Fine motor**: teach typing and introduce a computer as early as possible.	
	• **Curriculum**: modify requirements for activities so your child can participate with a minimum of fine-motor manipulation, e.g., instead of making an igloo with sugar cubes, she does a book report on igloos.	• **Acknowledgment**: search for those non-motor activities in which your child's gifts will shine.
• **Tactile**: use deep pressure prior to specific motor games to prepare your child for movement activities.		
• **Proprioceptive**: provide passive stimulation and activities that put pressure on your child's joints and muscles, e.g., pushing, pulling, running, jumping, especially before she goes into activities that require skilled motor responses.		

Postural Disorder: The "Other" SBMD

"Good posture" is the visible evidence of normal vestibular and proprioceptive processing. When good postural control is present, children are able to reach, push, pull, and resist force as needed to accomplish everyday tasks. Their bodies provide a stable yet mobile base for movement of their heads, eyes, and limbs.

Children with postural disorder have problems with body stability and mobility. Without good stability, they can't exert or resist force effectively and have trouble moving their arms and legs with skill. They usually have difficulty automatically adjusting and sustaining their body position to allow them to perform tasks efficiently. For example, if assigned to draw a large circle on butcher paper, they're more likely to stand up and walk in a circle around the paper while holding their pencil to the paper than to shift their body weight and rotate their arm as needed to complete the circle while sitting down.

Children with postural problems usually have poor strength in the abdominal muscles and the muscles on the dorsal side of the body (back of the torso and legs), weaknesses that combine to make such routine motor activities as sitting up straight and walking upstairs difficult. They tend to move very slowly because they're always struggling to overcome poor muscle tone, and they tire easily. As infants these children do not use their fingers to play with their toes because their abdominals are too weak to hold their knees up when lying on their backs.

Abby has trouble with *planning* her body's movements. Children with postural disorder have trouble *doing* the movements. If Abby had dyspraxia and a postural disorder, in addition to having trouble copying problems from the chalkboard, she would be slumped over the paper, perhaps with her head on her arm as she wrote. She might even have trouble lifting her head to look up at the board.

Postural disorder frequently occurs in children who have other patterns of SPD. In particular, children with dyspraxia, under-responsivity, and Sensory Discrimination Disorder often have postural disorder as well (see Chapter 12, "Beyond the Types").

Intervention to improve postural responses is usually quite successful in children with postural disorder. Grandma was right: Kids can be taught "good" posture.

I began to notice small hairs growing on Daniel's chin just after he turned sixteen. I waited several weeks and then asked if he noticed that he was beginning to grow hair on his face. "Yeah," is all he said. I went out and purchased a very safe and quiet electric razor for him. I waited until the weekend, showed it to him, and explained how it worked and how easy it would be. I felt so proud. I turned on the razor and Daniel immediately stepped back. Not only did the noise bother him, but when I showed him how it would not cut skin by running it over my palm, he refused to touch it. "Turn it off, turn it off!" he insisted.

CONTRIBUTED BY VICKI SIEGEL AND SON DANIEL

Chapter 10

As Sensational Children Grow Up

Parents of young children diagnosed with Sensory Processing Disorder often ask me, "What does the future hold?"

Although no longitudinal research has been done to tell us what happens to children with SPD as they grow older, the therapeutic community has considerable anecdotal experience, both with children whom therapists have followed from early childhood and with teenagers and adults who seek therapy later.

What experience tells us is that even if their movement from one developmental stage to the next is more complicated than it is for typically developing kids, children with SPD can and do grow up to enjoy fulfilled and productive lives.

A number of factors influence the likelihood that your child will overcome the sensory problems that disrupt his life in early childhood:

- *The age at which the disorder was detected and treated*
  The earlier the diagnosis and intervention, the more likely some or all of the sensory issues will be resolved and secondary problems avoided. If diagnosis and intervention are delayed and serious secondary problems such as depression, anxiety, poor self-confidence, or others have developed, the challenge becomes much more complex. Even if the sensory issues are resolved, the residual secondary problems may persist.

- *The pattern/subtype and severity of the disorder*
  In general, Sensory-Based Motor Disorders (dyspraxia and postural disorder) are less limiting for adolescents and adults than Sensory Modulation and Sensory Discrimination Disorders. In addition, less severe symptoms of any pattern or subtype can be addressed more easily and resolved more permanently than severe ones.

- *Your child's personality and temperament*
  Children who are resilient, motivated, flexible, and easy-going typically move through developmental challenges more smoothly than children who are rigid or apathetic.

- *Support for treatment from family and school*
  Children whose parents and teachers actively apply therapeutic principles at home and school usually do better than those without such support.

The importance of reinforcing at home the appropriate sensory-based treatment cannot be emphasized enough. Sensory issues may create some limitations in career choices, life skills, or recreational pursuits in later life, but with help, even children with severe SPD can learn strategies that will enable them to fit in, succeed, and enjoy productive lives. In particular, parents who use and teach their children to use the clinical reasoning strategies of A SECRET foster in their children the life skill of finding their own just-right fit as they grow up and move away from home.

Those children who do not receive timely intervention are at greater risk of reaching adulthood with sensory issues that continue to be disruptive. Unless she resolves her aversion to being touched, an over-responder like LaTanya could have serious problems with physical intimacy. If he doesn't learn to arouse his sluggish systems, an under-responder like Tam could become one of those workers who chronically runs late and falls short on the job. A sensory seeker like Ben could end up seeking stimulation from unhealthy sources like substance abuse, gambling, or promiscuous behavior. Meanwhile, a dyspraxic child like sunny, talented Abby could opt out of higher education and a career if she failed to develop the self-confidence and self-esteem needed to strive.

All children have to climb a developmental stairway to reach adulthood, and each new step—toddlerhood, preschool, kindergarten, elementary school, middle school, high school, and all the rest—always introduces new demands. Sensory issues complicate meeting these demands because they introduce an additional challenge the child has to juggle. Anticipating the challenges and preparing for them in advance can help.

A detailed discussion of the specific issues that children with each subtype of SPD experience as they move through adolescence and into adulthood would be a good subject to investigate in another book. Here for now are some general observations and keys to success for children like Abby, Ben, Tam, and LaTanya.

Abby and Children with Dyspraxia

"Drop the reins and reach for the sky!" All the horseback-riding students followed their instructor's directions, balancing precariously in English saddles on the first day of horseback riding therapy. "Hippotherapy," I had heard, was designed to help kids with all sorts of disabilities learn how to ride horses. After trying many sports, this was the first one that had my twelve-year-old son Sean feeling good about himself. One time, he was trying to stand up in the stirrups for a few seconds, then sit down. At first, he was having difficulty, which was usually the signal for him to give up after one or two tries. But I heard him say, "I didn't get it that time, but I can try again." I don't recall my son ever saying the word "try" before this. He sat straight and tall in his saddle and his balance improved tremendously. As he laughed and waved at me, I gulped back tears.

CONTRIBUTED BY ANDREA MILLER AND SON SEAN

With treatment, many children with a motor-planning disorder like Abby's find that their sensory difficulties actually become *less* problematic as they grow older. This occurs in part because the number of required school activities for which good motor planning is essential—recess, art, PE—shrinks, while at the same time the number of activities that rely on strengths such as cognitive skills and verbal ability expands. What's more, with computers and voice-recognition software, even the worst scribblers can turn out legible written assignments, demonstrate their academic prowess, and earn good grades.

Accommodations may continue to be necessary for timed tests, but as time goes on, children who have dyspraxia without other SPD symptoms need fewer accommodations because they become so good at adapting and compensating for their sensory issues. Often bright, verbal, and/or socially adept, these children are well-equipped to negotiate the obstacle course of sensory challenges in life. The world generally expands for them as they leave the sandbox and the playground behind.

Besides appropriate treatment, the key to the future for children with dyspraxia is self-esteem. When parents and others keep these kids focused on all the things they *can* do—which are many—instead of the ones they *can't*, children with dyspraxia are able to emerge from childhood with the confidence necessary to act on their abilities, make and keep friends, and reap the benefits that come from being accepted and appreciated by others. With their strong verbal skills and the problem-solving techniques they learn in therapy, they become good advocates for themselves at school, in social settings, and on the job, and this further reinforces their sense of competence, control, and satisfaction.

On the other hand, if the dyspraxic child's sensory and motor issues are not addressed and she grows up feeling incompetent and unhappy with herself and her abilities, the picture dims considerably. Anxiety, depression, and other mental health disorders are common risks for untreated dyspraxic children during adolescence and adulthood. If handwriting issues have not been addressed, especially slowness, these children may struggle academically with written assignments and timed tests. When "bossiness" or other destructive social-emotional behaviors have not been overcome, social acceptance and professional advancement may be hampered. Additionally, new motor-planning demands—learning to drive, organizing and keeping a dorm room or an apartment, fulfilling on-the-job requirements—will occur and can cause setbacks.

As long as kids with dyspraxia stay focused on their abilities instead of their disabilities and feel good about themselves, they can enjoy their teens and move into a successful adulthood. Abby might not grow up to be an architect or a jeweler or an artist because of the motor-planning requirements of those careers, but many options will be open to her in work and in life.

Ben and Sensory Seekers

It would be twenty-four hours of testosterone-flying, dirt-smearing, high-energy fun—or so I thought as I signed myself and my son up for Boy Scout camp one June. Mac was bursting with excitement when we arrived, but problems soon erupted. He impulsively dialed 911 from a pay phone and the sheriff called back. Playing with a flashlight around the campfire, he bonked another boy in the face. The next day he turned on all the faucets in the bathroom and water spewed everywhere. Every hour seemed to hold a new disaster, and I began to wonder how I ever thought this would work. The den leader warned we would have to leave if there was one more episode. Then came the advanced obstacle course—a fifty-foot slide extended to the other side of a chasm. The boys tried to grab a large metal triangle and slide across to the other side. Aaron tried . . . nope. Jon tried . . . nope. Paul tried . . . nope. I could hear Mac's shrill "I wanna try! I wanna try!" Mac tried . . . and sailed across the huge chasm twenty times. Maybe Boy Scout camp wasn't a complete mistake after all.

CONTRIBUTED BY SONJA ROSE AND SON MACKENZIE

If the key to the dyspraxic child's future is self-esteem, the key for sensory seekers is self-regulation. With treatment, sensory seekers like Ben learn how to satisfy their hunger for sensation so they can self-regulate, which allows them to enjoy considerable success in later childhood and their adult years.

As adolescents, many sensory seekers find a socially approved outlet for their sensory appetites in sports competition, which pays dividends of social approval, social acceptance, and self-esteem. If they have learned to satisfy their sensory needs sufficiently to master fine-motor activities such as handwriting and to pay attention in class, they are able to succeed academically, which opens educational and career avenues. Those sensory seekers who channel their extraordinary energy into creative and original projects also may discover a personal strength that can lead to inventive and entrepreneurial careers. In some professions, the fact that they're tireless gives them an edge over the competition.

The danger for children like Ben comes when they don't learn to satisfy their sensory appetites and achieve self-regulation. The social rejection and public disapproval that results from unregulated behavior can produce a negative self-image. If low self-esteem lessens the motivation to meet social and cultural expectations, these kids can easily slide into a pattern of making bad choices. If they find social acceptance only among other rejected kids, they can end up in a crowd whose search for stimulation includes antisocial and self-destructive activities.

Sensory-seeking children who learn self-regulation and avoid a downhill track in adolescence become good candidates for physically demanding professions that put a premium on speed and zest for change. Ben would probably make a great firefighter, athletic coach, or emergency-room doctor. Like other sensory seekers, he might continue to stand a step too close to people or speak a few decibels too loud or pound folks on the back when a gentle pat would do. But, in an adult who otherwise regulates his behaviors and who constructively taps into the deep reservoirs of energy that sensory seekers enjoy, these are likely to be viewed merely as forgivable idiosyncrasies.

Tam and Children with Under-Responsivity

When my son with sensory issues was in preschool, he made one friend who had sensory problems similar to his own. Even though the boys went to different schools from kindergarten on, they remained best friends for years. Both of them felt safe knowing they could struggle openly without feeling "weird" or worrying about losing the other's friendship. The other mother, Rose, and I cherished our sons' rela-

tionship as well as our own. We all found in each other the priceless friendship where quirks are not only tolerated but lovingly accepted. Our parallel friendships—the boys' and the moms'—were sturdy little boats that carried us all through some very rough seas. Twenty years later, we live miles apart, but we all treasure our shared past and still see each other whenever we can.

CONTRIBUTED BY DORIS FULLER AND SON GREG

Children with under-responsivity who receive appropriate treatment learn to seek out and find the sensory stimulation they need to rouse themselves to action, which enables them, too, to enjoy academic, recreational, and professional success. As teens, under-responders might not choose to audition for the lead in the school play, but they could become adept and happy on the crew that handles the lights or runs the sound system. As adults, the hurly-burly of courtroom law might exert problematic demands on their slow sensory-processing system, but working as a research lawyer in a law library could be just right. Any career with automatic components and routine will be a better fit for under-responders in adulthood than careers that rely on quick responses and involve constant change. Working on an assembly line or in a tollbooth would fit far better than waiting tables or working as a short-order cook.

A key to life satisfaction for children with under-responsivity is social participation, which is so crucial during the adolescent years. Because these kids don't automatically get involved with what's going on around them, it's easy for them to become isolated and withdrawn. Even if they perform acceptably at school or at work, being isolated places them at higher risk for alcohol and/or drug abuse, depression, and suicide, as both teens and adults. Friends make all the difference. With friends come the emotional and social benefits of belonging and a reduction in overall risk.

The happy reality is that adult life holds plenty of opportunities for low-key people like Tam. Employers need workers who thrive in more subdued and solitary settings just as they need people who do well in chaotic and social ones. With early intervention and a friend or two, grown-up Tam will find many opportunities to fit in and enjoy himself as an adult despite his sensory issues.

LaTanya and Children with Over-Responsivity

> *I remember the days when a cheering crowd and a pat on the back were painful for my son. I remember the years of isolation, earplugs, desensitizing massages, avoiding exciting events because of the commotion and noise, and the struggles to brush his teeth and wash his face. I still tense up remembering the endless struggles with social interactions, the fear of balloons, fireworks, Halloween masks, etc., but now I also feel joy over the accomplishments Daniel has achieved through tenacity and encouragement.*

CONTRIBUTED BY VICKI SIEGEL AND SON DANIEL

There are many keys to helping a child with over-responsivity find a brighter future. Besides appropriate treatment, a child like LaTanya needs self-esteem as much as Abby does, self-regulation as much as Ben does, and social participation as much as Tam does.

Children with severe over-responsivity who have not received effective treatment are likely to continue struggling with their sensory sensitivities through middle and high school because the situations that are most challenging for over-responders—transitions, unpredictability, sensory overstimulation—reach a crescendo during the teen years. Loud concerts, movies and parties, crowded malls, driving a car in traffic, or even riding in a car where a boom box is throbbing or the windows are down and the wind is rushing in generates one sensory assault after another. Self-care activities that are distasteful or un-comfortable because of their sensory sensitivities (shaving, putting on makeup, hair care, wearing deodorant) become essential to social sur-vival and can lead to social stigma if the teen refuses to perform them. Children with over-responsivity who withdraw in order to escape the commotion and mess of the teen years are at risk of becoming socially isolated loners. Depression, anxiety, low self-esteem, and other be-havioral and emotional difficulties can result.

Nonetheless, things often improve dramatically once the teen years are over. As adults, over-responders at last gain control over many of the situations most likely to inflame their sensitivities. They can choose food that feels and tastes acceptable, buy clothes that are comfortable, take a job with fewer sensory elements, avoid people who are loud or physical or unpredictable. If they have learned A SE-CRET or its equivalent, they can manipulate the elements of daily life to make it more predictable and enjoyable even though their sensi-tivities may persist.

As over-responders achieve control over the outside elements of their context, self-regulation usually becomes easier and self-esteem can flourish. They learn to avoid getting into situations in which they're likely to fall apart and end up feeling bad about themselves. Maybe they never become comfortable cheering the Colorado Rockies to victory on a summer afternoon at Coors Field, but they can hap-pily watch the game at home on TV with a small group of equally mild-mannered friends and the volume turned low. With self-regulation, self-esteem, and friends, options open and life satisfac-tion grows.

Planning for the Future

Every child's path to adulthood will be different. However, children with Sensory Processing Disorder all benefit when their parents anticipate the issues each developmental step brings and prepare both themselves and their children for its challenges. Abby Hudson's parents knew that dyspraxic children who are unathletic and overweight can become isolated and unhappy in the social jungle of middle school. Long before reaching that developmental step, they began providing their daughter with a balanced diet and devising plenty of calorie-burning physical activity for her. For a dyspraxic child like Abby, a magnet school for theater or language or academic excellence might provide a more suitable environment than a mainstream middle school. Doing some advance research on educational alternatives is another way the family can prepare for the middle-school transition.

Dramatic changes are not always necessary, but for children with SPD, adaptations at each developmental stage are almost inevitable. Looking ahead and planning for developmental obstacles *before* you and your child reach them are essential. Sensational children *can and do* grow into sensationally happy and successful adults. With planning and support along the way, your child can be one of them.

> *Daniel has participated in many sports, including soccer, Little League baseball, tae kwon do, tennis, and golf, but he has finally found his niche in bowling. At the age of sixteen, after bowling for only three years, he was nominated to be a People-to-People Sports Ambassador for the United States in the sport and was chosen after a rigorous selection process to represent the United States in London. To get there, Daniel had to travel alone as far as New York—connecting through domestic and international terminals in Atlanta—and then meet sixty strangers who would share the journey. I was home pacing the floors, but he managed it all. Ten days later, he placed fifth overall and was invited back next year to compete in Australia and New Zealand! Wow. What a long way from our struggles through the preschool, middle school, and early high school years.*

CONTRIBUTED BY VICKI SIEGEL AND SON DANIEL

PART III

Beyond the Basics

Research into the causes, mechanisms, symptoms, and treatment of Sensory Processing Disorder has entered an explosive growth period, with studies under way by scientists from multiple disciplines nationwide and around the world. The following are ten truths researchers already have established.

Ten Fundamental Facts About Sensory Processing Disorder

- Sensory Processing Disorder is a complex disorder of the brain that affects developing children.
- Parent surveys, clinical assessments, and laboratory protocols exist to identify children with SPD.
- At least one in twenty people in the general population is affected by SPD.

- In children with ADHD, autism, and fragile X syndrome, the prevalence of SPD is much higher.
- A significant difference exists between the physiology of children with SPD and children who are typically developing.
- A significant difference exists between the physiology of children with SPD and children with ADHD.
- SPD has unique sensory symptoms that are not explained by other known disorders.
- Heredity is implicated as one cause of SPD.
- Laboratory studies suggest that the sympathetic and parasympathetic nervous systems are not functioning typically in children with SPD.
- Preliminary research data support decades of anecdotal evidence that occupational therapy is an effective intervention for treating the symptoms of SPD.

Almost twenty years ago, when our son was diagnosed with Sensory Processing Disorder, I was uncertain. Neither in medical school nor in postgraduate training—both at well-known academic institutions—had I ever heard of SPD. My wife, my son, and I were amazed at the effect of the OT he received and how quickly it targeted his difficulties. What was this all about? What were the underlying mechanisms of the disorder? How could this therapy, which looked like play and sounded like fun, make such a difference? What neural mechanisms were involved in his changes? What was the etiology—was it genetic?

For the remainder of his childhood, our son was the beneficiary of educational plans and therapies of various kinds, both in and out of school, but the original OT assessment proved to be the backbone of his diagnosis and the foundation of his treatment. I have followed with interest the developing science of this field because, whatever the answers are, it has definitely made a difference for our son, for us, and for so many affected families. I am thrilled at the emerging awareness of Sensory Processing Disorder as a distinct diagnostic and therapeutic entity.

CONTRIBUTED BY NICK SCHARFF, M.D.

Chapter 11

The Science of SPD

One of the reports I sometimes hear from families and teachers of sensational kids is that they've been told Sensory Processing Disorder is "just a theory," that it "hasn't been proven," or that it "makes sense but doesn't have any research behind it." The fact that the disorder is not yet listed in the *Diagnostic and Statistical Manual* adds to the confusion. Parents urgently want to know: *Is SPD recognized in any of the diagnostic manuals? Is assessment valid? Does therapy work?*

My answer to these questions is *yes, yes,* and *yes.*

Families, educators, physicians, and others who live and work with these children can be confident that rigorous scientific research into the causes, mechanisms, symptoms, and treatment of the disorder is being conducted and published across the country and around the world. Yes, additional research is still needed—but the same can be said of countless other human disorders, syndromes, diseases, and maladies. True, inclusion in the *DSM* and most other diagnostic reference books has not yet occurred,* but the same was long true for many conditions that are now universally recognized.

More important, after a hiatus following Dr. Ayres's death in 1988, research into SPD has entered a massive growth phase. The sensory-processing abilities of hundreds of children are being tested in multiple laboratories, providing the replicate data that are the cornerstone of scientific credibility. Research scientists from numerous, diverse disciplines are conducting primate studies, rat studies, anatomic studies, electroencephalographic and other psychophysiological studies, plus studies of twins, studies of family links, and much more. Results are being reported in peer-reviewed professional journals where research must meet exacting standards to be published.

Scientists are hard at work on questions such as:

● What's going on in the brains of these children? (Or, in technical language: What are the underlying physiologi-

---

* Regulatory-Sensory Processing Disorder is recognized as diagnostic code 201–207 in Greenspan, S.I., S. Wieder, eds., *Diagnostic Manual for Infancy and Early Childhood: Mental Health, Developmental, Regulatory-Sensory Processing and Language Disorders and Learning Challenges (ICDL-DMIC).* Bethesda, MD: Interdisciplinary Council on Developmental and Learning Disorders (ICDL), 2005. Regulatory Disorder of Sensory Processing is recognized in *Diagnostic Classification: 0 to 3.* Washington, D.C.: Zero to Three, 2005.

cal, neurological, and biochemical mechanisms implicated in SPD?)

- How is SPD similar to and different from other disorders? (Or: What is the concurrent and divergent evidence that SPD is a valid separate syndrome and not just a set of correlated symptoms within ADHD, autism, fragile X syndrome, or another disorder?)
- What does SPD look like? (What is the behavioral phenotype of SPD?)
- Does treatment work? (What empirical evidence documents the effectiveness of occupational therapy and/or other treatments in ameliorating SPD as well as in changing self-regulation, self-esteem, and social participation in children with the disorder?)
- How many people have SPD? (What is the prevalence of SPD in the typically developing population and in populations that have disabilities?)
- Where does SPD come from? (What is the etiology of SPD?)
- Is heredity a factor? (Is there a familial component to SPD?)

This chapter and the three that follow outline some of the discoveries scientists have made and directions in which they are searching for more answers.

"What's Going on in the Brain of My Child?"

The scientific question, "What are the neurophysiological mechanisms of Sensory Processing Disorder?" translates into everyday language, "What's going on in the brain of my child?" To address this question, multiple research programs nationwide* have set a broad agenda that includes studying markers of brain activity in children with Sensory Processing Disorder.

The initial collective focus of this work has been on studying sensory over-responsivity. Over-responsivity was selected because the behavior problems associated with it tend to be severely disruptive and readily identifiable and frequently result in referral for evaluation. Since the behaviors are consistently fight/flight responses, a decision was made to start looking at the autonomic nervous system (ANS), known from animal studies[1] to be the source of fight/flight behaviors.

Two systems within the ANS were identified for study: the sympathetic nervous system, which is responsible for the fight/flight reaction, and the parasympathetic nervous system, which is responsible for restoring calm.[†] Ideally, these two systems work in partnership: The sympathetic system alerts us to potential danger when we encounter a new or threatening stimulus, and the parasympathetic system helps us retain or regain control so the fight/flight instinct doesn't override reason. Although the relationship between the two systems is, of course, more complex than this, the partnership analogy captures the essence of it. If you're walking down a dark alley at night and hear a loud crash, your sympathetic system alerts you to possible danger—making your heart race and your palms sweat—and then your parasympathetic system returns your physiology to normal when you look around and see a cat dashing away from an overturned garbage can.

---

* One program was initiated at the STAR Center in Denver and subsequently expanded to seven other sites coast to coast. Called the SPD Alpha Research Project, the initiative utilizes the Sensory Challenge Protocol described later in this chapter to study markers of brain activity in children in the laboratory. The second initiative is the SPD Scientific Work Group, a consortium of NIH-funded scientists from multiple fields working to broaden SPD research into medicine and developmental neurobiology. See Appendix I for a roster of researchers participating in the two initiatives.

† This calm or regulated state is called homeostasis. A third system of the ANS, the enteric nervous system (the nervous system responsible for reactions in internal organs such as the stomach and intestines), was not studied because no pragmatic way was found to measure it in the laboratory.

The behavior of children like LaTanya, in whom the fight/flight reaction is exaggerated and the calming reaction is often delayed or absent, suggests that the neurological partnership in the ANS is not working as it should in children with over-responsivity. In a landmark study, researchers set out to test this hypothesis.

First, prior research of the autonomic nervous system in children with other types of disabilities[2] was analyzed. Methods that had been found effective for measuring high arousal in these children were identified and from them the Sensory Challenge Protocol,[3] a new psychophysiological laboratory procedure, was developed to measure sensory over-responsivity. During the sensory protocol, a child is seated in a room designed as a pretend "spaceship." A short clip of the film *Apollo 13* is shown in which the astronauts are being attached to electrodes. While the child watches the movie-astronauts being hooked up with electrodes, electrodes that will measure two types of physiological response in the "little astronaut" are attached to the child.

The first of these measured responses is electrodermal activity, from the root "electro," for electric, and "dermal," for skin. Electrodermal activity (sometimes abbreviated "EDA") is an electrical change in the skin that can be measured by the sweat on the hands. Measuring the magnitude of electrodermal activity indicates the intensity of the sympathetic nervous system reaction to a stimulus.[4] The second measured response is vagal tone, a measurement of heart rate variability. In several populations,[5] vagal tone has been established as a reliable measure of regulation by the parasympathetic system.[6]

Once the electrodes are in place, the child is told that he will soon see, smell, hear, and feel some "funny things." Then a series of sensory challenges—eight each of six different stimuli*—is presented with a lapsed time of ten to twenty seconds between each sensation.

---

* The smell of wintergreen, the sound of a school bell and the sound of a one-note tone, the sight of a strobe light, the touch of a feather, and the feeling of a chair tipping abruptly backward.

The two figures below provide a sample of the information generated by the protocol.

In Figure 11.1, a typically developing child seated in the "spaceship" has just felt his chair tip backward fifteen degrees and then return to upright. The vertical lines indicate each of the chair's tip-back mechanical movements during the test; the wavy lines represent the child's reactions to tipping backward.

Look at the initial reaction after the first vertical line. The wavy line rises and then falls smoothly, making a little hill shape. This indicates the child noticed (known as "oriented to") the sensory message. After orienting, the child's physiological reaction swiftly returns to baseline, which indicates he correctly interpreted the movement as being not dangerous. Later, when the chair tips backward a second and third time, you can see from the wave form that the physiological re-

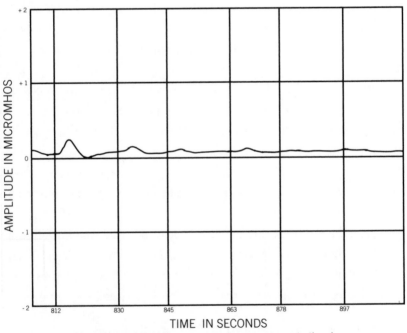

TIME IN SECONDS

*each vertical line represents a movement stimulus

Figure 11.1. Sympathetic system reactions in typically developing children

action gets smaller and smaller until it eventually disappears. This indicates that the child compared the later sensory messages with the first one and continued to correctly interpret them as "same-old, same-old," resulting in successively smaller physiological reactions. Scientists call this process "habituation," one sign of normal sensory processing.

Figure 11.2 paints a very different picture. This shows the physiological reactions of a child with sensory over-responsivity. What a difference! The chair's movement triggers a much more intense reaction, which is represented by a higher wave form, and the child responds multiple times to the same sensation (see the multiple peaks after the first event). What's more, the physiological reactions do *not* decrease when the movement is repeated. The child's brain continues to signal, "Something's wrong here! Stay alert! Possible danger!" even after experience should have assured him the situation is safe. He does not habituate, which helps explain why a child like LaTanya flinches,

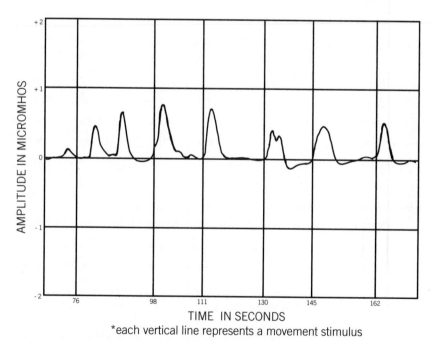

TIME IN SECONDS
*each vertical line represents a movement stimulus

Figure 11.2. Sympathetic system reactions in children with sensory over-responsivity

cringes, and sometimes breaks into tears when she's jostled unexpect-edly on the school bus, in the classroom, and on the playground.

Hundreds* of children have been tested using the Sensory Challenge Protocol since its initiation in 1995, producing a wealth of promising information about what's happening in the brains of chil-dren with SPD. In one of these studies, the autonomic nervous sys-tem activity of typically developing children was compared to that of children diagnosed with fragile X syndrome, a genetic condition in which sensory over-responsivity almost invariably occurs.[7] Figure 11.3 shows the findings. The "log magnitude of peak" on the left of the chart is the scale for the electrodermal response. Each of the numbers across the bottom of the graph represents a set of sensory stimuli. For example, 1 shows the average size of electrodermal response for the first trial of all sensations (i.e., average of first smell + first sound + first sight, etc.); 2 is the average response size for all the second trials; 3 is the average of the third trials, and so forth.

Again the results are dramatic. The children with fragile X and sensory over-responsivity exhibited significantly larger responses to the sensory messages than did the typically developing children. Additionally, the sensory over-responders continued to respond strongly with each sensory event while the responses in the typically developing children diminished and habituation occurred. In other words, the brains of children with fragile X and sensory over-responsivity reacted differently to sensory stimulation than the brains of typically developing children, supporting the thesis that sensory problems have a physiological basis.

The responses of typically developing children were also com-pared with those of children who had been evaluated and found to have sensory over-responsivity but who had no other known disorder.[8]

---

* At the time of publication, more than four hundred children and two hundred adults had been tested in the original sensory protocol laboratory. Currently, an additional six sites are conducting research—expanding the size of this sample and increasing the number of ques-tions that can be answered.

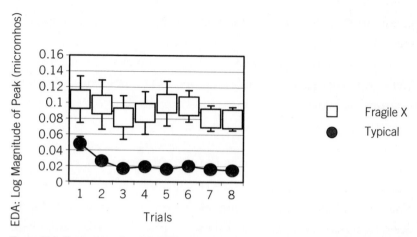

Figure 11.3. Electrodermal activity (EDA) of typically developing children compared to children with fragile X syndrome

Figure 11.4 shows that the comparison again found dramatic and statistically significant differences. Whereas the sympathetic reactions were significantly greater among the over-responsive children than among the typically developing children, the parasympathetic reactions were significantly less.[9] This may be an indication that the

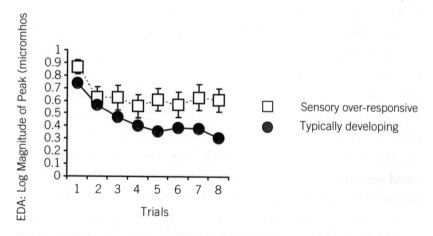

Figure 11.4. Electrodermal activity of typically developing children compared to children with sensory over-responsivity and no other diagnosis. Findings presented the first laboratory evidence that children with SPD are physiologically different than typically developing children.

parasympathetic system was not doing its job of putting the brakes on the fight/flight reaction.

Considered together, these data suggest two possible causes of the highly reactive behaviors seen in sensory over-responsivity: too much sympathetic activity or too little parasympathetic activity.

Research Implications

The implications of these studies are enormous. The partnership of the sympathetic and parasympathetic systems is basic to coping with all the changes and transitions that occur in daily life. Establishing that the regulatory partnership within the autonomic nervous system of children with sensory over-responsivity may not be working helps us understand the extreme fight/flight behaviors in this population. The data also offer empirical evidence validating the physiological basis of SPD.

Studies like this one hold immediate relevance for parents and others who live and work with sensational children by suggesting promising directions for intervention. If kids with sensory over-responsivity are handicapped by underactive parasympathetic systems, they will benefit from the application of and instruction in calming techniques that help them lower arousal and achieve self-regulation. Self-regulation is essential if a child is to move on to higher-level activities such as social participation, academic accomplishment, and a healthy sense of self-worth. Therapies that improve self-regulation increase a child's ability to manage the fight/flight reaction and to function in situations where overreaction would hamper development. In other words, what scientists are learning about the brains of children with over-responsivity can lead to techniques that will help your own over-responsive child succeed at home, school, and in the community.

Even though initial studies of the autonomic system's functioning have focused on children with over-responsivity, it's quite possible that the same systems are responsible for the poor awareness in children with under-responsivity. If LaTanya's over-responsivity is caused by too much sympathetic activity and/or too little parasympathetic activity, it seems possible that Tam's under-responsivity is caused by the opposite—too much parasympathetic or too little sympathetic activity.

The research design examining this and many other hypotheses has been tested in small studies. "All" that's missing to carry out definitive research is funding. As this funding becomes available, more and more of the questions that parents, educators, therapists, and scientists are asking about the disorder will be answered.

The heartening news now is that while the list of questions remains long, answers *are* being found. With each scientific step comes better understanding, more effective treatment, and a brighter future for sensational kids everywhere.

Ultimately we learned that OT is about understanding ourselves. We are all sensory beings, with specific sensory-driven needs that must be addressed in order for us to function at our best. Learning about sensory processing not only helps the child to understand his own body as it relates to the world around him, but also gives parents and those who care for the child an understanding of their own sensory needs. We all feel calm and safe when our sensory systems are organized and when our sensory needs are being met. We can trust what we feel, so we can move past survival mode into learning.

CONTRIBUTED BY MARIE RAWLINSON AND SON DAVID

What Can I Do to Help?

The world of Sensory Processing Disorder advocacy is huge and we need *you!*

There are many ways in which parents, extended family, therapists, and concerned citizens can help in getting SPD recognized as a diagnosis, in supporting parents of children with SPD, and in advancing research into the underlying mechanisms and effectiveness of treatment for SPD. Here are just a few of the opportunities:

Parent Support
- Start a parent support group in your city. Successful groups have been begun by experienced and novice parents alike. SPD Parent Connections is about parents getting together to support one another. (Visit www.KIDfoundation.org/parentconnection or contact the KID Foundation for more information.)

Education
- Read about Sensory Processing Disorder. In Appendix A you'll find a list of good books about SPD in people of all ages.
- Contact Sensory Resources or another conference organization and find out when a conference is planned in your area. If none is on the schedule, ask the organization staff to consider holding one. Companies that sponsor educational programs and provide other educational resources are listed in Appendix A.

Advocacy
- Assist with the petition to have SPD formally recognized as a diagnosis. Information is available at www.KIDfoundation.org/advocacy.
- Contact your state or federal legislator and make an appointment to explain SPD. Legislators can provide vital support, particularly in influencing the National Institutes of Health to fund research related to SPD.

Research

- Participate in a research project. Current projects are listed at www.KIDfoundation.org/research.
- Shopping online through the KID Foundation's affiliate program. This costs you nothing and directs 5 percent of your purchases to the Foundation's research efforts. Just go to the KID's website and click through to Amazon, Expedia, eBay, or one of dozens of other affiliated online stores.
- Donate directly. Individual, family foundation, and corporate support make possible much of the work described in *Sensational Kids*. Make contributions at Help Support the KID Foundation on the KID website at www.KIDfoundation.org/help.
- Introduce the KID Foundation to philanthropists and charitable organizations you know or let us know about the movers and shakers in your community whom you think we should contact about getting involved.

NOTES

1. Cannon, W. B. *The Wisdom of the Body.* New York: Norton, 1932.

2. **Down syndrome**: J. Clausen, A. Lidsky, and E. A. Sersen. "Measurement of autonomic functions in mental deficiency." In R. Karrer (ed.), *Developmental Psychophysiology of Mental Retardation.* Springfield, IL: Thomas, 1976; J. M. Martinez-Selva, F. A. Garcia-Sanchez, and R. Florit. "Electrodermal orienting activity in children with Down syndrome," *American Journal on Mental Retardation* 100.1 (1995): 51–58; R. M. Wallace, and F. S. Fehr. "Heart rate, skin resistance, and reaction time of mongoloid and normal children under baseline and distraction conditions," *Psychophysiology* 6 (1970): 722–31. **Schizophrenia**: D. K. Kim, Y. M. Shin, C. E. Kim, H. S. Cho, and Y. S. Kim. "Electrodermal responsiveness, clinical variables, and brain imaging in male chronic schizophrenics," *Biological Psychiatry* 33 (1993): 786–93. **ADHD**: D. C. Fowles, and A. M. Furuseth. "Electrodermal hy-

poreactivity and antisocial behavior." In D. K. Routh (ed.), *Disruptive Behavior Disorders in Childhood.* New York: Plenum Press, 1994 (181–205); R. H. Rosenthal, and T. W. Allen."An examination of attention, arousal, and learning dysfunctions of hyperkinetic children," *Psychological Bulletin* 75 (1978): 689–715; J. H. Satterfield, and M. E. Dawson. "Electrodermal correlates of hyperactivity in children," *Psychophysiology* 8.2 (1971): 191–97. **Conduct Disorder:** T. P. Zahn, and M. J. P. Kruesi. "Autonomic activity in boys with disruptive behavior disorders," *Psychophysiology* 30 (1993): 605–14. **Autism:** S. Stevens, and J. Gruzelier. "Electrodermal activity to auditory stimuli in autistic, retarded, and normal children," *Journal of Autism and Developmental Disorders* 14.3 (1984): 245–60.

3. L. J. Miller, D. N. McIntosh, J. McGrath, V. Shyu, M. Lampe, A. K. Taylor, F. Tassone, K. Neitzel, T. Stackhouse, and R. Hagerman. "Electrodermal responses to sensory stimuli in individuals with fragile X syndrome: A preliminary report," *American Journal of Medical Genetics* 83.4 (1999): 268–79; L. J. Miller, J. E. Reisman, D. N. McIntosh, and J. Simon. "An ecological model of sensory modulation: Performance of children with fragile X syndrome, autism, attention-deficit/hyperactivity disorder, and sensory modulation dysfunction." In S. S. Roley, E. I. Blanche, and R. C. Schaaf (eds.), *Understanding the Nature of Sensory Integration with Diverse Populations.* San Antonio, TX: Therapy Skill Builders, 2001: 57–88.

4. J. L. Andreassi. "Concepts in psychophysiology." In J. L. Andreassi (ed.), *Psychophysiology: Human Behavior and Physiological Response.* Lawrence Hillsdale, NJ: Erlbaum Associates, 1989: 393–422; M. E. Dawson, A. M. Schell, and D. L. Filion. "The electrodermal system." In J. T. Cacioppo, and L. G. Tassinary (eds.), *Principles of Psychophysiology: Physical, Social, and Inferential Elements.* New York: Cambridge University Press (1990): 200–23; D. C. Fowles. "The eccrine system and electrodermal activity." In M. G. H. Coles, E. Donchin, and S. W. Porges (eds.), *Psychophysiology: Systems, Processes, and Applications.* New York: Guilford Press, 1986: 51–96.

5. **High-risk infants:** J. A. Doussard-Roosevelt, S. W. Porges, J. W. Scanlon, B. Alemi, and K. B. Scanlon. "Vagal regulation of heart rate in the prediction of developmental outcome for very low birth weight preterm infants," *Child Development* 68.2 (1997): 173–86. **Adults with head injuries:** Y. Donchin, S. Constantine, A. Szold, E. A. Byrne, and S. W. Porges. "Cardiac vagal tone predicts outcome in neurosurgical patients," *Critical Care Medicine* 20 (1992): 942–49. **Individuals with delayed cognitive development:** J. A. DiPetro, S. K. Larons, and S. W. Porges. "Behavioral and heart rate pattern differences between breast-

fed and bottle-fed neonates," *Developmental Psychology* 23 (1987): 467–74. **Individuals with social problems**: J. A. Doussard-Roosevelt, S. W. Porges, J. W. Scanlon, B. Alemi, and K. B. Scanlon. "Vagal regulation of heart rate in the prediction of developmental outcome for very low birth weight preterm infants," *Child Development* 68.2 (1997): 173–86.

6. J. Hayano, Y. Sakakibara, A. Yamada, M. Yamada, S. Mukai, T. Fujinami, K. Yokoyama, Y. Watanabe, and K. Takata. "Accuracy of assessment of cardiac vagal tone by heart rate variability in normal subjects," *American Journal of Cardiology* 67 (1991): 199–204; S. W. Porges, and J. A. Doussard-Roosevelt. "The psychophysiology of temperament." In J. D. Noshpitz (ed.), *Handbook of Child and Adolescent Psychiatry*. New York: Wiley, 1997.

7. See note 3 above.

8. D. N. McIntosh, L. J. Miller, V. Shyu, and R. Hagerman. "Sensory-modulation disruption, electrodermal responses, and functional behaviors," *Developmental Medicine and Child Neurology* 41 (1999): 608–15.

9. R. C. Schaaf, L. J. Miller, D. Sewell, and S. O'Keefe. "Children with disturbances in sensory processing: A pilot study examining the role of the parasympathetic nervous system," *American Journal of Occupational Therapy* 57.4 (2003): 442–49.

Parenting my daughter can make me laugh or cry, depending on the day, the hour, the minute, really. My beautiful daughter Briana ("Breezy") turned four this past July. She is an engaging, charming, and endearing little girl. At the same time, she can be inconsolable, stubborn, willful, and controlling. She can cheer me up when I am feeling down with her innocent yet amazingly insightful comments about her world. And she can make me cry when I watch her struggle to make friends at the playground, learn how to ride a bike, or struggle to make herself do new things.

CONTRIBUTED BY MAUREEN HERNON-THISTLE

AND DAUGHTER BRIANA

Chapter 12

Beyond the Types

The children—all imagined—whom we spent a day following in Part II exemplify four specific subtypes of Sensory Processing Disorder. LaTanya, Tam, Ben, and Abby are all "model" children created to show how subtypes of SPD affect kids' everyday lives. If these were real children, the picture we'd see would be more complicated, with overlapping and fluctuating patterns of behavior that might change from day to day or even hour to hour, the way Breezy's seem to.

If you are the parent of a child with SPD, you know what I mean. Perhaps your child has been evaluated and you've been told he has a modulation *and* a discrimination disorder or dyspraxia *and* postural disorder. Or maybe he's been given a single diagnosis but sometimes has symptoms that seem inconsistent with it. Perhaps you're like the mother who wanted to know why her over-responsive son was so sensitive to touch that he couldn't stand the feel of water washing his face and yet could stay in a swimming pool for hours. Possibly you can identify with another parent whose son was diagnosed with sensory under-responsivity yet made a habit of running into her hard enough to leave bruises, a symptom normally associated with sensory seeking.

Many inconsistencies in behavior can be explained by the SECRET elements of context I've discussed. Take a sensory seeker who routinely goes and goes—and then sinks into such a completely passive state that he appears under-responsive. A closer look at the child's context might reveal that, when he crashes, all his sensory needs have been met (the sensory element changed) or that another child has come onto the scene and caused him to withdraw (the relationship element altered) or that he has lost interest in the activity (attention changed). Usually behavioral shifts are not random, spontaneous fluctuations without an explanation, and very often the explanation is a change in context.

The Prevalence of Combination Disorders

Studies confirm that it is possible for a child to have only one classic pattern or subtype of Sensory Processing Disorder. Nonetheless, many children *do* have symptoms of more than one subtype of SPD, giving them what I call a "combination disorder." In one study analyzing the phenotypes of SPD, two hundred children ages three to twelve were observed.* Figure 12.1 depicts the relationship found among the three subtypes of Sensory Modulation Disorder: sensory over-responsivity, sensory under-responsivity, and sensory seeking. In all,

---

* Miller, L. J., J. Coll, J. Koomar, T. May-Benson, S. Schoen, B. Brett-Green, and M. Reale. "Relations among subtypes of Sensory Modulation Dysfunction." Manuscript in progress.

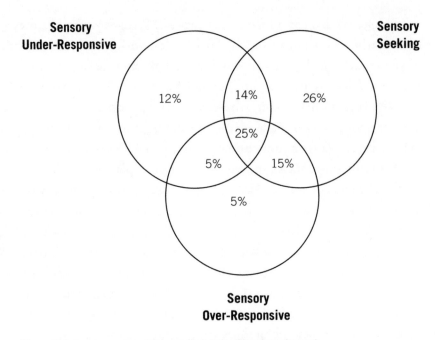

Figure 12.1. Co-occurrence of Sensory Modulation Disorder subtypes*

34 percent of the children had symptoms of two of the subtypes and another 25 percent had symptoms of all three, for a total of 59 percent of the children with combined subtypes.

Figure 12.2 reveals even more dramatic evidence of co-occurrence "beyond the types." In this illustration, the relationship among the three classic patterns of SPD—Sensory Modulation, Sensory-Based Motor, and Sensory Discrimination—is depicted. While 30 percent of the children had symptoms of only one of the three classic patterns, 43 percent had symptoms of two patterns, and 27 percent had symptoms of all three. Taken together this suggests that a huge percentage—70 percent—of the children had combination disorders, a result that validates long-standing clinical belief that combinations may be the rule rather than the exception.

* Due to arithmetic rounding, percentages exceed 100 percent.

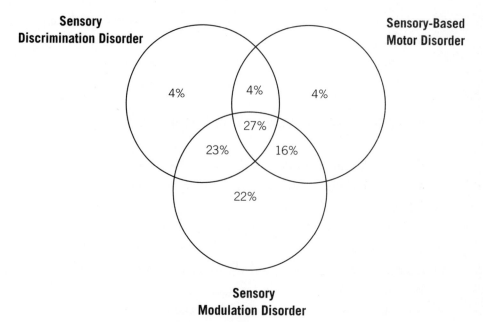

Figure 12.2. Co-occurrence of SPD classic patterns

The frequent occurrence of combination disorders is most likely a result of the brain's structure. The brain's systems are interrelated, which means that a physiological or biochemical problem in one area can affect operations in another area. Any traveler who has ever suffered through a weather disruption can imagine how this works. When thunderstorms shut down Chicago O'Hare Airport, even distant airports are affected because air traffic is an interrelated system. A neurological disorder is the brain's equivalent of a thunderstorm in a key hub. Although disruption can be limited to a single area, it's common for multiple parts of the system to be disturbed.

Since any of the three classic patterns of SPD and their subtypes can combine, it might seem that a mind-boggling number of combination disorders would be possible. In reality, relatively few combinations account for most of the co-occurrence of SPD. Three of these combinations merit special attention:

- sensory under-responsivity with postural disorder
- dyspraxia with postural disorder
- dyspraxia with sensory seeking

Sensory Under-Responsivity with Postural Disorder

Children with sensory under-responsivity who do not feel their bodies well and have poor muscle tone and strength may be diagnosed with both sensory under-responsivity and postural disorder.

If Tam had this combination disorder, he would exhibit the same under-responsivity we've already seen, but would have additional difficulties related to posture, muscle tone, and motor control. The chronic under-arousal already causing problems for him would be compounded in physical activities, especially those requiring endurance. For example, he would probably have trouble walking long distances and lifting heavy objects. It is also likely he would have oral-motor problems such as difficulty sucking, swallowing, and/or taking deep breaths.

The co-occurrence of sensory under-responsivity and postural disorder complicates treating either pattern. As long as a child's body remains under-aware of sensations, it is difficult for him to acquire the sensory information he needs for good postural control; but as long as postural control is poor, obtaining adequate sensory input is problematic. Treatment of this combination disorder typically involves giving the child enough stimulation to achieve optimal arousal and then building postural stability based on this increased sensory awareness.

Dyspraxia with Postural Disorder

Because the sensory and the motor systems are involved in both praxis and posture, dyspraxia and postural disorder frequently occur in combination. Children with this combination disorder do not feel their bodies well and have trouble with both planning their movements and moving with accuracy.

Chatty little Abby had the motor-planning problems common to dyspraxia and also displayed some symptoms of postural disfunction. If she had enough symptoms to qualify for postural disorder, she would have the same troubles with motor planning she does now and additionally be insecure with movement, which would make her cautious, passive, and even more reluctant to engage in gross-motor play than she already is. She would insist on watching TV or reading or playing on the computer and would hate PE more than she does now. In chaotic, sensory-rich environments, she would be fearful because her balance would be challenged, making her motor-planning problems even more evident. Disneyland would definitely be a big no-no. What's more, her appearance would be slouchy whether she was sitting or standing—she would slouch at her desk, slouch through recess, and slouch at the TV or computer back at home.

Children who have dyspraxia combined with postural disorder tend to have visual-motor problems, too, and poor control of eye movements, which require a stable head position. Visual-motor problems make activities such as hitting a moving ball or transferring words or numbers from the blackboard to paper difficult. Children with visual-motor problems can have difficulty with scanning and depth perception.

The basis of the combination of dyspraxia and postural disorder is believed to be a simultaneous dysfunction in the tactile and proprioceptive systems. For this reason, the core activities in treatment usually incorporate both touch and proprioception.

Dyspraxia with Sensory Seeking

Children with a third common combination pattern, dyspraxia with sensory seeking, seek out movement the way that busy little Ben did in Part II but are not the natural athletes he is. Instead they tend to be clumsy and have poor timing and sequencing skills.

Children with this combination disorder are harder to diagnose because their problem is subtle. They love movement, but on closer analysis their movements are not smooth. They're the crash-and-bash kids—flinging themselves out of a swing the way Ben would but without the rhythm and timing to jump at the right time and land smoothly. In fact, they tend to get hurt a lot and are often labeled "accident prone." They may be "class clowns" because they appear to be doing things on purpose to make other children laugh—like falling out of their chairs or stumbling over cracks in the sidewalk. In reality they are unable to coordinate their movement with their sensory appetites. They may also have trouble planning and producing the necessary movement to complete actions in a changing environment. For example, if you say, "I am going to roll this ball and I want you to run up and kick it," they can't time their movement so as to intersect with the path of the moving ball.

The basis of the sensory seeking/dyspraxia combination is believed to be a simultaneous dysfunction in the vestibular and proprioceptive systems. Again, treatment often involves providing proprioceptive input, typically in combination with vestibular input in activities that help the child learn how to think about and plan actions.

Other Combination Patterns

Other combinations can occur beyond the types.

Children with sensory under-responsivity nearly always have Sensory Discrimination Disorder in one or more senses. This is probably because they have trouble feeling sensations and consequently have trouble discriminating what they sense.

Children who have only sensory over-responsivity often have symptoms in more than one sensory system. Like LaTanya, they might be oversensitive to touch, sound, and taste or to any mixture of sensory symptoms. However, when over-responsivity occurs in combination with another pattern or subtype (e.g., over-responsivity and postural disorder or over-responsivity and SDD), the sensory over-responsivity may be limited to the tactile system, with no sensitivities in the other systems.

In what can seem contradictory, symptoms of sensory over- and under-responsivity are sometimes observed in the same child, such as when a child is over-responsive to touch and under-responsive to movement. One baffled set of parents wanted to know why their son's pain tolerance was so high that he could take a five-foot fall and stand up giggling yet become agitated when he touched slimy or gritty textures or someone hugged him.

Until more research is done, the underlying mechanisms that produce such combinations will remain unknown. In the meantime, whatever the combination of symptoms "beyond the types" you see in your child, it is essential to seek professional advice to sort among them. Effective intervention results when each source of dysfunction is accurately identified and appropriately addressed. Without the "right" diagnosis, the "right" treatment becomes a matter of chance.

The SPD–ADHD Connection

We just got back more test results on our son Lee. Along with SPD, he has ADHD, Specific Learning Disabilities, Mood Disorder, and a Central Auditory Processing Deficit. As I have progressed through this maze of testing during the last couple of years, I'm now amazed to hear from the specialists how common it is for all these to be present in one child. As a parent who considered herself pretty well informed and connected, I am astonished that no one ever told me in the beginning to look at all these other conditions!

CONTRIBUTED BY ROIANNE AHN, PH.D., AND SON LEE

Combination patterns are not limited to the classic patterns and subtypes of Sensory Processing Disorder. Scientists are also finding that SPD occurs in tandem with a number of nonsensory disorders.* When I met Roianne Ahn, she was a star doctoral student who'd been reduced to despair because of the baffling array of diagnoses given to her son and the daunting challenge of how to meet so many competing needs. Her dilemma illustrates why the study of coexisting disorders is a vital area for sensational kids and their families. If a child like Lee has SPD *and* one or more other disorders, his parents, his teachers, and the clinicians treating him need to identify *all* the conditions in order to find the intervention that is most likely to improve his functioning.

One connection that is already the subject of considerable study is the relationship of SPD to Attention Deficit Disorder, often called Attention-Deficit/Hyperactivity Disorder or ADHD. Ben, the sensory-seeking preschooler we followed in Chapter 8, offers a perfect illustration of why the SPD–ADHD connection is of keen interest to researchers and families. With his nonstop motion, inattentiveness, and chronic disorganization, a sensory seeker like Ben can look a lot like a child with the hyperactivity subtype of ADHD. In fact, misdiagnosis and mislabeling of the sort that Ben's mother, Nancy, routinely encountered is common.

Figure 12.3 shows how researchers approach the question of how two (or more) disorders might be related. Each set of circles depicts one of four relationships the disorders might have.

- They are different and do not overlap.
- They are different but do overlap, with some children having both disorders.
- One disorder is actually a variation or subset of the other.
- The disorders are identical.

* When two disorders coexist, the phenomenon is known as "comorbidity."

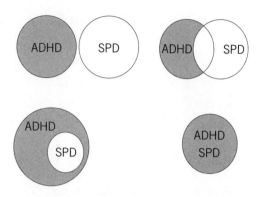

Figure 12.3. Four scenarios for the association of SPD and ADHD

In the case of SPD and ADHD, several colleagues and I conducted a nationwide study in an effort to find out which of these relationships most accurately describes the connection between SPD and ADHD. In the study, parents of 2,410 typically developing children participating in the development of a standardized IQ test were surveyed with a questionnaire that screens for both the attentional symptoms of ADHD and the sensory symptoms of SPD. The survey asked the parents to respond to statements like *My child responds by withdrawing when touched unexpectedly* and *My child is so easily distracted that he can't sit through dinnertime*. Children scoring in the lowest 5 percent on the Impulsivity, Activity Level, and Attention subtests were classified as having ADHD symptoms, while children scoring in the lowest 5 percent on the Sensitivity and Regulation subtest were classified as having SPD symptoms. Then we compared the ADHD group to the SPD group.

What we found was that about 7.5 percent of the children in the general population had symptoms of either SPD or ADHD, or both disorders (see Figure 12.4). In just about a third of those children, *only* symptoms of ADHD were reported by the parents. In slightly under a third, *only* symptoms of SPD were reported. Notably, 40 percent of the children with distinct symptoms of one disorder had symptoms of the other disorder as well.

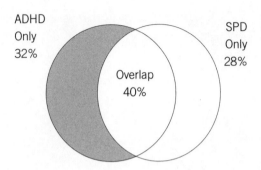

Figure 12.4. Co-occurrence of SPD and ADHD in a national sample

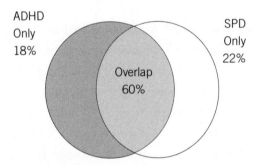

These data are derived from a national stratified sample of 2,410 children.

Figure 12.5. Co-occurrence of SPD and ADHD in children referred with either disorder

As researchers, we knew we were on to something, so we recruited a second group of children in order to take a closer look at the SPD–ADHD connection. In this study, we focused on children who had been referred to us with a preexisting diagnosis of either SPD or ADHD.* In this group of children, 60 percent of the kids—six out of every ten—were reported with symptoms of both ADHD and SPD

---

* We knew that when children are referred for services, most of them will have more than one diagnosis. This phenomenon, called "Berkson's bias," is well established: Children who are already within a clinical setting with one diagnosed disorder are more likely to have two or more disorders than children in the general population who are not receiving services.

(see Figure 12.5).* More important was that about 20 percent had *only* SPD and about 20 percent had *only* ADHD, signifying that the two disorders were not identical.

Before this research, skeptics often claimed that there was "no such thing as SPD—it's really just a subset of ADHD." For the first time, we had evidence that the two disorders were unique, but we needed to know more. Both of these studies were based on parent reports. Now we had to go further and determine whether the parent observations corresponded to the brain function of children.

We designed a new study to investigate the physiological differences in the brain function of children with SPD and those with ADHD. On the basis of previous doctor referrals, 130 children were sorted into four groups: those with (1) SPD, (2) ADHD, (3) both disorders, or (4) neither disorder. Then all the children were given the Sensory Challenge Protocol in our "spaceship" laboratory, and their physiological responses were compared.

You can see the dramatic results in Figure 12.6. (The horizontal line shows the break point between the upper half and the lower half of the children; the box shows the range of children falling from the 25th percentile to the 75th percentile.) Of the children with disorders, children with ADHD alone had the lowest responses to the sensory stimuli, similar to those of typically developing kids. But children with SPD or those who had ADHD *and* SPD exhibited far more responses than other children. This suggested that the brains of children with ADHD alone process sensory information in a fundamentally different way from how the brains of children with SPD or with SPD and ADHD process that information.[†]

---

* Miller, L. J., J. Coll, B. Brett-Green, S. Schoen, and M. Reale. "Comparison of electrodermal responses in children with ADHD and Sensory Processing Disorder." Manuscript in progress.

† This finding needs to be replicated before it is accepted as fact.

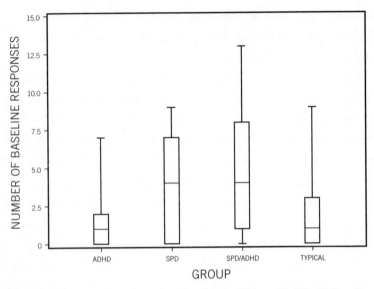

Figure 12.6. A comparison of the electrodermal activity in children with SPD, ADHD, and typical development

In the laboratory where test data is analyzed, we were tantalized. At last, a physiological distinction between ADHD and SPD had been identified. If our results could be replicated by other researchers using the same protocols, then parents and teachers wondering, "Is this SPD or ADHD?" might someday find the answer in a laboratory test. A direction worthy of further study had been identified.

What's more, the findings raised our hopes for improving the treatment of children with one or both disorders. In practical terms, if children with SPD and children with ADHD have measurable physiological differences, it follows that the interventions most appropriate for each disorder will be different, too. Currently, the standard treatment for ADHD is medication, which may have undesirable side effects that parents understandably wish to avoid. The standard intervention for SPD is occupational therapy. When the disorders occur together, both medication treatment and occupational therapy may be useful. However, misdiagnosis may result in a child's receiving an inappropriate intervention.*

The search for answers to your child's behavior can produce a collection of diagnostic labels that baffles and discourages you as it did Roianne Ahn. If that happens, *don't* give up. Continue your quest for answers until the information you receive "fits" your child. Only a complete understanding of your child will permit you to find the interventions that will help him the most.

SPD and Other Disorders

My daughter Regina has an anxiety disorder and selective mutism as well as sensory over-responsivity. When she is in an uncomfortable setting such as school, she becomes speechless. Just imagine how it feels being bombarded by stimuli in the classroom and being unable to tell anyone because you can't speak. Imagine how powerless she must feel. Children with SPD are so busy trying to deal with the environment that they can barely stay ahead of themselves, and children with anxiety disorders feel as if the whole world is crushing them. The sensory problems feed the anxiety, and the anxiety feeds the sensory problems. Around and around they go, but there's nothing very merry about this merry-go-round.

CONTRIBUTED BY REGINA'S MOTHER

Besides the SPD–ADHD connection, additional studies are looking into the relationship of Sensory Processing Disorder and Tourette's syndrome, Obsessive-Compulsive Disorder, and many other neurological conditions.

---

* Much further study into the underlying neurological mechanisms of SPD and ADHD is needed to understand these matters.

Tam, the under-responsive child in Chapter 7, illustrates why the relationship of SPD and high-functioning autism and Asperger's syndrome is another subject of interest to scientists and families. Studies to date suggest that children with autism divide into two groups: children with high arousal and children with low arousal. Those who have low arousal can behave somewhat like Tam, requiring a great deal of stimulation before they become alert and active. Those with high arousal may look more like LaTanya—overly sensitive to stimulation.

In one study, forty children with high-functioning autism or Asperger's syndrome were tested for physiological responsivity and given the Short Sensory Profile used to screen for SPD. Among these autistic children, 78 percent were found to have significant symptoms of Sensory Processing Disorder* (see Figure 12.7). The reverse was not true. In a separate study of more than one hundred children referred for Sensory Processing Disorder, the incidence of autism was zero, i.e., none of the children referred for SPD had autism.[†]

Like the studies of the connection between SPD and ADHD, this research strongly suggests that while SPD and autism may have some overlapping behaviors or symptoms, the two conditions are distinct disorders. A diagnostician or team skilled in evaluating sensory disabilities will be able to distinguish whether a child's symptoms result from SPD, autism, or another comorbid disorder. Again, since appropriate intervention depends upon accurate diagnosis, such an evaluation is essential to helping your child.

---

* Miller, L. J., S. Schoen, J. Coll, B. Brett-Green, and M. Reale. Final report: Quantitative psychophysiologic evaluation of Sensory Processing in children with autistic spectrum disorders. Los Angeles, CA: Cure Autism Now, February 2005.

† Miller, L. J., J. Coll, J. Koomar, T. May-Benson, S. Schoen, B. Brett-Green, and M. Reale. "Relations among subtypes of Sensory Modulation Dysfunction." Manuscript in progress.

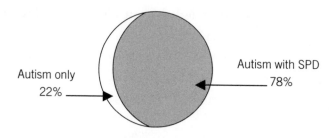

Figure 12.7. Co-occurrence of SPD and autism in referred children

Subjectivity in Diagnosis

Although accurate diagnosis is critical to appropriate treatment, there doesn't yet exist a blood test or a urine sample or a brain scan that a psychiatrist or psychologist can order from the lab to tell you, "There it is! Proof positive! Your child has _____" and then fill in the blank. Most neurological disorders, developmental disorders, and many mental health problems are diagnosed in both children and adults primarily on the basis of observed or reported behavior, an innately subjective—not objective—technique. Although the classifications in the *DSM-IV* make diagnosis more systematic than it once was, ultimately, the classifications themselves are typically the product of subjective judgments based on personal observation of behavior by the clinicians.

Just as a stomachache can signal food poisoning, colitis, appendicitis, or a twenty-four-hour bug, a child's atypical behavior could have multiple explanations. When diagnoses appear to conflict, the conflict generally stems from a difference in training by the professionals who are observing and making the judgment calls. The Sensory Challenge Protocol is one of the new objective methods that have emerged recently to take understanding and diagnosis of SPD to the next level. However, until the protocol and other objective measures are used more widely, differences of opinion will remain inevitable, and universal diagnostic agreement will be hard to come by.

> *Since OT, Breezy has been much better able to focus at school and home. She sits in circle time, plays next to her peers, and is beginning to play cooperatively as well. At home, she seldom crashes and bumps. She gave up diapers within one month of therapy—just like that! She is more organized and calm, and her hour-long tantrums are a thing of the past.*

> CONTRIBUTED BY MAUREEN HERNON-THISTLE
> AND DAUGHTER BRIANA

Often when parents discover their child has a neurological problem, they find that the problem runs down the family tree. As the mystery of Heather's sound sensitivities unfolded, I found a name for sensory disturbances I'd experienced since childhood. I'd sought help earlier for myself and now for my daughter, but none of the diagnoses ever seemed right. They certainly didn't lead to any useful treatment for either of us. One psychiatrist became so frustrated that she said she thought that whatever was wrong should be named the "Jo Disorder" after our family. Very flattering—ha-ha.

CONTRIBUTED BY JENNIFER JO, PH.D.,

AND DAUGHTER HEATHER

Chapter 13

Causes and Prevalence

When a child with Sensory Processing Disorder is surrounded by typically developing children, it's easy for sensational families to throw up their hands and cry, "Are we the only ones?"

The answer is easy: *No!*

Parents and professionals used to estimate that 5 to 15 percent of *all* children have some form of Sensory Processing Disorder, and that 40 to 85 percent of children who have other disabilities (e.g., ADHD, autism, fragile X syndrome) have sensory-processing problems as well. To establish empirical data on prevalence, one group of Colorado re-

searchers* surveyed the parents of nearly 1,800 incoming kindergartners in a large public school district. The survey found that the children in almost 14 percent of the 703 returned surveys had symptoms
of SPD significant enough to warrant a full evaluation for SPD.

Researchers used the extremely conservative assumption that none
of the roughly 1,100 surveyed children whose parents did not complete
the questionnaire had symptoms of SPD. They found that slightly more
than 5 percent—one in twenty children—of all the incoming kindergartners warranted evaluation based on the screening. If this prevalence
rate held true for the total population of the United States, this survey
suggests that at least fifteen million children and adults would have
symptoms of SPD, approximately 220,000 of them kindergartners. If
the actual rate of occurrence is closer to the 14 percent incidence in the
returned surveys, these numbers would more than double.

While we're all waiting for additional prevalence studies, parents
of children with SPD can be assured of one thing: You are most certainly *not* alone.

Whose Fault Is It, Anyway?

Besides being reassured that they're not alone, parents whose children
are diagnosed with SPD nearly always want to know, "Is it something
I did?"

Again, the preliminary research is reassuring. The exact cause of
Sensory Processing Disorder—like the causes of ADHD, autism, and
so many other neurodevelopmental disorders—has not yet been identified. However, preliminary studies and research suggest some leading contenders.

---

* Ahn, R., L. J. Miller, S. Milberger, and D. N. McIntosh. "Prevalence of parents' perceptions of sensory processing disorders among kindergarten children." *American Journal of
Occupational Therapy* 58.3 (2004): 287–302.

Heredity

The most promising explanation to date is heredity. Perhaps you have intuitively noted the similarities between your child's behaviors and behaviors you or your spouse have or recall from childhood. Like Jennifer Jo, you may have come to the conclusion that the symptoms "run in the family." Initial research indicates that your intuition is probably sound.

One small pilot study* explored family links between twenty-seven children (eighteen boys and nine girls) with SPD and their biological parents. Often in heredity studies, researchers have to go back several generations to uncover evidence of an inherited trait. In this case, the correlation was so pronounced that tracing the disorder through multiple generations proved unnecessary (see Figure 13.1). Ninety-two percent of the sample children—all except one boy and one girl—had at least one parent with SPD symptoms. The association was highest when the mother had SPD symptoms (40 percent) and only slightly lower when the father had symptoms (37 percent).

This pilot study was not large or complete enough to establish definitively that SPD is inherited, but the evidence certainly suggests a link. Reinforcing this research, a study analyzed the occurrence of SPD symptoms in twins† raised in the same home. In this study, parents were surveyed about a variety of behaviors in their toddlers, about half of whom were identical twins and half fraternal. Identical twins were found to be much more likely to have the same sensory symp-

---

* A pilot study is one in which the researchers are trying to establish whether there is enough evidence to conduct a large-scale research project. Pilot studies often have limited sample sizes.

† "Twin Studies of Tactile and Auditory Defensiveness," a presentation by H. Hill Goldsmith, Ph.D., Leona Tyler Professor of Psychology, University of Wisconsin-Madison, reported at the Sensory Processing Disorders Scientific Work Group meeting, Boulder, Colorado (2004). A summary of the study appears at www.KIDfoundation.org/research/SWG.goldsmith. Dr. Goldsmith is completing a larger research study to evaluate twins further.

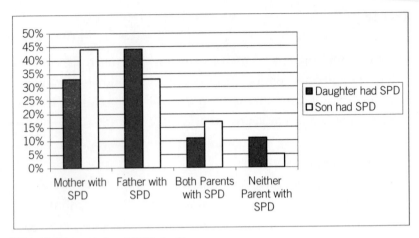

Figure 13.1. Transmission of SPD in families

toms than nonidentical twins, again suggesting that the traits seen in SPD are genetic.

Findings such as these don't mean that every child who has SPD inherited it from a parent. However, documenting inherited traits in close family members is the crucial first step scientists have to take before investigating whether more sophisticated genetic studies are warranted. Larger studies already have been funded and begun.

Prenatal Conditions and Birth Trauma

Another suspected cause of SPD are prenatal and birth complications.

In one study,* researchers analyzed three hundred children up to age sixteen receiving treatment in a large occupational therapy practice in Massachusetts. Data were evaluated to find out how many of the children had had birth complications such as prolonged labor, breech birth, prematurity, or fetal distress. Most birth complications

* Miller, L. J., principal investigator. "Outcome of sensory-based intervention after birth trauma." National Institutes of Health (R-21 HD/AR41614: 2001–2003; study site: OTA Watertown, Massachusetts).

occur in less than 10 percent of all live births, the exceptions being cesarean section and induced labor, which occur in approximately 20 percent of the general population. As Figure 13.2 illustrates, among the studied children with sensory symptoms, some complications (prolonged labor, fetal distress, forceps/vacuum delivery, and jaundice) occurred at a much higher rate than in the general population.

Further studies of prenatal and birth complications are likely to confirm additional associations between prenatal/birth factors and SPD. For example, sensory issues are frequently seen in infants with very low birth weight (less than 1,500 grams) and/or who have been exposed to alcohol or other drugs before birth. In addition, while this particular study did not find an association between SPD and a gestational age of less than thirty-seven weeks, it is widely recognized that extremely premature babies (born after less than thirty-two weeks of gestation) often have sensory-processing issues. Whether sensory difficulties are caused by premature birth, by the lengthy hospitalization that typically follows such births, or by other factors altogether remains to be determined.

In any case, none of the findings to date tell us what percentage of children who have birth complications go on to develop sensory issues. What they do indicate is that some prenatal and birth risk factors occur in children with SPD far more often than among typically developing children. Such disproportion suggests that investigating the role of birth complications will be another fruitful direction as the hunt for what causes SPD continues.

Environmental Factors

A third suspect in the search for causation is childhood environment.

Studies of children living in Romanian orphanages find strong associations between later sensory problems and the low levels of sen-

Birth complication	Occurrence in all live births (nationwide)	Occurrence in SPD sample	Difference between SPD and national samples	Number of children in SPD sample
Prolonged labor	<1 %	7.7%	>7.7%	23
Fetal distress	3.9	10.8	6.9	32
Jaundice	16	21.2	5.2	63
Forceps/vacuum delivery	9	12.8	3.8	38
Five-minute Apgar ≤ 7	1.4	1.7	.3	5
Breech presentation	3.8	3.7	-.1	11
Cesarean section	21.2	21	-.2	63
Meconium	5.5	2.3	-3.2	7
Preterm <37 weeks	11.6	8.1	-3.5	24
Induced labor	19.2	5.7	-13.7	17

Figure 13.2. Birth risk factors and SPD

sory stimulation, environmental complexity, and interaction with people and the environment prevalent in these institutions.* Many adoptive parents of these children report symptoms of over-responsivity that evolve over time into sensory-seeking patterns. The symptoms appear to be more severe the longer the child was institutionalized, suggesting that the institutional environment is a causative factor.

Similarly, children who have experienced severe physical or sexual abuse often become extremely defensive to touch and loud sounds. Like LaTanya, who woke up in a panic when her brother slammed his bedroom door, children who develop Post-Traumatic Stress Disorder as a result of abuse often become overly vigilant, apparently as a form of self-defense. The explanation for the similar symptoms seen in children with SPD and children with PTSD is another potentially fruitful direction for scientific inquiry. Additional environmental "suspects" in the search for what causes SPD include poverty-related risks, lead poisoning, and newborn hospitalization for medical conditions. Early behavioral patterns such as "colicky baby," "fussy baby," or regulatory difficulties with eating and sleeping disorders may turn out to be "precursors"—early indicators of a sensory problem but not causes. If confirmed to occur disproportionately in children with Sensory Processing Disorder, they may become additional red flags that justify early evaluation, diagnosis, and intervention.

Much more research is needed before the causes of Sensory Processing Disorder will be conclusively identified. Nonetheless, enough is known today for parents of children with SPD to be reassured: Your child's sensory issues are not a symptom of "bad parenting" on your part.

---

* Lin, S. H., S. Cermak, W. J. Coster, L. Miller. "The relation between length of institutionalization and sensory integration in children adopted from Eastern Europe." *American Journal of Occupational Therapy* 59.2 (2002): 139–47.

Ira was born under difficult conditions after a forty-three week pregnancy. He was five pounds at delivery and the umbilical cord was wrapped around his neck. His Apgar score for the first five minutes was low. By the age of fifteen months, he was head banging out of frustration, and his development was lagging in fine- and gross-motor skills. His language and communications were nonexistent. The progress he made with various therapies is encouraging, but we will always believe his birth difficulties led to the sensory problems he later experienced.

CONTRIBUTED BY CHRIS AND TERESA HEIN AND SON IRA

The first OT practice we took Ralphie to was very small and without much therapeutic equipment. The therapist was a bit gruff, though bright and helpful. There weren't many other kids getting therapy there and we felt it wasn't much fun for our son so we switched to a place that specializes in sensory-based treatment. What a difference! It seemed more like a circus camp. One activity had four kids in a huge tire swing, swinging around in the dark and through bubbles. What a blast they all had.

CONTRIBUTED BY CATHY MAHONEY AND SON RALPHIE

Chapter 14

Intervention Methods and Treatment Effectiveness

No "cure" for Sensory Processing Disorder is known. However, occupational therapy with a sensory integration approach has been in use for more than forty years and has produced countless success stories in which sensational children and their families emerged with a higher quality of life.

Like Cathy Mahoney, parents whose children have been diagnosed with SPD and who seek direct occupational therapy services in a private setting are often surprised by what they find. First, there's the environment. Intervention takes place in a large room that looks more like a supersized McDonald's Playland than a clinical office. The OT gym, as the treatment room is sometimes called, is full of fun toys and equipment and all sorts of things hanging from the ceiling—a trapeze, nets, ropes, various types of swings. There are barrels for rolling, a ramp for scooterboarding, and therapy balls of every possible size and color.* Puzzles, games, and other playthings are also on hand in the gym for work on academic goals and other functional skills.

The Role of Play in Therapy

The reason the setting for occupational therapy resembles a "circus camp," as Cathy saw it, is that OT for children is accomplished through sensory play. Of the occupations of childhood, play is the principal one, which makes it a natural medium for enticing kids to do the hard work required to improve their abilities. OTs use play to present children with demanding but achievable goals that require them to make an "adaptive response"—an action beyond the limit of what comes easily and automatically but close enough that the child can reach it with the right support.

In Ralphie's case, intervention began after a diagnostic evaluation determined that he was a sensory seeker with some tactile over-responsivity, a combination disorder that had produced fine-motor delays such as poor handwriting and was increasingly causing him social problems like the ones we saw with Ben, the whirlwind in Chapter 8. At a pivotal preschool conference, one aide labeled Ralphie "a pest" and another called him "odd." "Maybe there's a sensory issue," one of the teachers suggested. Although the Mahoneys eventually withdrew Ralphie from the preschool, they credit the teachers there with pointing them in the right direction by noticing he had sensory problems.

Ralphie qualified for public school services, which his parents

---

* Dr. Ayres first began developing sensory equipment to treat children in the 1960s. Now a number of inventive and reliable specialty companies offer clinical and home versions based on her ideas. See Appendix A for a list of resource companies.

supplemented with one-on-one private therapy. During goal-setting with the OT, priorities such as helping Ralphie socialize better and learning to write his name were identified. To begin working toward these goals, the first session of therapy began with the OT gym hung with only one of its many swings and no other children present. Ralphie was drawn into slow forward-and-backward swinging tasks in a subdued environment with the lights dimmed and a soothing CD playing in the background, measures designed to help him work on self-regulation.

In subsequent sessions, Ralphie's therapist consistently "upped the ante"—increasing the stimulation in the environment by hanging more swings and introducing other stimuli that challenged Ralphie to satisfy his sensory appetite for movement while maintaining a regulated state with the OT's support. At the same time, the therapist taught Ralphie and his mom calming activities and clinical reasoning strategies to help the little boy avoid overarousal when his proprioceptive and vestibular senses were stimulated. To a stranger passing by these OT sessions, it might have appeared that the boy and his therapist were simply having fun. In fact, every piece of equipment available and all the activities that took place were contrived to fill Ralphie's quota of vestibular stimulation and to promote greater self-regulation while reducing his tactile sensitivities.

Once Ralphie's self-regulation had increased, more children were incorporated into the second half of his treatment sessions. Eventually, the little boy was dubbed the "social director" by other therapists, who sought him out as a playmate for the children they were treating because of his sensitivity and outgoing personality.

Depending on the child and therapist, OT may incorporate make-believe as well as active play. Fantasy engages children's imaginations and encourages them to accept challenges they might avoid if they were doing exercises instead of playing. It may have looked like Ralphie and the other kids in the giant tire swing were just moving through bubbles, but they were really piloting a rocket ship to the moon through a meteor shower. To save the ship, Ralphie had to burst as many of the bubble/meteors as possible, a challenge that forced him to organize and self-regulate during what could have been an over-arousing movement activity.

"Brushing" and Other Complementary Therapies

A number of complementary and alternative therapies have been developed to treat children with Sensory Processing Disorder. One example is the Wilbarger protocol, commonly called "brushing." This therapy includes a structured program of applying deep pressure and proprioception at prescribed times during the day to children who have tactile and/or other sensitivities. The Wilbargers recommend that only one type of brush, a specific bristle brush manufactured by a single producer, be used in this process and that only their specific method of applying deep pressure and proprioceptive stimulation with the brush be used.*

The Wilbarger protocol, craniosacral manipulation, acupuncture, and other alternative and complementary therapies may have a role within a comprehensive treatment program. However, empirical research has not yet demonstrated their effectiveness. These and all therapies should be used only by a qualified therapist who carefully monitors the effectiveness of the interventions on an individual basis. They should *never* be used as stand-alone techniques or by anyone who has not received specific training in the method. In the future, effectiveness research will verify whether these techniques provide valuable enhancements to traditional therapy programs.

Sensory Processing Disorder is a complex neurological im-

---

* Wilbarger, J., and P. Wilbarger. "The Wilbarger approach to treating sensory defensiveness." In A. C. Bundy, S. J. Lane, E. A. Murray, eds., *Sensory Integration: Theory and Practice* (2nd ed.). Philadelphia: F. A. Davis Company, 2002: 331–38.

pairment. As appealing as simple, isolated treatments may be, they are not a substitute for sound clinical reasoning and comprehensive family-centered intervention.

The Parent's Role in Therapy

Ralphie's achievements in OT demonstrate a good reason for you to be in the therapy session with your child. You don't want to miss his successes!

Besides, you want to see for yourself the techniques the therapist uses. Cathy knew Ralphie often became overaroused during physical play; it was part of why he became so aggressive with his preschool playmates. By observing the therapy sessions, she could see how the therapist presented her son with progressively harder but achievable assignments, manipulating his context to make sure he was never allowed more movement than he could manage without risking a meltdown. As Cathy watched, she learned how to provide Ralphie with the just-right amount of sensory input herself, which helped her learn how to prevent meltdowns at home and elsewhere.

With very few exceptions,* there is much more to be gained from parents being in their child's therapy session rather than outside in the waiting room. Parents who are in the treatment room to observe and participate can see clinical reasoning at work and learn when and how

---

* One exception applies to children who are so dependent and clingy that they have trouble separating from their parents. Since one of the goals for this child is likely to be learning to separate, the therapist will work with the family to arrive at a method that will enable the parents to wait outside the therapy room during the session. Another exception is when parents with children who have similar problems are in treatment at the same time and place. The spontaneous support and information exchange that can blossom among parents in the hour while their children are in a session can outweigh the benefits of observing the therapy session. For additional details on parent support in the waiting room, see Cohn, E. S. "From waiting to relating," *American Journal of Occupational Therapy* 55.22 (2001):168–75.

to adjust the elements of A SECRET. They also learn when and what kinds of discipline and reward work best with their child.

The Effectiveness of Therapy

Parents sometimes express surprise that their children show improvement in areas that appear totally unrelated to what goes on in the therapy sessions. At the beginning of treatment, Ralphie could only scribble on paper. Though he never practiced writing during therapy, he could write his name and draw a person by the time he completed OT, and it wasn't long before he came to love other fine-motor activities like building with Legos. What happened was that the therapist worked on filling the boy's quota of movement and proprioceptive input, which satisfied his sensory appetite. With his sensory appetite quenched, Ralphie was able to begin mastering the fine-motor and thinking tasks he had previously been too disorganized to execute.

Although treatment success stories like Ralphie's abound, few empirical studies exist to show why it is effective, for whom, and under what conditions (e.g., How many sessions a week? In sessions of what length? With or without parents involved?). In an effort to address such questions using rigorous scientific methods, two pilot treatment studies have been conducted at the STAR Center in Denver.

In one study, thirty-two children were evaluated for physiological and behavioral responses to sensation, social-emotional factors, and attentional abilities. Individualized goals were established before treatment, then the children received twenty sessions of occupational therapy (twice-weekly sessions for ten weeks). The evaluations administered before treatment were given again after the twenty sessions were concluded.

Significant improvements were found after treatment in a variety of subtests used to assess the children's functioning. Figure 14.1 shows some of the results. Improvement was observed in attention, cogni-

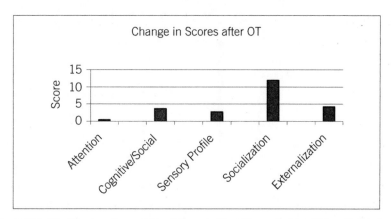

Figure 14.1. Effectiveness of occupational therapy with children who have SPD: a pilot study

tive/emotional areas, perception of sensation, socialization, and externalizing (e.g., aggression).

Because there was no control group (i.e., children receiving a different form of therapy or no therapy at all), the study could not conclude decisively that treatment produced the improvement seen in the sample children. To address this limitation, a pilot randomized controlled trial (the gold standard of treatment methodologies) was conducted in which children received either occupational therapy, an alternative treatment, or no treatment for ten weeks, twice a week.

Children were evaluated before and after the ten-week period and the results from the three treatment groups were compared.

Figure 14.2 shows some of the results. The black bars indicate change after the alternative treatment (called "activity protocol" or "AP"). The gray bars indicate the change after OT, and the white bars indicate the change for those who were on the wait list and received no treatment. The picture that emerges is impressive. The children receiving the alternative protocol (AP) had change scores from −0.6 to +6.2, with a total cumulative improvement of 10.8 points. The children in the wait-list group who received no treatment had change scores from −1.6 to +4.8, with a total cumulative change of 6.6 points. The children who received OT had change scores from +1.6 to +6.0,

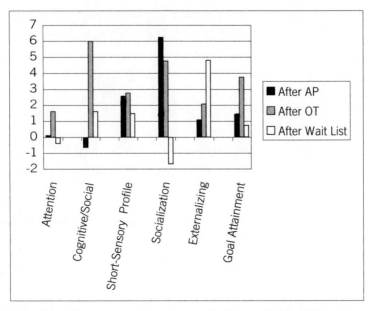

Figure 14.2. Effectiveness of occupational therapy with children who have SPD: a pilot randomized controlled trial

for a total cumulative score of 20.9 points. At least in this study, the children in the group treated with occupational therapy clearly made the most progress.

During the second ten-week period, the results virtually reversed. The children receiving OT increased their performance by fourteen and eleven points, while the group that shifted into the alternate treatment decreased by six points.

Although large-scale treatment effectiveness research is needed to validate the findings of these pilot studies, parents can take heart that preliminary research using state-of-the-art techniques indicates that forty years of success stories like Ralphie's can be verified with measurable evidence that treatment does indeed work. This particular study indicates that as few as twenty sessions of therapy over ten weeks can make important differences.

While I was struggling to understand a neurological diagnosis that I tripped over trying to pronounce, I had no idea that a bright room with swings, ball pits, tunnels, bouncing balls, and Play-Doh was "brain work." Luckily for our family, we found many kind and extraordinary OTs who would have a profound impact on our child, who had problems with extreme impulsiveness and distractibility and sensory defensiveness as well. Each breakthrough gives our family hope that as Hayley's brain learns so many of the things that come without thought for most of us, she will become skilled at experiencing things without fear and have a happy and productive life.

CONTRIBUTED BY CARRIE FANNIN
AND DAUGHTER HAYLEY

A Personal Message to Parents

At only six years old, our son has "graduated." One by one, the horrible symptoms caused by his sensory disorder have faded and some have ceased to exist. It didn't happen overnight, but it happened, and he became stronger, more confident, happier. Today, Michael is whole, strong, composed, and ready to face the world.

How do we say "thanks" for giving our child his life back? For changing a dark future to a bright one?

CONTRIBUTED BY MICHELLE MORRIS AND SON MICHAEL

D o you remember frail little Rachel Hurt from Chapter 3, the girl whose mouth was so sensitive to sensation that she couldn't eat? The same Rachel who had a gastrointestinal tube implanted in her stomach to get food into her tiny body?

Here's an update her mother, Cindy, sent me.

"Today Rachel is in first grade. While she is still somewhat picky about what she eats, she tolerates many foods and her feeding tube was removed over a year ago.

"At the end of last year, her teacher brought each child to the front of the class and said something special about them. At Rachel's turn, the teacher said, 'What's special about Rachel is her smile.' I could hardly believe she was talking about a child who used to cry all the time, who would push her head into my leg if I tried to leave her, who would scream when a siren went by, close her eyes in sunlight, and be generally miserable all day. And now she was known for *smiling*? 'Rachel smiles all the time and her smile is infectious,' the teacher continued. Then she turned Rachel around to face the audience. Rachel smiled . . . and the whole audience started smiling back at her.

"I have never felt such a moment of intense joy in my life. My daughter has made the most important change any child could make. She has gone from being miserable to smiling all the time. It seems like a miracle, but Rachel is a happy girl with a lifetime of smiles instead of misery ahead of her."

At the outset of the journey that families like the Hurts have made, parents often despair that such a day will ever come for their child or themselves. If you are one of those parents, hold tight to the picture of Rachel smiling. Like Michael Morris and Emma Reinhart and Jake Renke and Daniel Siegel and dozens of other children in this book, Rachel didn't find her smile overnight, but she found it.

Teachers, if you see behavior or other problems that could have a sensory basis, you have an opportunity to change a child's life. Talk to the parents. Refer the child for screening. Because you see so many children, you are a pivotal resource in an ideal position to recognize red flags that others miss. When you see them, sound the alarm.

Parents, if you recognize red flags, trust your intuition. Nobody knows your child better than you do. Find health care providers who will listen to you. They do exist. Seek well-trained evaluators who can get to the bottom of your child's issues. You will never be sorry. Feel good about the values and priorities you have for your child and your family. They are legitimate and important and deserve attention. Grant yourself time away from your wonderful but challenging youngsters. You work hard and you deserve a break—often! And if the challenges are putting stress on your child's siblings, your marriage, your extended family, your friendships, or other relationships, know that you are not alone. Seek support and connection through resources such as SPD Parent Connections and wherever you can find it.

You were already an expert on your child when you picked up this book. I hope you're a better-equipped expert now that you've finished it. Use this knowledge. When you see the familiar signs that a meltdown is taking shape, remember A SECRET and modify the situation to let the steam out of the buildup. If you encounter a skeptic who says, "There's no research about this disorder," feel free to say, "That is *so* nineties." Combat skepticism with data. Read and network to stay abreast of the new findings being made all the time.

Ask questions. Find answers. Hope. Persevere.

Whether you are a family just starting on the journey of discovery and mending or a family whose journey is already at or near its end, tell your story. Tell it to confused parents and despairing parents. Tell it to hopeful and encouraged parents. Tell it to teachers and doctors and neighbors. Tell it to me.

But tell it.

It's sensational, just like your child and you.

> *Every morning now, my boy hits the ground running. Gone are his meltdowns, his terror, and his sadness. Michael now believes the world is a friendly place. He can express his wants and needs. He rides a bike, collects bugs, helps me cook, tends his garden, catches fish, goes to movies, and plays ball with his papa. He doesn't run into walls, choke on food, or cry at lights and sounds. He no longer fears new places and people. He is able to learn. We buzz and brush, squash and jump. Our days are joyful, and we can't wait till tomorrow! Michael has become . . . himself. We live. We laugh. We love. I couldn't ask for anything more.*
>
> CONTRIBUTED BY MICHELLE MORRIS AND SON MICHAEL

I am collecting stories of sensational children and their families for my next book. If you have a story, please send the story, your full name, address, telephone number, and e-mail address to the KID Foundation, 5655 South Yosemite, Suite 305, Greenwood Village, Colorado, 80111 or to (stories@ sensationalkids.org).

—LJM

ACKNOWLEDGMENTS

I always start my presentations with a slide that says, "It takes a village to do a research project." I have been lucky enough to live in a large and support-filled village—so large that I could not possibly list by name each villager who has shared part of my thirty-year professional journey. I trust that all of you know how much you have contributed to the work that led to this book and how deeply I appreciate each and every one of you.

The most important contributors to this work are my teachers: the children and families from whom I learn more every day about Sensory Processing Disorder (SPD). An extra special thanks goes to the parents and children who shared their personal stories for this book (alphabetically by first names): Andrea and Sean Miller; Carrie and Hayley Fannin; Cathy and Ralphie Mahoney; Chris, Teresa, and Ira Hein; Cindy and Rachel Hurt; Dawne and Brad Roy; Doris and Greg Fuller; Ida and Jacob Zelaya; James Jonas III and William James Jonas IV; Jamie and Jakob Riddick; Jennifer and Heather Jo; Karen and Tanner DeWoody; Kathy and Connor Hutton; Laura and Brogan Heneghan; Laurie and Jake Renke; Lori and Jordan Fankhanel; Marie and David Rawlinson; Maureen and Briana Hernon-Thistle; Michelle and Michael Morris; Nick Scharff; Pamela and Jack Cardin; Raena and Thomas Rawlinson; Roianne and Lee Ahn; Sonja and MacKenzie Rose; Terri and Emma Reinhart; Valerie and Joshua Dome; Vicki and Daniel Siegel; Vicky and Sammy Mylenic. Particular thanks go to all the parents hosting SPD Parent Connections worldwide (www.KIDfoundation.org/parentconnection), and especially the executive committee: Raena Rawlinson, chair, and Ida Zelaya, Jamie Riddick, and Melissa Zacheryl.

I will also be forever indebted to Dr. A. Jean Ayres, my first teacher and lifelong model, who developed the theory of sensory integration and infused me with her passion to learn everything possible about the disorder. Other great teachers who have guided and shared with me along the way include: Anita Bundy, Ann Grady, Barb Hanft, Beth Osten, Bud White, Deanna Sava, Diana Henry, Erna Blanche, Florence Clark, Georgia DeGangi, Grace Baranek, Heather Miller-

Kuhaneck, Jan Hollenbeck, Janet Wright, Jean Dietz, Judy Kimball, Judy Reisman, Julie Bissell, June Bunch, Kathleen Morris, Marie Anzalone, Moya Kinnealey, Ric Carrasco, Sharon Cermak, Sharon Ray, Shay McAtee, Shelly Lane, Shula Parush, Stacey Szklut, Sue Kratz, Wendy Coster, and Winnie Dunn.

The knowledge about SPD that is ours today would not have been possible without the hardworking occupational therapists who participated in the studies mentioned in this book: Becky Greer, Clare Summers, Correen Jack, Julie Butler, Julie Wilbarger, Nicki Pine, Robin Seger, Sharen Trunnell, and Tracy Stackhouse. Also invaluable have been the advice and support of other staff and faculty at the Children's Hospital and the University of Colorado Health Sciences Center: Bob DiLaura, Bob Emde, Danny McIntosh, Dennis Matthews, Ed Wills, Joann Robinson, Joe Coll, Joy Browne, Jude McGrath, Marianne Wamboldt, Mark Laudenslager, Marty Reite, Mary Klinnert, Paul Fennessey, Ray Merenstein, Robin Gabriels, Sally Rogers, and Susan Hepburn. Meanwhile, my fellow founding members of the Alpha research group are breaking vital new ground as the first group of occupational therapy collaborators investigating SPD: Barb Brett-Green, Diane Parham, Ellen Cohn, Susanne Smith Roley, Jane Koomar, Janice Burke, Roseann Schaaf, Sarah Schoen, Stacey Reynolds, Teal Benevides, Teresa May-Benson, and Zoe Mailloux.

The current and past KID Foundation board and staff members have a special place in my heart. They have provided support and encouragement since 1978 and been a steady and thoughtful source of guidance throughout: Andrea Loveridge, Barry Gore, Bill Whalen, Bridget Bax, Chris Auer, Cindy Hurt, Ed Goldson, Ellen Toomey, Greg Eurich, Jan Ingebritson, Joe Betts, Judy Benzel, Karla Johnson-Grimes, Kathy James, Katy Miller, Kevin Pratte, Linda Williams, Marie Verrett, Mary Jo Houser, Roianne Ahn, Teri Heinz, Sandra Rojas, Scottie Taylor Iverson, Susan Labagnara, and Tammi Fowler.

My colleagues on other major projects—Bridget Piernik-Yoder, Dave Herzberg, Gay Lamey, Nancy Flores Castilleja, and Tom Oakland—deserve a prize for waiting so patiently for me to finish this book and return to their fold. And while I was engrossed in this writing, the research conducted by fellow members of the Sensory Processing Disorder Scientific Work Group—Barb Brett-Green, Barry Stein, Bill Gavin, Dave Pauls, Ed Levin, Gene Arnold, Hill Goldsmith, Margaret Bauman, Mary Schneider, Mike Kisley, Patti Davies, and Sinclair Smith—continued expanding knowledge far beyond what I alone could have accomplished.

The professional staff of STAR (Sensory Therapies And Research) Center have joined the village to put into practice the discoveries about SPD that research is continually making: Andrea Stoker, Cheryl Mock, Kate O'Brien Minson,

Lee Tarsitano, Marianne Reale, Randall Redfield, Ron Minson, Sarah Schoen, and Sue Coffaro.

As vital as all these contributors have been, our understanding of SPD would not have reached the point it has today without the generous financial support of the Wallace Research Foundation, the Heneghan Family Foundation, the Tuckman Family Foundation, the Brout Family Foundation, the American Occupational Therapy Foundation, David Brown, Joe Tirella, and Patti Marashian of Sensory Resources, Andy Roussey of Southpaw, Troy, Herb, Scott, and Gary Pfefferle of PlayAway, Sue Wilkinson and Peter Savitz of Abilitations/Integrations, and Sue Seiler of KidAbilities. These supporters are as golden as the contributions they make.

My coauthor, Doris, and I are grateful to our literary agent, Jody Rein, who believed in the importance of this book and brought us together for the great adventure of writing it, and to our editor, Christine Pepe, who loved *Sensational Kids* from the start.

Family members and friends who have lifted me up and kept me from faltering include Katy Miller, Bruce Pennington, Carol Stock Kranowitz, Jennifer Brout, Randi Hagerman, Roianne Ahn, Jane Koomar, Shelly Lane, Marshall Haith, Nedra Gillette, Mary Schneider, Mary Evert, Nick and Jacki Scharff, and Karen Zareck.

And of course, our immediate families—Bill, Coles, and Marita Whalen; Ken Sanger and Greg and Natalie Fuller—have been indispensable. Each one has encouraged, supported, and loved us through our countless hours of conferencing and preoccupation as they waited and waited and waited for us to finish.

Without all of these villagers, this book would still be a dream. Thank you.

APPENDIX A

Resources for Parents, Teachers, and Therapists

Below you will find some suggestions for reesources that may prove helpful on your SPD journey. This is just a partial list, as new organizations are founded every day.

Additional resources may be found at *www.SPDnetwork.org/other*.

The KID Foundation: *www.KIDfoundation.org*—Focuses on parent support, research, education, and advocacy for recognition of Sensory Processing Disorder.

SPD Network: *www.SPDnetwork.org*—Provides a vast array of information about SPD as well as easy access to many SPD–related resources for both parents and professionals.

SPD Parent Connections: *www.KIDfoundation.org/parentconnection*—A network that provides support, information, and understanding to anyone who lives with a child who has SPD or wants to learn more about these developmental disorders.

SPD Resource Directory: *www.KIDfoundation.org/directory*—A directory of occupational therapists, physical therapists, speech/language pathologists, physicians, mental health providers, eye care providers, dentists, and educators with a special interest in SPD. Also lists facilities and community resources nationwide.

Organizations and Websites

American Occupational Therapy Association: *www.aota.org*—Information about the occupational therapy profession and links to your state's organization, which may direct you to occupational therapists who specialize in sensory-based issues.

Association for the Neurologically Disabled of Canada: *www.and.ca*—This nonprofit organization describes what Sensory Processing Disorder is and provides a checklist of symptoms.

SPD–Related Listservs:

Occupational Therapy Internet World: *www.ability.org.uk/ergo.html*— Occupational therapist links, newsletter, directory, chat room, and other websites.

Sensory Integration and Autism: *www.autism.org/si.html*—An occupational therapist offers an explanation of sensory integration and autism.

Yahoo Groups: *http://groups.yahoo.com*—A listserv that facilitates e-mail–based discussion and support. To find a discussion group, type in "Sensory Processing Disorder" and hit *Search.*

Equipment and Products

Abilitations: *www.abilitations.com* (800) 850-8603—Catalog of special-needs equipment, focusing on movement, positioning, sensorimotor abilities, exercise, aquatics, and play.

Achievement Products for Children: *www.specialkidszone.com* (800) 373-4699— Products for home, school, and clinic that make life more comfortable for children with sensory problems.

Common Senses: *www.commonsenses.ca* (905) 951-2804—An online sensory toy shop dedicated to offering affordable sensory toys to children from 5 to 105—the "perfect shop for anyone who colors outside the lines."

Harcourt Assessment and PsychCorp: (800) 211-8378—Publisher of six of Lucy Jane Miller's nationally standardized tests: Miller Assessment for Preschoolers; Japanese MAP; FirstSTEP—Screening Test for Evaluating Preschoolers; Primer Paso; Toddler and Infant Motor Evaluation; and Miller Function and Participation Scale. Also publishes other OT assessments and books and psychological assessments.

Henry OT: *www.henryot.com* (623) 933-3821—Videotapes and books for students, teachers, and families; application of Sensory Processing Disorder principles for school/home are included.

In Your Pocket: *www.weightedvest.com* (800) 850-8602—Variety of weighted vests and sewing patterns for children with Sensory Processing Disorder.

Integrations: *www.integrationscatalog.com* (800) 850-8602—A catalog of sensory equipment for home, school, and therapeutic settings. The format includes special informational tips about how to use the equipment. A mainstay of every professional setting that uses a sensory-based approach to remediation.

Jump-In Products: *www.jump-in-products.com* (810) 231-9042—Products for sensory processing and physical restoration.

Kidzplay: *www.theragifts.com* (603) 437-3330—Catalog includes sensory motor products, toys, and gifts for children who have Sensory Processing Disorder, autism, learning disabilities, or other conditions.

Learning Gear Plus: *www.learninggearplus.com* (866) 280-2769—Educational products including pencil grips, shoelaces that don't need tying, and foam coverings for utensil handles.

PDP Products/Professional Development Programs: *www.pdppro.com* (651) 439-8865—Toys/games, equipment, videos, and books for enhancing sensory processing and oral-motor development.

Pippen Hill Designs: *www.pippenhilldesigns.com* (410) 451-1331—The official website for the Dream Kuddle Pillow, a helpful resource for children with sensory challenges.

PlayAway: *www.playawaytoy.com* (715) 752-4565—Indoor equipment that can be used for therapy and play.

Pocket Full of Therapy: *www.pfot.com* (800) PFOT-124—Therapeutic games, books, and equipment for promoting fine-, gross-, and oral-motor development.

RehabToys.com: *www.rehabtoys.com* (407) 322-3962—A therapist-owned company serving the needs of parents, teachers, and therapists. Balls, books, music, professional resources, sensory room furniture, suspension products, and videos are a few of the products offered at this site.

Sensory Comfort: *www.sensorycomfort.com* (888) 436-2622—Clothes, including seamless socks, and household products for children and adults with sensory processing differences.

Sensory Tools: *www.genjereb.com* (608) 819-0540—Music CDs and other music resources for therapists, educators, and parents of children with Sensory Processing Disorder, Attention Deficit Disorder, and autism.

Sensory Resources: *www.sensoryresources.com* (888) 357-5867—Resources for raising children with sensorimotor, developmental, and/or socio-emotional challenges; also produces conferences nationwide.

Southpaw Enterprises: *www.southpawenterprises.com* (800) 228-1698—Equipment for occupational therapy, including bolster swings, inflatable balls, swings, weighted vests, and suspension structures.

Sportime: *www.sportime.com* (800) 444-5700—Equipment for physical activities, including mats, tunnels, and obstacle course items.

Therapro: *www.theraproducts.com* (800) 257-5376—Catalog of sensory motor products for children, including books, chairs, and games.

The Therapy Shoppe: *www.therapyshoppe.com* (800) 261-5590—Books, cassettes, weighted vests, oral-, fine-, gross-motor toys, and therapy equipment.

TherapyWorks: *www.alertprogram.com* (877) 897-3478—Books and leader's guide for "How Does Your Engine Run?" program for children with self-regulation problems.

Western Psychological Services: *www.wpspublish.com* (800) 648-8857—Publisher of Dr. A. Jean Ayres's tests and other tests used in the evaluation of SPD. Provides names of occupational therapists certified to administer the Sensory Integration Praxis Test (SIPT) by WPS/USC.

Books: Activity Guides

Arnwine, Bonnie (2005)
Starting Sensory Integration Therapy
Fun activities that won't destroy your home!

Kranowitz, Carol Stock (1995)
101 Activities for Kids in Tight Spaces
Activities for the doctor's office, on car, train, and plane trips, home sick in bed.

Kranowitz, Carol Stock (2003; revised 2006)
The Out-of-Sync Child Has Fun: Activities for Kids with Sensory Integration Dysfunction
A companion to *The Out-of-Sync Child: Recognizing and Coping with Sensory Integration Dysfunction*; presents activities that parents and kids with SPD can do at home.

Books: General Interest

Ayres, A. J. (1972)
Sensory Integration and Learning Disorders
Classic text written by the occupational therapist/psychologist who developed sensory integration theory and intervention.

Ayres, A. Jean, Philip R. Erwin, and Zoe Mailloux (2004)
Love, Jean: Inspiration for Families Living with Dysfunction of Sensory Integration
The story of Philip Erwin, a young man who had sensory-processing difficulties, and his aunt, A. Jean Ayres, Ph.D., OTR, the scientist who pioneered the diagnosis and treatment of the disorder. The story, presented in letters from "Aunt Jeanie," details Philip's struggle, as well as the criticism and scholarly exile that Ayres suffered in professional circles.

Ayres, A. Jean (1979; revised 2005)
Sensory Integration and the Child: Understanding Hidden Sensory Challenges
Written for families and teachers by the theoretician and therapist who formulated sensory integration theory and therapy; provides a great understanding of SPD.

Biel, Lindsey, and Nancy Peske (2005)
Raising Your Sensory Smart Child: A Parent's Guide to Sensory Integration Dysfunction
An informative book written by a parent of a child with Sensory Processing Disorder and a pediatric occupational therapist; provides a practical, hands-on guide with many ideas for activities; operates an informative website for parents, addressing questions such as how to find an occupational therapist.

Heller, Sharon (2002)
Too Loud, Too Bright, Too Fast, Too Tight: What to Do If You Are Sensory Defensive in an Overstimulating World
An overview of sensory defensiveness and an examination of treatment options, including diet, medication, and relaxation techniques. Appendices list alternative treatments and resources.

Kranowitz, Carol Stock (1998; revised 2005)
The Out-of-Sync Child: Recognizing and Coping with Sensory Integration Dysfunction
Written by a former preschool teacher with a special background in movement education, this highly acclaimed book describes how problems processing touch-pressure and movement stimuli affect a child's performance in school and at home; includes detailed checklists and resources.

Kranowitz, Carol Stock (2004)
The Goodenoughs Get in Sync
A delightfully illustrated "chapter book" for eight- to twelve-year-olds that tells a
charming story about five family members who each have a different sensory-pro-
cessing challenge, their naughty dog, and how they get in sync after a tough day.
Winner of the iParenting Media Award and a finalist for *ForeWord* magazine's
Book of the Year in Children's Nonfiction.

Orloff, Susan (2001)
Learning Re-enabled
April Edwards, the parent of a child who has been served by occupational therapy, says: "Orloff's book is informative and practical, providing encouragement to
parents and children. It defines professional terms and physiological functions af-
fecting learning."

Schneider, Chemin (2001)
Sensory Secrets: How to Jump-Start Learning in Children
Addresses how to use information from all the senses to develop the skills necessary for growing, learning, decision making, and communication; a guide to promote successful learning and positive behavior in people of all ages.

Trott, Maryann Colby, Marci Laurel, and Susan Windeck (1993)
SenseAbilities: Understanding Sensory Integration
A sixty-nine page booklet that uses case examples to help families and teachers understand SPD; includes suggestions for adapting playground equipment, bedtime,
clothes, communication, and travel. Sold in packages of five booklets with one set
of unbound pages.

Books: Teachers

Bissell, Julie, Jean Fisher, Carol Owens, and Patricia Polcyn (1998)
*Sensory Motor Handbook: A Guide for Implementing and Modifying Activities in the
Classroom* (2nd ed.)
Suggestions for classroom, physical education, and recess for children K–3. Authors
have extensive experience providing occupational therapy using an SPD approach
in the schools.

Henry, Diana (1996)
Tools for Teachers Plus Other Useful Tools for Parents, Teachers, Teenagers, and Others
Explains the impact of sensory-processing problems in the classroom and illustrates

how to adapt the school environment to help students with hyperactivity, distractibility, and sensorimotor delays, including poor handwriting; shows how movement and sensory experiences are vital for learning.

Hickman, Lois E., Rebecca Hutchins, Jennifer Ellen (2002)
Seeing Clearly (2nd ed.)
Fun activities to improve visual skills.

Kashman, Nancy, and Janet Mora (2005).
The Sensory Connection
An OT and speech-language pathologist team approach to treating sensory and communication disorders.

Kranowitz, Carol Stock, Deanna Iris Sava, Elizabeth Haber, Lynn Balzer-Martin, and Stacey Szklut (2001)
Answers to Questions Teachers Ask About Sensory Integration
Carol Stock Kranowitz and expert occupational therapists have assembled an extensive and easy-to-use set of checklists and other tools that are invaluable to every teacher and parent who has children with sensory-processing challenges.

Kranowitz, Carol Stock (2005)
Preschool Sensory Scan for Educators (Preschool SENSE)
A valuable new tool that occupational therapists can provide to teachers who are striving to help preschoolers with Sensory Processing Disorder.

Szklut, Stacey, Carol Stock Kranowitz, and David Silver (1999)
Teachers Ask About Sensory Integration
Carol Stock Kranowitz, author of *The Out-of-Sync Child*, interviews occupational therapist Stacey Szklut about how to teach children with Sensory Processing Disorder; includes a sixty-page reproducible booklet with classroom checklists, resources, idea sheets.

Books: Textbooks on Theory and Intervention

Ayres, A. Jean (1972)
Sensory Integration and Learning Disorders
Classic text written by the occupational therapist/psychologist who developed sensory integration theory and intervention.

Blanche, Erna, Tina Botticelli, and Mary Hallway (1998)
Combining Neuro-Developmental Treatment and Sensory Integration Principles: An Approach to Pediatric Therapy
Treatment for children 0–12 years with sensory processing and movement disorders such as SPD, cerebral palsy, autism, fragile X syndrome, and Down syndrome.

Bundy, Anita C., Elizabeth Murray, and Shelly Lane, eds. (2002)
Sensory Integration: Theory and Practice
Textbook of sensory integration theory and application for advanced knowledge related to Sensory Processing Disorder. Also available in a 418-page edition (2002).

Case-Smith, Jane, ed. (1996)
Occupational Therapy for Children (3rd ed.)
This 846-page textbook includes a chapter on SPD theory and intervention; also provides a summary of all research by A. Jean Ayres, Ph.D., OTR, written by SPD experts Diane Parham, Ph.D., OTR, and Zoe Mailloux, M.A., OTR.

Case-Smith, Jane, ed. (1997)
Pediatric Occupational Therapy and Early Intervention (2nd ed.)
This textbook includes two excellent SPD chapters focused on young children: "Sensory Integration Assessment and Intervention," by Susan Stallings-Sahler, Ph.D., OTR, and "Early Emotional Development and Sensory Processing," by Elise Holloway, M.P.H., OTR.

Smith Roley, Susanne, Erna I. Blanche, and Roseann C. Schaaf, eds. (2001)
Understanding the Nature of Sensory Integration with Diverse Populations
An excellent resource in paperback for people who want more advanced information.

Yack, Ellen, Shirley Sutton, and Paula Aquilla (2002)
Building Bridges Through Sensory Integration
Innovative strategies and practical advice for managing behaviors, improving muscle tone, developing social skills, creating sensory diets—and more!

Music

The Wiggly Scarecrow products
Coles Whalen (words and music)
www.KIDfoundation.org (2005)
Fabulous, fun CD of fifteen songs created expressly for children with SPD. CD

includes a printable guide "How to Use These Songs to Move, Think, Relate and Rest." You will love this CD.

28 Instant Songames—CD with booklet (2005)
MaBoAubLo and Barbara Sher
Includes games of body awareness, movement play, feeling identification, and self-expression, as well as imagination games that encourage expressive language play.

The Children's Group Inc.
www.childrensgroup.com
Classical music for children, parents, grandparents, and teachers. Products include Don Campbell's *The Mozart Effect* recordings and the *Classical Kids* series.

Danceland—CD with booklet (2002)
Kristen Fitz Taylor and Cheryl McDonald in collaboration with Lois Hickman, Aubrey Lande, and Bob Wiz
Fun songs and activities to improve sensory skills.

Marvelous Mouth Music—CD with booklet (2002)
Suzanne Evans Morris, Ph.D., with Aubrey Lande and Bob Wiz
Bring speech development to life through musical play.

Songames for Sensory Integration—2-CD set with booklet (2001)
Aubrey Lande, Bob Wiz, and friends
Offers a world of developmental play activities for young children.

Soothing the Senses (2005)
Fred Hersch
Luxuriously gentle and lyrical selections to relax and soothe the senses.

Video

Getting Kids in Sync (2002)
Carol Stock Kranowitz
Demonstrates appropriate, fun, and easy sensorimotor activities to help children integrate their senses and develop their bodies.

The Out-of-Sync Child (2001)
Carol Stock Kranowitz
Will help anyone understand the many ways Sensory Processing Disorder affects children and what others can do to help.

APPENDIX B

ICDL Diagnostic Classifications For SPD*

200. Regulatory-Sensory Processing Disorder
Sensory Modulation Challenge (Type I)
201. Over-Responsive, Fearful, Anxious Pattern
202. Over-Responsive, Negative, Stubborn Pattern
203. Under-Responsive, Self-Absorbed Pattern
 203.1 Self-Absorbed and Difficult to Engage Type
 203.2 Self-Absorbed and Creative Type
204. Active, Sensory Seeking Pattern
Sensory Discrimination Challenges (Type II) and Sensory-Based Motor Challenges (Type III)
205. Inattentive, Disorganized Pattern
 205.1 With Sensory Discrimination Challenges
 205.2 With Postural Control Challenges
 205.3 With Dyspraxia
 205.4 With Combinations of 205.1–205.3
206. Compromised School and/or Academic Performance Pattern
 206.1 With Sensory Discrimination Challenges
 206.2 With Postural Control Challenges
 206.3 With Dyspraxia
 206.4 With Combinations of 206.1–206.3

* From Greenspan, S. I., and S. Wieder (eds). *Diagnostic Manual for Infancy and Early Childhood: Mental Health, Developmental, Regulatory-Sensory Processing and Language Disorders and Learning Challenges (ICDL-DMIC).* Interdisciplinary Council on Developmental and Learning Disorders (ICDL): Bethesda, MD, 2005. Work group members: Lucy J. Miller, Ph.D., OTR; Marie Anzalone, ScD.,OTR; Sharon A. Cermak, Ed.D., OTR/L; Shelly J. Lane, Ph.D.; Beth Osten, M.S.,OTR/L; Serena Wieder, Ph.D.; Stanley I. Greenspan, M.D.

207. Mixed Regulatory-Sensory Processing Patterns
    207.1 Attentional Problems
    207.2 Disruptive Behavioral Problems
    207.3 Sleep Problems
    207.4 Eating Problems
    207.5 Elimination Problems
    207.6 Elective Mutism
    207.7 Mood Dysregulation, including Bipolar Patterns
    207.8 Other Emotional and Behavioral Problems Related to Mixed
        Regulatory-Sensory Processing Difficulties
    207.9 Mixed Regulatory-Sensory Processing Difficulties where Behavioral or
        Emotional Problems Are Not Yet in Evidence

APPENDIX C

The Language of Sensory Processing Disorder

Diagnostic language in any health field tends to evolve over an extended period of time during which scholars test and discard many terms before a universally accepted vocabulary finally "sticks."

The childhood disorder we recognize and accept today as Attention-Deficit/Hyperactivity Disorder (ADHD) was first identified as "chronic brain syndrome" in 1952 and subsequently called "hyperkinetic syndrome," "hyperactive child syndrome," "minimal brain damage," "minimal brain dysfunction," and "minor cerebral dysfunction." Only in 1980 did the term "Attention Deficit Disorder" (ADD) reach the top of the vocabulary heap, and then it was another seven years before the refinement of "Attention-Deficit/Hyperactivity Disorder" became widely used.

Autistic Spectrum Disorder (ASD—more commonly, "autism") went through a similar long development, beginning as "schizophrenic reaction, childhood type" in 1952, and then "infantile autism" and "schizoid disorder of childhood or adolescence" in 1980 before becoming "Autistic Disorder" in 1987 and finally ASD.

The terminology related to Sensory Processing Disorder and its treatment is evolving just as those of ADHD and ASD did. Dr. Ayres originally used the term "sensory integration dysfunction," which many people abbreviated SID. Thirty years later, colleagues and I promoted the term "dysfunction in sensory integration" (DSI) to avoid confusion with the widely used acronym for Sudden Infant Death Syndrome (SIDS). However, misunderstanding persisted. Although occupational therapists usually understand one another when using the term "sensory integration dysfunction," scientists, physicians, and other health professionals unfamiliar with the theory, assessments, and intervention frequently do not share the same knowledge base and often hold a more neurobiological view of the term. "Sensory Processing Disorder," the term used in this book and increasingly in clinical reports, was developed to distinguish the disorder from its theory, assessment, and treatment and to differentiate it from the neurobiological function already known as sensory integration.*

Paralleling evolution of an accurate, easily grasped name for SPD has been the evolution of a nosology for the subtypes of the disorder. For example, "over-responsivity" was first used by Dr. Ayres to describe over-sensitivity to touch; she called the condition "tactile defensiveness." Her original concept was later expanded to include over-sensitivity in sensory systems other than touch and became known as "sensory defensiveness," which later evolved into "sensory modulation dysfunction" and "sensory modulation disorder (SMD)." Now SMD, along with three subtypes that include "sensory over-responsivity," is increasingly recognized as a "classic" category within the larger framework of Sensory Processing Disorder. "Tactile defensiveness" is seen as one of many symptoms of sensory over-responsivity.

The umbrella term "Sensory Processing Disorder" and the terminology used in this book to describe the classic patterns and subtypes of SPD have been formally recognized in the *Diagnostic Manual for Infancy and Early Childhood,* developed and published by the Interdisciplinary Council on Developmental and Learning Disorders (ICDL) and the *Diagnostic Classification: 0 to 3 (DC:0–3),* the reference for physicians and mental health practitioners working with children aged three years and under.† Nonetheless, recognition of the nosology is not consistent even within the occupational therapy profession. Acceptance of a universal language for SPD will be facilitated when the disorder is recognized in additional standard reference works used in diagnosing childhood disorders, e.g., *The Diagnostic and Statistical Manual-IV* (currently in its fourth edition and commonly called the *DSM-IV*), the standard reference source for all mental health disorders, and the *International Classification of Diseases* (the *ICD-10*), the standard reference for physicians.

With official recognition and the increased study, awareness, and diagnosis that always follow recognition, the terminology of SPD, its subtypes, and its symptoms is expected to stabilize. More than forty years after Dr. Ayres first began writing about the disorder, parents, teachers, physicians, therapists, friends, and family can look forward to discussing SPD with a common language.

---

* A more complete discussion of the concepts behind the new nosology can be found at http://www.spdnetwork.org/aboutspd/defining.html.
†For more information, visit http://www.icdl.com.html.

APPENDIX D

Eligibility Requirements
for Screening/Evaluation Under IDEA

At preschool ages, your child must meet your state's eligibility requirements to receive services. Generally children are eligible who have medical, physical, neurological, cognitive, or behavioral diagnoses. Although SPD is *not* currently accepted as a diagnosis, children may be eligible if they have a general developmental delay due to Sensory Processing Disorder. Additionally, a recognized non-sensory problem that is comorbid with the SPD or that produces symptoms similar to SPD's may be used to justify screening. Referral for screening will typically lead to a more comprehensive evaluation. Evaluations are usually conducted under the special education department and are provided by the school team, free of charge to the parents. Your insurance may be billed.

If your child is school age, you may request a special education evaluation in writing through your teacher, local school administrator, or the school district special education department. The school will then screen your child for eligible diagnoses (as explained above) and determine whether the diagnoses are impacting school performance. If this criteria is met, your child is eligible for a comprehensive evaluation with a focus on determining eligibility for services and, if the child qualifies, developing an Individual Education Plan (IEP). The IEP typically includes accommodations and services to support the child's school participation. Evaluations and services are provided at no cost to the family.

If your child is found to have a diagnosis that does not impact academic performance and is not eligible under IDEA, he may still be eligible for evaluations, accommodations, and services covered by Section 504 of the Rehabilitation Act. Section 504 is a civil rights law that mandates that children have the support needed to participate in all aspects of school activities. Services tend to be more related to adapting the school environment than to direct intervention, but intervention is sometimes provided. These services are provided at no cost to the family.

More information about school services is available at the following sites:

- *www.taalliance.org*: The Technical Assistance Alliance links to the parent training and assistance site in every state.
- *www.wrightslaw.com*: Wright's Law provides current, accurate information about special education law and advocacy for children with disabilities.
- *www.KIDfoundation.org/other*: The KID Foundation provides information and links to other resources. Click on Special Education Law and Advocacy.

CONTRIBUTED BY SHARON RAY, SC.D., OTR

APPENDIX E

Locating a Multidisciplinary Team

A number of strategies are effective to help you locate a multidisciplinary team qualified to evaluate your child:

- Ask your primary physician for a referral.
- Ask the school psychologist, social worker, counselor, or other school specialist for a referral.
- Call your local children's hospital and ask for a referral.
- Call a university with a clinical training program in the specialties you need and ask for a referral.
- Study the Yellow Page listings of professionals in one of the specialty areas that typically participates in multidisciplinary teams and seek out those practitioners who advertise working as part of a team.
- Network with other parents of children with Sensory Processing Disorder through SPD Parent Connections or another community-based support group.
- Consult the SPD Resource Network at www.SPDnetwork.org/directory, where providers of services for children with SPD are listed by city.

Professional collaboration will increase the chance that you receive an accurate diagnosis and a clear plan of action. Specialists working in isolation tend to see problems from a narrower perspective and may miss a diagnosis outside their experience. For example, a pediatrician might diagnose ADHD and want to prescribe one drug, a psychiatrist could identify Anxiety Disorder and want to prescribe another drug, and an OT might say the problem is sensory and doesn't require medication of any kind. It's possible all three diagnoses are correct, but none is complete. Treating just one condition is thus unlikely to solve all the child's symptoms.

APPENDIX F

What Will a Team Evaluation Cost?

A comprehensive multidisciplinary evaluation for Sensory Processing Disorder is not inexpensive. Several factors will determine what you pay for clinical assessment and diagnosis.

- *Where you live*

Costs vary by region and between urban and rural areas. If expert diagnostic services are not available where you live and you travel to where they are, your cost will be higher than if services are local to you.

- *Who evaluates your child*

The number of professionals in the multidisciplinary team, the comprehensiveness of the testing, and the specific professions involved will influence the cost of services. The fees for a full neurological evaluation, for example, are higher than the fees for a speech evaluation. Psychiatrists, who are physicians, typically charge more for services than other mental health professionals.

- *Whether your school district offers assessment services*

Public school districts are equipped to conduct some of the evaluations performed as part of a comprehensive assessment, providing your child qualifies. These services are often available even if your child has not reached school age. Since you do not pay directly for school services, having some evaluations administered through the schools may reduce your out-of-pocket costs for assessment. Information about the availability of school services can be obtained from your local school district, your state department of education, or your county's public health department. Whether an OT with training in sensory problems is included as part of the school evaluation team will vary by school district.

- *Whether you live near a teaching university or children's hospital*

Hospitals affiliated with medical schools, federally funded Association of University Centers on Disabilities, and universities that offer degrees in psychology, social work, occupational therapy, physical therapy, and/or other health care professions often provide assessment services at a reduced cost.

- *What your medical insurance (if any) covers (if anything)*

An enormous variation exists in whether and how much of evaluation services will be covered by insurance. Services by one evaluator may be covered and those of another not covered.

When it comes to the cost of evaluation, knowledge is power. Talk to other parents who have had evaluations and find out who provided evaluation services the parents found to be sensitive and accurate. Learn as much as you can *before* you begin so you do not pay for services you might obtain at little or no cost. Talk to your primary physician about your child's needs and your financial limitations. Additonal strategies that sensational families have found helpful include these:

- Call the special education office of your school district to find out the rules and regulations for obtaining school services in your area.
- Review your medical insurance coverage to identify those diagnoses covered by your plan.
- Ask the person performing the evaluation what they are assessing and what they expect to learn from specific tests before agreeing to have your child tested.
- Always try to determine if there is an occupational therapist or another person trained in sensory processing on the team before you begin.

APPENDIX G

Locating and Choosing a Qualified Occupational Therapist

Although you may encounter a qualified diagnostician in another health field, it is most likely that your child's sensory problems will be evaluated by an occupational therapist. The following strategies can help you find a qualified occupational therapist:

- Search the SPD Resource Directory at www.SPDnetwork.org/directory for occupational therapists in your area.
- Call your local hospital and ask to speak with someone in the occupational therapy department or the rehabilitation unit, then ask if a pediatric OT is available at the hospital. Ask whether this individual has experience diagnosing sensory problems. If not, ask for a referral to an OT in private practice.
- Call or e-mail an occupational therapy program at a university near you. Ask to talk with a faculty member who teaches pediatrics and/or SPD assessment and treatment. Ask that faculty person for a referral to a professional who specializes in pediatric OT.
- Seek local contacts in your area from the American Occupational Therapy Association. (An accredited university OT program can be found by going to the American Occupational Therapy Association's website at www.aota.org, clicking on "Academic Affairs & Accreditation," then on "Educational Programs." All programs are listed by state.)

When searching for an occupational therapist to evaluate your child for Sensory Processing Disorder, it is essential to ask specific questions about the therapist's expertise in diagnosing sensory problems. All OTs study sensory integration principles as part of their professional education, but only some pursue advanced training in SPD. Here are some questions to help you determine whether a therapist has the necessary background to accurately assess and diagnose sensory-based disorders:

• Do you have formal training in assessing and treating children with Sensory Processing Disorder? When and what form did that training take? Have you studied SPD in graduate school, professional seminars, and/or received individualized mentoring?

• How much experience do you have assessing children with developmental problems and sensory issues, particularly Sensory Processing Disorder? How many years have you been doing this, and how many children have you evaluated?

• What tests do you typically give in an evaluation for SPD, and were you specifically trained or certified to give them?

You should also determine whether your candidate is certified as an occupational therapist by the National Board of Certification in Occupational Therapy. If not, you may want to keep looking. An OT who is not certified has completed his or her education but has not yet demonstrated proficiency.

A careful process of finding and interviewing the OT who evaluates your child will ensure that you receive the best possible assessment for your child.

APPENDIX H

Sample Letter for Helping Others Understand Your Sensational Child

Writing and sharing a letter about life through the eyes of your child can be an effective way of explaining Sensory Processing Disorder to extended family, friends, playmate parents, and others. The following letter is adapted from one family's approach to fostering understanding of their child with a letter. It is shared for the use or further adaptation by other sensational families.*

Dear Grandma and Grandpa and Aunt Katy and Uncle Greg:

I have heard that we will be staying with you again for Christmas this year! I know you have noticed that visits away from home are very hard for me, so I decided to write you and give you some ideas for making my time with you a lot better than it was last year.

I know Mom has told you about my "hidden handicap" called Sensory Processing Disorder. People sometimes call the disability "SPD" or "sensory integration dysfunction," too. SPD is a neurodevelopmental disorder that affects my brain and makes it different than your brain.

SPD is a complicated disorder and research is only just starting to come out about it. What we know already is that kids with SPD are not all the same. Some kids are over-responsive to sensations, which means they find a lot of sensations offensive. This causes them to have a "fight/flight" reaction to messages from their senses. Other kids are sensory under-responsive, which makes them seem not to feel sensations much at all. Some of these kids don't feel pain or they can swing or spin for hours. Other kids are sensory seekers. These kids get called "hyper" a lot because they're in constant motion and seem obsessed with touching things. Still another kind of SPD makes children look clumsy and awkward, which causes

---

* A letter prepared by a client of Rosemary White, OTR, and a story by parent Dannelle Liddell about her son Gavin inspired this letter.

people to make fun of them for being "klutzy." Most of us with SPD have pieces from several of these subtypes mixed together.

When kids have SPD, you can usually tell because of what they do. Sometimes it shows in the way they move (tripping, falling, getting lost, having trouble organizing stuff) and sometimes it shows in the way they act (aggressive, withdrawn, sad, no energy, thinking they are bad or weird, having no friends).

I'm the over-responsive/sensory defensive type of SPD. My SPD makes it hard for me to correctly interpret the sensations I feel. I'm sure you remember last year when someone pushed the ice maker button on the refrigerator when I didn't expect it, and I had what Mom calls a "meltdown." It just seemed to me that the noise was dangerous, like a bomb or something. I am much better now at controlling my emotions, but I still get scared and act weird when there is a loud sound that I didn't know was coming.

One sound that bothers me a lot is people singing. That's why I don't like to be in the room when you guys are singing carols. Also, I just hate it when anyone comes up and pats me on the back or squeezes my cheek. It makes me want to pull away, even if it is a light touch.

You're going to notice this year I have some really dark sunglasses and that Mom and Dad let me wear my cap even inside the house. That's because my eyes are sensitive to bright lights, and I feel so much better when I have my sunglasses or hat on.

Another thing. Please don't be critical of the way I dress or disappointed that I'm not dressed up at parties where everyone else is. Mom knows I feel so much better with a certain kind of sweatpants and T-shirt. It's more important to be in control than to look the "right" way.

Now about eating. Mom still says I am a very picky eater even though I don't seem picky to me. It's just that the smell and feel of certain foods in my mouth bother me so much. Lots of time I gag when I taste weird things or smell stuff that other people don't even notice. Please just let me eat what I want to; Mom is bringing extra snacks for me in case there's nothing that I can eat at some meals.

Sometimes people think that if I don't join them at the meal table it's because I am being rude. People even say mean things to Mom and Dad like, "Why is Joshua misbehaving? Don't you have any control over him?" Sitting still is just hard for me, and the smells, sounds, and people get to me, too. I start to feel like *I have to* move around or I'll explode. Don't ever hold up your meals for me—just go on without me. My parents are used to this, and they'll help us all handle the situation. They always figure out a good way for me to get food and stuff like that.

As far as activities go, I've learned a lot this year about myself. I know it makes me crazy to go to a mall or a big party or any busy environment. In fact, places like that usually make me fall apart because I feel like the whole environment is out to get me. Mom says that I'm having fewer meltdowns than I used to. Part of why is that I work hard to contain my feelings and another part is that we try to avoid busy places. If you have some holiday plans that are in noisy and busy places, please don't take it personally if I don't go along. I really will be fine with my puzzles and books and toys back at the house. Please don't try to persuade me to come because it isn't fun for me.

I'll apologize in advance because I know that I am sometimes bossy and controlling. When I get everything around me organized I can handle the world better. When things don't surprise me, I'm more like a regular kid.

You know what's most important to me? It's that you don't judge my parents' efforts. Everyone is always giving them advice about me—like *they* know better how to handle me than Mom and Dad. But nobody else lives with me, and it's really hard on my parents when people who don't live with me try to tell them how to do it. They know you have the best intentions but, honestly, we have been through so much already and they are so familiar with me and my needs. I know they are human, but sometimes I think they must be angels. They are such great people and they need your support.

It might sound like I'm asking you to change yourself, but I'm really not. I just want to ask you to be patient with me and understanding with my parents. I am trying hard to cope with everything, and they're doing their best to help me.

Do you think you see the world now a little bit like I do? That's what I hope. I am just me. I am like you in lots of ways and I'm different in other ways. There will be a place for me in the world, and I plan to do great things when I grow up. But in the meantime, at this family celebration, we'll all have a better time if you can take the time to imagine how I feel, to realize that I want to be "good" and participate, and I am doing the best I can!

See you soon!

Love,

Joshua

APPENDIX I

Roster of Research Collaborators

1. Sensory Processing Disorder Scientific Work Group (SPD-SWG)

The SPD-SWG is a multidisciplinary consortium of scientists studying Sensory Processing Disorder from numerous neurobiological disciplines. Among other subjects, the work group is conducting pilot studies of primates, rats, anatomy, electroencephalographic activity, twins, and familial links. The following list includes professionals who attended one or more SPD-SWG annual meetings:

Chair

Lucy Jane Miller, Ph.D., OTR, associate clinical professor of rehabilitation medicine and pediatrics, University of Colorado Health Sciences Center, Denver

Members

Enid Ablowitz, director of advancement, Coleman Institute for Cognitive Disabilities, University of Colorado, Boulder

Margaret L. Bauman, M.D., associate professor, Department of Anatomy and Neurobiology, Harvard Medical School, Boston

Barbara Brett-Green, Ph.D., assistant clinical professor of rehabilitation medicine, University of Colorado Health Sciences Center, Denver

Patricia L. Davies, Ph.D., associate professor, Colorado State University, Fort Collins

William Gavin, Ph.D., research associate professor for the University of Colorado

H. Hill Goldsmith, Ph.D., Leona Tyler Professor of Psychology, University of Wisconsin–Madison, Department of Psychology, Madison

Edward Goldson, M.D., professor of pediatrics, University of Colorado Health Sciences Center, Denver

Marshall M. Haith, Ph.D., professor of psychology, Department of Psychology, University of Denver, Denver

Michael A. Kisley, Ph.D., assistant professor of psychology, University of Colorado at Colorado Springs, Department of Psychology, Colorado Springs

Sherry Leonard, Ph.D., associate professor, University of Colorado Health Sciences Center, Departments of Psychiatry and Pharmacology, Denver

Edward D. Levin, Ph.D., professor of psychiatry, Duke University Medical Center, Department of Psychiatry, Durham, NC

Michael Merzenich, Ph.D., professor, University of California San Francisco, San Francisco

David L. Pauls, Ph.D., professor of psychiatry (genetics), director, Psychiatric and Neurodevelopmental Genetics Unit, Harvard Medical School, Charlestown, MA

Mary L. Schneider, Ph.D., professor of kinesiology, Harlow Primate Lab, University of Wisconsin–Madison, Madison

Sarah Schoen, Ph.D., OTR, assistant clinical professor, Department of Pediatric Rehabilitation, University of Colorado Health Sciences Center, Denver

Sinclair A. Smith, Sc.D., assistant professor, Neuromuscular Function Laboratory, Department of Occupational Therapy, Temple University, Philadelphia

Mark Stanton, Ph.D., associate professor, Department of Neuroscience, University of Delaware, Newark

Barry E. Stein, Ph.D., professor and chairman, Wake Forest University School of Medicine, Department of Neurobiology and Anatomy, Winston-Salem, NC

Linda Williams, M.D., Executive Director, KID Foundation, Greenwood Village, Colorado

2. Alpha Research Group

The Alpha Research Group is a consortium of occupational therapy scientists funded with federal and private grants to study Sensory Processing Disorder utilizing the Sensory Challenge Protocol developed in Denver. This work will investigate the validity of the Denver findings at multiple independent research sites.

In addition, each principal investigator noted below will explore additional research questions related to SPD.

Denver, Colorado	Lucy Jane Miller, Ph.D., OTR, principal investigator
	Barbara Brett-Green, Ph.D., neuroscientist
	Sarah Schoen, Ph.D., OTR, research associate
Augusta, Georgia	Susan Stallings, Ph.D., OTR, principal investigator
	Lynne Jaffe, Ph.D., OTR, research associate
Los Angeles, California	Diane Parham, Ph.D., OTR, principal investigator
Philadelphia, Pennsylvania	Roseann Schaaf, Ph.D., OTR, principal investigator
	Janice Burke, Ph.D., OTR, research associate
	Teal Wisniewski, M.S., OTR, research associate
Richmond, Virginia	Shelly Lane, Ph.D., OTR, principal investigator
	Stacey Reynolds, M.S., OTR, research associate
Torrance, California	Diane Parham, Ph.D., OTR, principal investigator
	Zoe Mailloux, M.A., OTR, research associate
	Suzanne Smith-Roley, M.S., OTR, research associate
Watertown, Massachusetts	Jane Koomar, Ph.D., OTR, principal investigator
	Teresa May-Benson, Sc.D., OTR, principal investigator
	Ellen Cohn, Sc.D., OTR, research associate

INDEX

Page numbers in italic indicate figures.

ABOUT THE AUTHORS

Lucy Jane Miller, Ph.D., OTR, is an occupational therapist and research scientist who in 1999 received a National Institutes of Health career award to investigate Sensory Processing Disorder (SPD). Dr. Miller directs STAR (Sensory Therapies And Research) Center in Denver, and founded and serves as research director of the KID (Knowledge in Development) Foundation. She is an associate clinical professor of rehabilitation medicine and pediatrics at the University of Colorado Health Sciences Center. In 2005, Dr. Miller received the Martin Luther King Jr. Humanitarian Award from the State of Colorado and the American Occupational Therapy Association's highest national award—the Award of Merit—for her contributions to assessment, clinical practice, and research. She has authored seven nationally standardized assessment and screening tests for children and more than one hundred professional articles and chapters during a thirty-year career devoted to the study and treatment of SPD. Dr. Miller is a native of Denver, where she continues to live and work.

Doris A. Fuller is an award-winning journalist who spent most of her reporting career at the *Los Angeles Times*. She has coauthored several books, including *Promise You Won't Freak Out* (Berkley, 2004), which she wrote with her teenaged children, about raising and being teens. *Promise* was a Books for a Better Life finalist in 2004 and was named the Best Parenting Book of 2004 by Amazon.com. Doris is a former Coloradoan now living and writing in northern Idaho.